SMART
—MONEY—
STRATEGY

SMART
—MONEY—
STRATEGY

YOUR **ULTIMATE GUIDE** TO
FINANCIAL PLANNING

LUKE SMITH

WILEY

First published in 2023 by John Wiley & Sons Australia, Ltd
Level 4, 600 Bourke St, Melbourne, Victoria 3000, Australia

Typeset in Jansen Text LT Std 11pt/14pt

© John Wiley & Sons Australia, Ltd 2023

The moral rights of the author have been asserted

ISBN: 978-1-394-17694-6

 A catalogue record for this
book is available from the
National Library of Australia

Cover design by Wiley

Disclaimer
The material in this publication is of the nature of general comment only, and does not represent professional advice. It is not intended to provide specific guidance for particular circumstances and it should not be relied on as the basis for any decision to take action or not take action on any matter which it covers. Readers should obtain professional advice where appropriate, before making any such decision. To the maximum extent permitted by law, the author and publisher disclaim all responsibility and liability to any person, arising directly or indirectly from any person taking or not taking action based on the information in this publication.

SKY77B77650-F00E-4C81-BEFB-500D3474B69C_020323

To my wife Peggy and to my daughters.
You remind me daily what's most important,
and without your support, I couldn't do what I do.

CONTENTS

ACKNOWLEDGEMENTS

I would like to acknowledge all those throughout my career who I have learned from and those who have inspired and encouraged me to start my own financial planning business—one that reflects my values around being easy to understand, being reliable and being trusted to look after my clients' personal financial planning advice needs. I also would like to thank my support staff who assist me every day in this endeavour. Finally, I thank my friend Peter Bowman for his ongoing support while I was writing this book. Without his involvement, the ideas in this book would have remained chatter over a coffee rather than something that people could benefit from in the future.

ABOUT THE AUTHOR

Luke Smith is The Strategy Stacker.

Luke is also a financial planner and the Director of Envision Financial, a financial planning advice business he founded in 2016 in Canberra, Australia.

Luke has been advising clients since 2004, working with individuals, couples, families, business owners and government employees to help them understand and make the most of their financial options.

Luke also appears weekly on local radio station 2CC Talking Canberra to discuss financial planning matters. A podcast of the show is available on Apple Podcasts, Spotify and other podcast platforms: search for 'The Strategy Stacker—Luke Talks Money' to find each episode.

For years, Luke has witnessed endless changes to investment and superannuation legislation, changes to the way people are taxed. There has also been changes to the rules around how people retire, which has caused confusion and uncertainty. In an age where life is meant to be easier, Luke believes that financial complexity is instead on the rise. He sees through the lives of his own clients. There's complexity around all aspects of money and when coupled with a distrust of banks and other financial institutions, it creates a challenging environment for people to move forward.

The gap in financial education is on show right now as we become a society of haves and have-nots and Luke believes the key to closing the gap is financial planning education. While there are some general books about budgeting, saving and investing, there's been nothing available to genuinely educate and inform Australians around the *real* financial strategies that financial planners use with their clients and how to put them together. This is the reason Luke wrote *Smart Money Strategy*. His down-to-earth approach breaks down complex financial planning strategies into everyday language and provides insights into how to put strategies together. The book can also be used to have more productive conversations with a financial planner, if you decide to seek personal financial advice.

To find out more and access additional smart money strategy tools, please visit thestrategystacker.com.au.

HOW TO USE THIS BOOK

As part of my ongoing philosophy to educate first and financial plan second, I have always had the belief that I have a duty to inform and educate my clients. This book is an extension of my financial planning firm's ongoing education program radio show on 2CC in Canberra (that was created to try and demystify industry-specific terminology and jargon, and to explain key financial concepts in plain English), and it is designed to give you the background to some key financial strategies—considering when and how to use them, and how 'stacking' these strategies can accelerate the probability of reaching your goals and the objectives of your 'why'—hopefully building in some tax deductions along the journey.

This book is designed to answer another question I get asked all the time: 'Where do you go to learn this stuff, because we didn't get any of it in school?' Another regular message in the Q&A box in our office is: 'Once your working life starts, you just don't have time to figure it out by yourself.' By sharing the information in this book, I hope that I can help you find the answers to the questions you have about money and personal finance, as well as provide a starting point for you to create a financial plan that works for you. I have designed this book for singles, couples, families and the young at heart. The strategies I share here can be applied no matter how old or young you are, and you will be surprised at how well some strategies stack with others, regardless of your goals and your starting position.

It is important to keep in mind that your financial journey is your own. It's not the same as your next-door neighbour, your work colleague, your brother or any another family member. Like most things in life, we all have different priorities and strive to achieve different things in different areas of our life. With this in mind, I have collated the key strategies in this book for you to consider, understand, apply and review along your journey. Not everything will be applicable to you, but a change in financial behaviour is a positive not a negative, and an informed change in your behaviour that is in line with your 'why' can be very powerful indeed.

Most importantly, this book is designed to be used with a qualified financial planner should you wish to seek personal advice. I cannot understand your specific personal situation or your life and financial goals through writing a book, so the information I provide here is 'general advice'. I can however hope to open your mind to the many useful financial planning strategies that are available and encourage you to seek personal financial advice for your own situation. I also want to share with you what's involved in the financial planning process and what goes into a personal financial plan (covered in Part IV of this book). I hope it alleviates any fear or apprehension you might have about seeking personal advice. You don't know what you don't know!

To the mums, dads, aunts, uncles, nanas and grandpas out there, I hope that you can take some useful strategies from this book and use them to help educate the next generation when it comes to saving, spending and other good behaviours that will stand them in good stead as they grow into adulthood. I honestly believe that the sooner they start learning about how money works—and even start to understand the smart money strategies in this book—the more confident and happy their financial lives will be. By the end of this book, I hope we'll agree on the value of sharing this information with the next generation too.

Wishing you strategy stacking success!

INTRODUCTION

I've been in the financial services industry for over 20 years, and it has always concerned me that I hear similar comments about money from a range of clients of all different ages: 'I wish I had known that five years ago' or 'I had no idea you could do that' (often followed by, 'I thought you could only do it *this* way'). When our finances are such a key component of our lives, it can be very sad to realise that so many people have these gaps in their financial knowledge.

Money is often a driver for some of the big decisions in our adult lives. New clients often end up in my office after taking a leap of faith, normally via a referral from an existing happy client. I spend some time with them talking through where they're at in their lives (including with their financial life), what they would like to achieve, and how we can take some financial steps together to keep them moving in the right direction or get them to where they want to go. It's especially important that I identify the strategies and options that they have. I also need to help my clients understand why the strategies I present to them are valuable, so they deepen their understanding about how smart money strategies can work for them.

I was brought up to hate waste—be it a waste of time, effort, money, talent, opportunity or knowledge. Hopefully by working your way through this book you can limit the times you say, 'I wish I had' and 'If only I had known', and increase the times you can say, 'Doing X has saved me Y' or 'Now we can do Z' in the future. There is no magic bullet and nothing about finance comes without risk, but over your work and retirement life there is always going to be give and take, and you can work with this flexibility: spend a little more now, work a little harder (or longer) later; save a little more now, work a little less later; and every other possible combination you can imagine. Along the way, you may find that making informed decisions about your money can help you save, build and grow what you are working with—affectionately known as your *resources*.

When you think about your resources, you probably think about the money you have in the bank or your super account. You might also think about the investments you hold—be they shares, property or some other kind of asset. What you also need to think about as a resource is *you*.

Your ability to earn an income is your most valuable resource. Your ability to manage your money is your second most valuable resource. Most people don't think like this. They forget about themselves and they dismiss their ability to make decisions for the betterment of their financial lives—which is often where a financial planner comes in.

A financial planner is a qualified professional who can help you identify your goals, understand financial strategies and options, create a personal financial plan and work with you towards achieving your goals. In short, a financial planner can provide you with personal financial advice.

It's also important to note that in Australia the terms 'financial planner' and 'financial adviser' are restricted terms by the *Corporations Act* 2001. This means that you can't just decide one day to call yourself a financial planner. To use either job title, there are certain legal requirements you need to meet, including being authorised by the Australian Securities and Investments Commission (ASIC). The Financial Advisers Register (managed by ASIC), which is published on the Moneysmart website, allows consumers to check their financial planner is authorised to provide advice and find out some more information about them.

Smart Money Strategy is designed to help you build your own knowledge and understanding about how financial planning strategies work. The book also provides a great platform for you to be better equipped when you walk into a financial planning meeting, should you decide to seek personal advice. By reading this book, it's my sincere hope that you can have more productive and engaging conversations with your financial planner to more effectively and efficiently achieve your goals.

Personal financial advice and general advice

It surprises me that within this age of information people still don't understand the value of personal financial planning advice. There's a big difference between *general advice* and *personal financial advice* when it comes to your financial planning, yet a recent study commissioned by ASIC found that many Australians couldn't tell the difference between general advice and personal financial advice.

So how can you tell the difference between the two?

The key difference comes down to whether a financial planner has considered your personal financial objectives, situation or needs. If no one has asked you about those things, the advice you are receiving is general advice. General advice is often seen in the media, within education tools and forums and in books like this. General advice provides information only, which may or may not be applicable to you.

Personal financial advice, on the other hand, is about you, and you alone. For example, you might be seeking personal financial advice for specific life issues, such as changes to your work situation (including a new job, redundancy or retirement), starting or selling a business, getting married or divorced, or having children. Almost everything we do in life has a financial consequence, so there are lots of reasons to seek personal financial advice.

At the heart of it, and in my view, personal financial advice involves:

- Understanding your starting position

- Exploring your 'why'

- Understanding the options specifically available to you

- Helping you implement healthier financial behaviours

- Creating a financial plan to help you meet your goals, and working with you to assess your progress towards those goals and recommending adjustments as may be required.

Personal financial advice is also about working with you over time to assess your progress towards your goals and changing and sustaining your financial plan as your life changes.

As I haven't asked you about your objectives, situation or needs, the advice in this book can't be considered personal financial advice as I don't understand anything about your personal financial situation and I haven't provided you with a financial plan that will help you achieve your goals. However, what I can do is give you general advice about how strategies and products work and how they can be used in different general situations. I find that even with my own clients, it often helps to explain things generally before exploring and assessing how a strategy might work within the context of their own situation and personal financial plans.

Let's consider these points about personal financial advice in more detail from the perspective of building your financial understanding.

It helps you understand your starting position

On any journey you take, it helps to know where you're starting from. In Chapter 6, I offer you a series of activities to help you explore and understand your own financial starting position. It's a really important step to know where you're at as it guides what you do next.

It helps you explore your own 'why'

A financial planner can help you by asking questions and acting as a sounding board to help you define your 'why'—the needs, wants and ambitions that determine how you might best structure your finances to achieve your goals.

If you've never thought about your own 'why', it might be hard to define what it means to you. You might be so busy with work or your family that you've never stopped to think about it. But knowing your 'why' gives you information and the motivation you need to create achievable goals for you and your family over time. Thinking about where you need to go will keep you engaged and motivated because even if it involves some sacrifices along the way, you know it will be well worth it in the end. Chapter 2 explores defining your 'why' in more detail.

A financial planner can help you define your goals and make them specific and measurable. A financial planner can also help you assess the goals you already have to ensure they're realistic and achievable.

It helps you build your knowledge so you can assess your strategy options

Although I may have never met you, the fact that you're reading this book tells me you're looking to build your knowledge and you're looking to create better financial outcomes for yourself and perhaps your family. Personal financial advice can help you identify and navigate the strategy options that are available and which ones are suitable specifically for you, and a financial planner can assist you along the way. You'll also learn a lot more about money than you probably ever have before and understand the risks that are involved too. Part III of this book introduces you to the key strategies you can 'stack' in different ways to meet your goals.

It helps you implement new behaviours

Knowledge is great, but good financial behaviour also matters in determining the outcomes that you achieve. You need to operate within a 'circle of safety'—that is, have good everyday financial behaviours. To some, this may sound boring—if that's you, please feel free to spice up your life through food, music, movies, a relationship or something else more exciting than money. The key takeaway here is that if your financial life is boring, you're probably on track in many regards!

Behaviour changes you can make to improve your financial fitness include:

- Being mindful of the foundations of money outlined in this book as you spend
- Introducing new behaviours to reduce debt, save or invest as a result of understanding your strategy options
- Implementing new behaviours as a result of building your own strategy stacks, and getting a series of strategies to work in your favour

- Being consistent. Consistency is vital to reaching your goals, while one-off, speculative opportunities are usually surpassed by long-term hard work in the end.

A financial planner can coach you along the way, helping you reinforce the good behaviours and identify the bad behaviours you may need to rethink. Chapter 3 encourages you to set some strong foundations for your financial life, so you give yourself the best chance of success. Make an agreement with yourself to put them into place before you start strategy stacking.

It helps you achieve your personal goals

Understanding your finances is not just about learning more and changing your behaviours, it's also about giving you the best possibility to achieve your desired outcomes, such as saving for a first home, reducing the mortgage and raising a family, or retiring comfortably and debt-free. Timing is also important, so consider your goals in terms of:

- Things you want to do right now (near-term goals)
- Things you want to do in one to two years (short-term goals)
- Things you want to do in three to five years (medium-term goals)
- Things you want to do in more than five years (long-term goals).

It's important to time frame your goals with the resources you have to work with. If you don't place time frames on the outcome you're seeking, it may actually change your goals and the strategies you use to achieve them.

You may be looking for an emotional outcome from your personal goals too, such as reducing financial stress or building financial confidence. If you've never had a financial plan in place, then you might never have really experienced a feeling of certainty or confidence in your financial life.

Ultimately, the value of any personal financial planning advice—as well as any general advice you explore to increase your financial understanding, such as by reading this book—that you receive will be determined by what you want to get out of it and what goals you set. It's also important to remember that it's not just about the goals and strategies—it's also about your own financial behaviours. A financial planner can't be present 24/7—and you probably wouldn't want them to be!

PART I
THE FOUNDATIONS

I know some readers will be keen to get to the financial planning strategies that appear later in this book and start stacking the odds in their favour. If that's you, cool your jets! I genuinely ask you to pause for a moment—it's not the right place to start. Just like building a house, and especially a stable structure that will do what it is meant to do over the medium and long term, you've got to spend some time looking at the foundations that you plan to build upon.

I think the wise place to start is to look at some truths about money. I want to encourage you to think about your attitudes to money over the years as well as your relationship with it. For many people, money is transactional—it comes and goes and comes again until the next lot of expenses come along. Reflection here may help us see what we might need to change or challenge if we really want to move forward—not just with money, but in many aspects of our lives. It might also influence what you see as important within your own financial life.

I also encourage you to create what I call your 'why', which are your short-, medium- and long-term goals. Without goals, we often flounder about, not sure where we're going. Sometimes we don't make the decisions that have our best medium- and long-term interests in mind. This is often the case when goals aren't set or we haven't given ourselves the opportunity to set them.

Taking the time to set strong foundations is essential, especially if you genuinely want to give yourself the best chance of success, and I conclude this part by establishing what I think are the five foundations you need to build your strategy stack.

CHAPTER 1

Five Truths about Money

Before we start talking strategy, I'd like to ask you to explore your own attitudes towards, and your relationship with, money.

Consider the following questions:

- When did you start learning about money?

- Has money ever stressed you—or someone you know—out?

- Has your relationship with money ever felt like a love-hate relationship?

- How have you been influenced by others in your own relationship with money?

- Are you prepared to change how you manage your money?

- Are you willing to equip yourself with knowledge or seek financial planning advice to have a better relationship with money?

A big issue people have to overcome in their relationship with money relates to the preconceived ideas and assumptions they bring to the relationship. Many of these beliefs are not based on fact, and these unhelpful beliefs can impact upon your decision-making in a negative way. For example, many people don't understand what happens to their super at retirement. Despite what some people believe, you don't have to withdraw all the money from your super account and close it; in fact, doing so might have negative retirement consequences.

The truth is that many people haven't taken the time to think about the relationship they have with money and how their financial knowledge and personal biases impact what they do with their money. So, let's take a few moments to look at five truths about money—and how they might be impacting your financial life right now.

Truth 1: Your education doesn't prepare you for your adult financial life

When most of us think about our school days, we probably think of our friends, the subjects we liked, that one teacher who actually cared—and maybe, for some of us, how we wanted to get out of there and into the adult world.

Sadly, much of our childhood and teen education doesn't prepare us for adult life, particularly our adult *financial* life. The problem is more than mathematics: addition, subtraction, multiplication, division and a reasonable understanding of percentages is as much as we actually need to make sense of our finances. The problem is more about life issues.

Here are just a few issues in your adult financial life that you probably wish you'd had the answers to before you left education:

- How do I budget?
- How much can I afford to save?
- How quickly can I pay off my home loan?
- How much superannuation do I need to live a comfortable retirement?
- How do I make the most of my financial options?

These aren't unreasonable questions; they deserve more time within school classrooms—not to place undue emphasis on the love of money or getting more than you need, but to give young people the opportunity to live their best lives, without the consequences of financial stress in adulthood. Think how much happier we would all be without financial stress!

Improving financial literacy for adult life in schools is my challenge to education bureaucrats around the country. Perhaps students would benefit from taking a new subject called 'Money and Life'. Perhaps we could have fewer elective classes and more of these kinds of practical classes. However, it seems that as a society, we're more interested in equipping our kids with mobile phones so they can call us if anything goes wrong than equipping them with the knowledge to manage their adult lives. I don't understand why.

Truth 2: Your parents probably didn't prepare you for your adult financial life

If we didn't learn about money at school, then maybe our parents taught us about money instead. Right? Well, that's not the case for the overwhelming majority of Australians.

Some of us may have received pocket money when we were growing up. Unlike many of the kids of today, however, we might have had to do something to earn it. When I was a kid, I had to make my bed, take the rubbish out, and feed and walk the dog to earn my $5 a week. I can't even remember what I spent it on: probably $5 worth of mixed lollies or trading cards from the corner store. I also had a money box (though after the lollies and trading cards, I may not have had much left to put in there). Earning pocket money and adding change to my money box would have been the extent of the knowledge about money my parents gave me to prepare me for my adult financial life.

Our culture teaches us that we hide money conversations: 'That's private; we don't want anyone else knowing what we earn or what we spend'; 'It's nobody else's business.' If someone wants to know about what you do with your money, the perception is they're being invasive and rude—even if it's family. Unsurprisingly, the way we teach our kids about money is probably the result of the attitudes *we* were taught about money—so our grandparents didn't teach our parents much about money, our parents never taught us much about money...and it's likely we'll continue the same behaviour with our own kids if we don't make the decision to break this cycle.

Considering your parents' finances when you were growing up, did you know:

- How your parents managed their own budget?
- How much they could afford to save?
- How quickly they were paying off their home loan?
- How much superannuation they needed to live a comfortable retirement?
- How they made the most of their financial options?

If you can say yes to any of these, I'll be quite surprised. If you're a parent yourself, you might think, 'I'm not sure I'm ready to share that with my kids.' It's not something you'd share with a five-year-old, but you might explain your financial strategies to a 15-year-old—even just the concepts, if not the specifics—which is 100 times more than you may have got from your own parents. And your kids are probably going to inherit your money one day anyway, so why not share a little more information to help them manage it wisely?

We can't blame our parents for not preparing us for our adult financial lives—we can't change the past, and they were probably doing the best with what they had. (As the father of two children, I wonder how good a job I'm doing at times!) However, we can create a better future.

If you work for your money, then you owe it to yourself to make the most of understanding your options and take control to achieve what you want. So, put your efforts there. Thank your parents for what they did and know you can and will do even better.

Truth 3: Most people plan for a tax deduction, not a lifestyle

'Hello, accountant.' Every year, we reach a time when we reluctantly gather our receipts and expenses out of a file or shoe box and take them to an accountant, along with the payment summary from our employer. Most of us, myself included, use the services of an accountant. (Of course, if you've got the time or the interest, you might do it yourself.)

For a good segment of working adults, their accountant is the person that sorts all the tax stuff out. Every year, like many, you probably ask the same question of your accountant: 'How can I pay less tax?'

But accountants are not financial planners; the role of an accountant is to help you pay your taxes rather than help you work towards your financial goals. By law, they're not allowed to provide you with personal financial planning advice because they may not be qualified or licensed to do so. And I am not being critical of accountants here—most, including my own, do a great job at completing Australia's tax returns. However, it's important to acknowledge the difference between accountants and financial planners; after all, you don't go to a plumber if you need electrical work done.

Over the years, you may have received some useful advice from accountants about how you might improve your financial situation, such as by negatively gearing a property investment so you can claim the interest on the loan as a tax deduction. But this advice only gives you a tax deduction, it doesn't tell you what to do with the money—it doesn't help you plan for your lifestyle, or the bigger picture. How do you choose the best option for your money, while saving for the life you want to live in retirement? You probably won't know all your options if you never receive proper financial advice.

Getting more tax deductions doesn't address the big financial picture. It doesn't help you get where you're going or tell you what you need to do across a variety of areas to get there.

If your accountant is out of ideas when it comes to getting more tax deductions, then perhaps it's time to think about the bigger picture. I hope this book provides a good place to start!

Truth 4: Nothing's going to change if you don't change

Humans are creatures of habit. It's hard to change. But it's easier to change when you've got a goal that you believe is achievable, a goal that excites you and gives you what you want, and a goal that won't cause you too much pain.

The reality is most adults have lost the ability to step outside their day-to-day lives, think about their daydreams — the things they'd rather be doing with their lives — and create plans to help them get there.

My father taught me to hate waste. He hated waste in all its forms, not just wasting money. As an elite soccer coach, he also hated seeing wasted talent. This was most prominent for him when some young players would just do the bare minimum to get by. They didn't commit to extra training or learning and, as a result, never fulfilled their total potential. He also really hated people wasting their time. I think waste of money, talent and time also apply to people not living their ideal lives. Today, this is part of my own core values and why I believe change is so important if you really want to get ahead in your own life.

Why is it so difficult to change? Excuses might include:

- I don't have time.
- I don't know where to start.
- I don't have the knowledge.
- I don't know how to keep motivated.
- I don't know if it is possible to live my ideal life.

If any of these excuses apply to you, then I encourage you to challenge the things that are holding you back and preventing you from making positive changes in your life. Remember, changes can be big or small; even small changes in behaviour can make a huge difference over time.

If you don't change, no one is going to change for you. Do you think the bank wants to help you pay off that credit card or mortgage faster? Do you think that your super fund cares enough to help you work out what you need to do to reach your retirement goal? Do you think that all the people who send you bills care about your financial wellbeing—or do they just want to be paid? If it helps you to get angry enough to make a change, then get angry! Sometimes pain is the motivator of change if your dreams aren't enough.

As an adult, taking control of your financial life is your own responsibility. If you don't take steps to set yourself some targets, no one is going to do it for you. Don't you think you owe it to yourself to try and live your ideal life? I don't know for sure, but I'm guessing no one ever laid on their death bed saying, 'I wish I had lived less of my ideal life.'

Truth 5: To change, you need to equip yourself—and that's where this book comes in

Only a few generations ago, the concept of money was very simple compared to what it is today. Back then, you got paid in cash and you spent your money as cash. You might not have even had a bank account. And the saying about hiding your money under the bed may have been your reality.

Just a generation ago, we were introduced to credit cards that made getting into debt so easy, while charging interest at high rates. Regardless of this, most adult Australians have them and use them weekly. Credit card interest rates remain excessively high, at around 10–15 times higher than the cash rate set by the reserve bank (depending on the card you have).

Less than a generation ago, superannuation became compulsory. Super is the biggest asset most people own outside their family home, and yet most people don't know how to make the most of it or what their exit price (the value of their super balance) needs to be in order to live the retirement that they want. And despite super being compulsory, you have probably never been formally educated about it and your super fund is unlikely to have done a great job in helping you get the most out of it, either. The industry has grown to hold over $2.8 trillion, and many super product providers have grown fat and lazy with their members' money.

And today, in our kids' generation, money has become virtually invisible. New technologies that allow you to pay using your smartphone, watch or a tap of your card do away with notes and coins altogether. How will kids learn about money when it isn't even a real, tangible thing anymore?

Without a doubt, most people's knowledge in relation to money, financial strategies and their financial options isn't where it should be in order to make good decisions about their financial lives.

You need to equip yourself with the tools and knowledge to achieve your financial goals. That's where I hope 'strategy stacking' can help you. Even if you take just a few ideas from this book, it's better to do something than nothing.

I will share with you a range of financial planning strategies and show you how they can be stacked together to increase the likelihood of achieving your goals. There are no get-rich-quick schemes here; if you're looking to make a quick dollar, then this book isn't right for you. In fact, I'd ask you to stop reading the book right now if that sounds like you because there's nothing for you here. This is a book about strategic financial planning for the medium to long term, with actions you can take right now.

I realise that some readers who are confident 'do it yourself' investors will use this book as general advice and information to help them with their own decision-making. Some people however might use this book with a financial planner to test and explore the options and strategies available to them.

If you don't have time to learn the strategies yourself, I recommend you work with a qualified, experienced and appropriately licensed financial planner. They can provide you with the information you need to understand your options and provide strategies to help you reach your goals. That's what I do with my clients every workday.

* * *

The five truths about money might be challenging to some readers, and that's okay. My clients often share their regret at not realising what they didn't know about money, and how much time they lost when they could have been making better financial planning decisions.

It's particularly hard for those approaching retirement—many have lost decades of opportunities to boost their super or take other financial actions that could have made a big difference to the outcomes they could have achieved. If that sounds like you, don't be disheartened. You still have options available, you just may not have the ideal amount of time on your side. I ask you not to regret the time you've lost; in fact, turn it into a positive and share your newfound knowledge with others, or buy a copy of this book for a friend or a younger person in your life. Tell them you want them to have a good financial life when you gift it to them.

Taking the time to set up your own financial plan for success pays dividends—and I'm not just talking about money from shares. Having a financial plan provides you with increased confidence and actionable steps you can take to put yourself in a better financial position.

CHAPTER 2

Your Adult Financial Life Starts and Ends with 'Why?'

Why?

It's the most challenging of all the questions we get in life. It requires us to provide more information and, in some cases, justify ourselves. In that context, being asked 'Why?' can sometimes be very confronting.

Let's give some 'why' questions a go:

- Why didn't you get up an hour earlier this morning and hit the gym?
- Why were you late to work?
- Why did you eat that second piece of cheesecake?
- Why do I keep asking these annoying questions?

Well, sorry to keep asking, but when it comes to your lifestyle goals and your financial wellbeing, it starts and ends with your 'why'.

Why is this, you might ask? That's a question that's easier to answer. It's because:

- Only you can answer it
- Only you can hold yourself accountable.

Your 'why' really reflects what your own needs, wants and future ambitions are. Sounds simple, right? Well, not really in my experience. We're complicated human beings and our decisions are based on lots of things, not necessarily all of them focused on our financial wellbeing. It's worth the effort to spend some time here on your own 'why'. Your 'why' will help you focus your attention on setting your goals and determining what your financial priorities are.

Figuring out your 'why'

A financial planner can assist you if you're open to seeking advice, but not even they can tell you what your 'why' is.

I have spent hundreds of hours helping my clients to figure out their own 'why'. I often start by asking them why they have the investments they have. Typically, I get one of four reasons:

- **The rational reason:** 'I thought it was a good investment providing a good return.' This investment decision appears to be based on *logic*.

- **The social/emotional reason:** 'My friend/relative was doing it, so I thought I'd do it too.' This investment decision appears to be based on *feelings*.

- **The process reason:** 'It seemed like the next step to take.' This investment decision appears to be based on a *process*.

- **The creative reason:** 'I had an idea and that's what I did.' This investment reason appears to be based on something that *inspired* them.

These are all reasonable answers. But the reality is not one of them really answered the question 'Why?'

Finding your 'why' is really about uncovering what's most important to you and the reasons behind it. It's about goal setting. Furthermore, it's about goal setting that has your honest needs, wants and desires at heart.

We're all different, so everyone's 'why' is going to be different. I've had clients tell me, in confidence, about all kinds of goals. Many of them have common themes and connect to important aspects of my clients' lives. Yet, for most of my clients, my question of 'why' is the first time they have stopped and thought about what matters most to them.

It's also essential to note that the 'why' should never be about money itself. That's because money isn't a real end within itself, in my opinion. Money is only ever a facilitator to doing what you actually want to do.

I can't tell you what your 'why' is, but hopefully I can inspire you to define it.

So, what is your own 'why' about? As a starting point, might it be:

- Comfortably meeting your day-to-day physical needs?
- Providing you with financial security, now and in the future?
- Being with the people you want to be with?
- Following an ambition you have, such as a career, activity or hobby?
- Solving a problem or challenge?

Maybe one of these suggestions has helped to lead you towards identifying your 'why', or perhaps it is something else I haven't covered here, but hopefully this list has given you a place to start. Remember, only you can answer your 'why'.

As an activity, by yourself or with your partner, I encourage you to write a list of your true needs, wants and desires. Together, these things represent your 'why'. Stick your list on the fridge for a month and think about it. Modify things. Cross things out. Add new things that you think of until you feel that your list is complete.

Challenging your 'why'

It's also helpful to challenge the things on your list to make sure they deserve to be there. How might you do this? One way is to imagine you're at the end of your life, thinking over all you have achieved. If you achieve everything on your list, do you think you would be happy? If not, what's missing? Are there some things on the list that really don't belong there? Might there be better pursuits you could be spending your valuable and finite time on?

Understanding your 'why' is the most important step of your adult financial life. By no means is it easy. We all have hopes and dreams. Equally, we all have fears. Navigating your way through these emotions isn't always a walk in the park, and finding your 'why' requires real effort.

When you find it though, for the first time in your adult financial life you'll be content. For the first time in your life, you'll have concrete reasons for getting out of bed and doing what you do. You'll be living your life with purpose.

Adding a time frame

When you know what your 'why' is, you then need to apply a time frame. Adding a time frame creates a motivation for you to get moving on your 'why'.

I encourage you to break down your 'why' into short-term, medium-term and long-term goals:

- **Short-term goals:** What needs to be completed in one to two years.

- **Medium-term goals:** What needs to be completed in three to five years.

- **Long-term goals:** What needs to be completed in six to 10+ years.

When you think about your 'why' in terms of time, make sure you pick an appropriate time frame for each of your goals. For example:

- You want to pay down your $4000 credit card debit—and you realise you can clear this over the next 12 months.

- You want to save $20000 to put towards upgrading your car—and you realise you can afford to do this over the next four years (saving $5000 a year).

- You want to retire at age 65 with $750000 in super—and you realise you can make contributions to super above what your employer contributes to help you achieve that outcome in 35 years' time by doing some retirement balance projections.

Of course, you can add as many short-, medium- and long-term goals to help you reach your 'why' as you need to. It's your 'why', after all, and financial planning at its core is about helping people achieve their own 'why'. This book gives you the tools you need to make these goals achievable, whatever your goal.

So, add a time frame to your goals too before you stick it on the fridge. It's a great reminder of long-term planning and helps motivate you beyond thinking about the short-term goals. There's a bigger picture at stake now, and you've got something concrete, meaningful and inspiring to work towards.

CHAPTER 3

Setting Strong Foundations

Now that you've established your own 'why', there are five foundational principles you need to think about if you're serious about achieving your goals and making changes that will impact your life.

The five foundations are:

- **Foundation 1:** Respect your earnings
- **Foundation 2:** Pay attention to your spending
- **Foundation 3:** The cost of money is interest
- **Foundation 4:** Be realistic
- **Foundation 5:** Reward yourself.

Just like footings underneath a house, the strength of these foundations will determine how well your 'why' holds up once you start to do what you need to do to achieve your goals.

In this chapter, we take a closer look at these foundations.

Foundation 1: Respect your earnings

For most of us, *earnings* (or income) are what we receive in return for going to work. Earnings also includes money you receive from other sources, such as dividends from shares, interest on term deposits, rent from a property investment or the income earned from any other investments you have.

You might think that bank interest or those share dividends aren't important, given they don't add much to your pocket. However, if you have \$75 000 in savings and you earn 4 per cent on that over a year, that's a \$3000 return!

Over two years, it's \$6000; over three years, it's \$9000; over four years, it's \$12 000; over five years, it's \$15 000.

If you were to reinvest the earnings each year, you'd also get interest on your reinvested earnings (this is called *compounding interest*). Over five years, that would lead to a \$16 248.97 return in total. I talk more about compounding interest in Foundation 3.

Earnings are not that insignificant at all really, when you look at it like that. I'm sure you could do a lot with \$16 000.

Why are earnings important?

Earnings are important for two reasons:

- Your earnings income funds your living needs for today.
- Your earnings have the ability to fund the goals that you want to achieve in the future; plus, income will be the backbone of your retirement planning and lifestyle in your later years.

Income is King when it comes to a strong foundation!

Things to be mindful of

While most of us think about the weekly and monthly income we get, we fail to see how important that income is over a working life. Income from your work is likely to be your biggest source of earnings. For example, \$1500 a week translates into an income of \$78 000 a year (\$1500 × 52 weeks). 'So what?' I hear you say.

Well, over a 45-year career (from ages 20–65), that \$78 000 a year is actually worth \$3.51 million. Shut the gate! Even to a person who has money, that's not an insignificant figure, yet most of us don't think about the long-term value of our incomes and what we might do differently in our lives if we were more aware of this number. That's because we're typically not very good medium- and long-term planners.

I want you to pause for a moment and open the calculator on your smartphone (or dig out your calculator from wherever it's hibernating). Work out your annual income number (weekly income × 52, or you can multiply your fortnightly income by 26 or your monthly income by 12) and jot it in the margin of this book (or on a piece of paper, if handy). Multiply the number of years you have left in the workforce by your current annual take-home pay. I bet the number surprises you.

Here's a quick example. Chris has 15 years left in the workforce. Chris earns $90 000 a year, which makes his number $1 350 000 (15 × $90 000). That number is significant, I'm sure you'd agree. What's your number?

When you understand your lifetime earnings, it becomes easier to respect those earnings and appreciate the importance of protecting them (which you can achieve with many of the strategies in this book).

Additionally, don't dismiss your investment earnings; instead, consider how you might reinvest them. Your superannuation account already does this for you, primarily because you're not able to access any of the money until retirement age. Many Australians are surprised that with some long-term planning, they can put a savings and investment plan together that replaces the income that they receive from going to work every day. By finding better ways to save and invest, and with the benefit of compounding interest, they see they might be able to give up work altogether and live off the nest egg they've created. This frees them up to be doing the things they'd rather be doing (or perhaps reduce their 38+ hour work week).

Of course, careers are rarely smooth in the modern age. While our parents and grandparents may have had a job for life, this isn't likely to be the case for us. Breaks in work to start families, redundancies and career changes can all interrupt our earnings.

On the plus side, promotions and pay reviews can positively increase our earnings. Changing jobs is one of the best ways to get a pay rise—you can often negotiate what you want on your way in, which is often harder to do after you've joined a business. Upskilling yourself through training (investing in yourself) is another a good way to get a pay rise. Also, I cannot stress enough the financial value of a good recruiter to help you plan your career and secure pay-rise opportunities.

Respect your earnings. Over a lifetime, they are significant. Most people only think about their 'today' needs, but your future needs are equally important if you genuinely wish to achieve your medium- and long-term goals. Don't just plan for the weeks or months, plan for the years too.

Foundation 2: Pay attention to your spending

For most of us, *spending* (or our *expenses*) is what we do with our income after we earn it. Expenses come in many forms, from groceries to petrol; from utilities like your telephone, internet, electricity and water to even bigger expenses, such as buying a car or home.

You might think some expenses aren't important—for example, that cup of coffee you grab on your way to work or that chocolate bar you pick up at the checkout each week when you do the food shopping run. However, sometimes it's the small things that we don't pay attention to that cost us more than we'd care to spend over the longer term—if we'd thought about it.

Imagine that daily workday coffee costs you $4 each day. Over five days, that's $20 (5 × $4). Over 48 working weeks, assuming you take four weeks' annual leave, that's $960 (48 × 5 × $4). Over five years, your workday coffee costs you $4800 (5 × 48 × 5 × $4). Is there something else you'd rather be spending that money on? Perhaps an overseas holiday?

How about that weekly chocolate treat? Each time, say it costs you $3. Over a year, it's actually costing you $156 (52 × $3). Over five years, it costs you $780 (5 × 52 × $3). Now, $780 isn't $4800, but if you have enough of these small, coffee and chocolate kinds of habits the money starts to add up.

Most adults make a plan to earn a certain amount of money—that's why they go to work every day. Most adults, however, don't make a plan for how to spend it. And just like thinking about your earnings over the longer term, it's also worth your while to think about your spending over the longer term too.

Technology today makes spending very easy. A swipe or tap of a card or phone and we've paid for something without having any emotional connection to the transaction or actual value. Technology is like kryptonite when it comes to budgeting and controlling your spending! So, you need to make a spending plan.

Why is spending important?

Spending is important as it directly impacts your ability to save money. Without the ability to save money, trying to achieve your lifestyle and financial goals would be like poking yourself in the face with a stick. Painful, a waste of time, and it would surely leave you uninspired!

Spending today, without adding to your savings, might be great for today in that you achieve your short-term goals. In a world of instant gratification, spending is easier than ever before with 'tap and go' technology. We don't even see the money anymore. However, if you make the choice to just spend to live for today, and don't add to your savings at all, it leaves you with nowhere to go in the medium and long term with your lifestyle goals. So, spending is an opportunity cost. This means you have the opportunity to get something now by spending, or you have the choice to not spend right now, and save for something in the future.

Things to be mindful of

Beware of those habitual purchases that don't seem like much at the time. Those habits, repeated frequently, may cost you more than you think over time.

That doesn't mean you can't have any treats or fun in the short term when you're trying to achieve your medium- and long-term lifestyle and financial goals—it's just about planning for what you actually want. If a daily coffee is something you don't want to give up altogether (or you'd struggle to turn into a treat rather than it being an everyday habit), look to save some money elsewhere—perhaps by reviewing your utility providers, so you can change providers to find savings. By finding savings in areas of your life that you're less attached to, you may find it easier to make the savings. Changing out utility providers or swapping some expensive grocery brands for cheaper ones might be more agreeable if you love your workday coffee!

There's a great blur today between our needs, wants and desires. In times past, needs simply included food, clothing and shelter. Today, your 'needs' might include the latest iPhone, a Spotify subscription, a daily coffee and access to the internet. One of my clients' kids told me that he thought free Wi-Fi should be a human right! Talk about blurred lines.

If you're serious about wanting to achieve your medium- to long-term lifestyle and financial goals, then you need to think more about how you spend and make a plan. It will give you the ability to focus on what's actually important to you. Small changes over the medium and longer term will help you achieve results. I'm not saying you give up your wants and desires altogether—that's actually been shown not to work (foundation 5 covers rewarding yourself in more detail).

The final part to spending I wanted to share with you was the idea of value-checking. When you go to make a purchase, whether it is a day-to-day purchase or a larger purchase, stop and give yourself some time to review your spending and think, 'Is this value for money?' Ask yourself, 'Do I need to buy the most expensive brand to get the value out of this purchase?' Probably not.

For the life of me, I can't get my head around some of my smart clients who buy shoes or handbags that cost between $1000 and $2500. I'm not going to mention any brand names as I think those providers are making a killing as it is. Clearly to me, it's not good value. There's only so much leather and material you can put into a pair of shoes or a handbag, and I don't need to pay for that label—which is what you're actually paying for. But if your goal is to own those items and you save and achieve your goal, then that's your choice—it's not for me or anyone else to say what your 'why' should be. It's your money, they're your goals, you've worked hard for that money, so go and spend it as you like!

Have a plan to spend and a plan to save. I've seen clients earning high six-figure salaries who still need to come back to these basics. Planning your spending is fundamentally important—it directly impacts your ability to save.

Foundation 3: The cost of money is interest

Most things we do in life have a price. When we go to the shop to buy something, it's going to cost us money. When we go for a walk or on a bike ride for exercise, it costs us time and calories. It's important to realise that money also has a price, which is called *interest*. I wish more people took an interest in the interest of money over their adult lives, as it has the ability to deliver financial outcomes without them having to work extra hours in their day job.

If you save money, you can earn interest. It's the income you earn for letting someone else use your money.

If you have debt, you will pay interest. It's the fee you pay for using someone else's money until the debt is paid back. Interest is essentially a tax on your patience. In a world of 'give it to me now', this can be a bigger issue than you may realise.

In days gone by (and before banks found a way to make money out of it), people would lend money themselves and charge the recipient interest. The terms might have been spelt out in an IOU (in other words, 'I owe you'). The person lending the money would make their own risk assessment about the likelihood they were going to get paid back, and use this assessment to set an interest rate based on the likely risk and time frame.

Today, the Reserve Bank of Australia sets the 'cash rate', which is the interest rate on overnight loans in the money market. This is meant to guide what banks and other lenders charge as interest for the debts they provide, and what they pay as interest on the savings they hold for others.

At the time of writing, the Reserve Bank of Australia has set the cash rate at 3.1 per cent. However, it has the ability to change the cash rate every month. Over time, the average interest rate has been much higher than at the time of writing—at an average of 4.12 per cent between May 1992 and May 2022. So, we can reasonably expect that interest rates will become higher, moving forward.

However, whether we're talking long-term averages or current values, our financial institutions have been charging these kinds of interest rates:

- Credit card interest rates of around 19 to 25 per cent (per annum), plus an annual card fee

- Home loan interest rates of around 3 to 6 per cent (per annum), plus fees

- Unsecured personal loan interest rates of around 5 to 9 per cent (per annum), plus fees

- Overdraft interest rates of around 16 to 18 per cent.

At the same time, these financial institutions are only paying between 0.15 to 3.5 per cent on our term deposits (typical at the time of writing for a 12-month term).

There's a big gap between the less than 3 per cent you can earn on your term deposit and the over 19 per cent you might be charged on a credit card. Where's that other 16 per cent return going? It's likely to be going straight into paying the bank's costs, and the rest is profit. The Royal Commission into the Banking, Superannuation and Financial Services Industry found in 2019 that consumers had next to no power to negotiate the terms on the financial products they use. The reality is this is unlikely to change, and while you might ask your bank if they can give you a better rate on your savings, chances are they won't.

Thankfully, interest doesn't just come out of bank term deposit products. You can receive a return on:

- Dividends through shares

- Distributions from managed funds

- Interest or dividends through exchange-traded funds (ETFs)

- Rent through property
- Distributions from listed property.

Distributions might be a new term to you. It simply means the payment made to the investor from the investment provider, and it reflects the income distributed from the asset over a specific period of time.

Why is interest important?

Getting a return (the interest) on your money is fundamentally important if you want to stop work one day or achieve your other medium- and long-term goals without working more hours in your day job.

It's also important because once you have the ability to save and you have earnings from your investments, you can reinvest your interest and earn interest on your interest. This is called *compounded interest*.

Here's how it works.

Imagine you invest $1000. You earn a 4 per cent return in a year, and for every year your money is invested.

After a year, you'll have earned $40 in interest. If you take those earnings and invest them back into the same investment, in year two you'll have $1040 to invest and you'll have earned $41.60 by the end of the year. If you reinvest those earnings again, you'll earn $43.36 in interest at the end of the third year.

Using small numbers like these means that might not look like much. But over time, and with larger sums of money, it can make a real difference.

Let's take a look with a larger number.

Imagine you invest $100000. In year one, you earn $4000 in interest. If you take those earnings and invest them back into the same investment, in year two you'll have $104000 to invest and you'll earn $4160 in interest. If you reinvest those earnings again, you'll earn $4336 in interest at the end of the third year.

Compounding accelerates the growth of your money because you're earning interest on your interest. It's one of the ways the wealthiest people sustain their wealth without taking too much risk. They have more than they need immediately available to them, and it just builds up over time without too much effort from them. As a result, I cannot stress enough the value of time and good financial behaviour!

You may be wondering, 'Is there an easy way to work out compounding interest?'

Well, yes and no. There is, and it's a formula that I challenge you to get your head around:

Future Value = P (1 + R)^N

Where:

- P stands for the principal, which is the amount of money you initially invest.
- R stands for the rate of interest you invest at as a decimal — for example, 5 per cent is 0.05 over the life of the investment.
- N stands for number, which in this case is the number of years over which the investment is made.

Let's look at an example, where the principal investment (P) is $50 000, the rate of interest (R) is 5 per cent (or 0.05 as a decimal) and the number of years (N) is 20 years.

Using the formula:

Future Value = 50 000 × (1 + 0.05)^{20}

$= 50\,000 \times 1.05^{20}$

$= \$132\,664.89$

If you've got a 'future value' financial goal in mind, you can use this formula to help you play with some numbers and work out your options.

Things to be mindful of

What goal might be achieved by getting into debt, and is there another way? Be aware that paying interest through holding any kind of debt is going to cost you.

Before you get into debt, regardless of how small or large, you need to make a plan to pay it back. Your plan might include interest-focused solutions, such as:

- Shopping around for the best interest rate you can get—you can even re-check the rates during the term of your loan (if it's a home loan/mortgage, for example). Paying more interest than you need to robs you of the opportunity to save more money for your other medium- and long-term lifestyle and financial goals. Banks don't deserve your loyalty. I've seen clients save tens of thousands of dollars by doing this.

- Considering how you invest to help you meet your medium- and long-term financial goals.

- Being prepared to put your money to work so it earns interest.

- Reinvesting those earnings over time so your money works even harder, earning interest on the interest.

These examples are by no means complete. There are more strategies in Part 3 of this book to help you think about what you can do with your money to help you reach your goals more effectively.

Interest and compounding interest aren't that exciting or sexy. But is that really what you want from your investments? Probably not, if you stop and really think about it.

Also consider seeking the advice of a mortgage broker to do the hard work for you. That's what they do—find better deals. A good mortgage broker also takes away the 'it's too hard' feeling you might have. To them, it's not.

Working with a broker to save money on your mortgage is one of the simplest ways to improve your cash flow. Pay less interest, save more money, buy more income-earning assets. There you go: you're making a strategy stack without even realising it, and someone else did the heavy lifting! In all my years, my bank has never called me to check I was on the best deal with them. Don't wait for that call—go and get a better rate!

Foundation 4: Be realistic

Being *realistic* means quite simply to 'keep it real'. Most people don't live life like they are a celebrity billionaire. And to be honest, would you really want to live like that, with everyone watching what you do all the time, and wondering if people really liked you or just liked the trappings of your money? So, be realistic when it comes to setting your own financial foundations.

I spend a great deal of my time as a financial planner talking to clients about what's really important to them, what they want from their lives now and in their life after work, and if what they want can be realistically achieved without them taking risks that they're not comfortable with taking.

Often the answer is yes. Their goals are realistic, especially if they've been sensible with their money.

Sometimes though, the answer is no. And it's normally because of one or more of these reasons:

- They've put themselves in a debt hole and they don't know how to get out.

- They're not being sensible with their money (and often there's great waste).

- They don't have the willingness to change.

- They don't want to set medium- and longer-term goals.

- They can't commit to their own goals.

- They want a quick fix when a quick fix isn't possible.

- They've left their planning too late and no longer have time on their side.

Money conversations about what's realistic and what's not can be highly emotional. I've had people in tears about their or their children's financial lives. I've had more than one client say to me, a year off retirement, that they wish they'd received financial planning advice 10 years ago: 'I wish someone had told me that.'

Why is it important to be realistic?

Some things in life are filled with emotion: things like the start of a relationship, getting your driver's licence, buying your first home, your wedding day or the birth of a child. However, you don't want to live an emotional financial life. Financial stress has been shown to physically impact your personal health and emotionally impact important relationships. I've seen people in bad situations, and it's not a place you want to be.

Certainty, which is partially provided by being realistic, can help you live a more stable and confident financial life. This is regardless of how old you are—and even in the face of other emotional situations.

Being realistic also helps keep you motivated to achieve your 'why'. If a goal is attainable then you're more likely to do what it is that you need to, in order to achieve it. Being realistic therefore means you take it a step at a time.

Time is the key when it comes to being realistic. My father once told me, 'You can't make jam out of pig poo, and it doesn't matter how you mix it.' He was right. But what you can do is fertilise those strawberry plants and grow strawberries, which you can then make jam from eventually. It involves different kinds of behaviour and being realistic with your time frame.

Things to be mindful of

Being specific about your 'why' is really important. The better you can define it, and the more realistic your goals are, the more you'll be focused on achieving your 'why', as well as focused on the reason it's important to you.

Remember: 'You don't know what you don't know.' There are gaps in all our knowledge, which is one of the reasons I'm writing this book. I know there might be ways of achieving your goals that you don't yet know about. Being realistic doesn't mean you become negative or limit yourself, but there might be a way to achieve what you'd like to achieve that you don't know about yet. I hope this book can help you on your journey towards discovering those solutions.

Like negativity, also be aware of being too positive. In recent times we've seen a positive movement that suggests life is all sunshine and ponies. It's the movement that gives our kids a medal for running in a race, regardless of when they arrived at the finish line. If you're a fan of this movement, all the best to you. I worry though that we're not teaching kids to be realistic and we're setting them up to be over-positive.

Logically, I think it's important to understand there are limitations and risks in everything we do. However, these limitations and risks don't have to stop us from achieving our goals. If you can identify the obstacles that might get in your way, you can also make plans to deal with them. This is where I see financial planning strategies coming in, both singularly or stacked, as they can do all sorts of things to help you achieve your 'why'.

Foundation 5: Reward yourself

The idea of *rewarding yourself* means that you don't make achieving your 'why' an absolutely painful chore—instead, you remember to make time to celebrate along the way.

So, when do you reward yourself? It's a long time to wait to reward yourself for a three- to five-year goal, or an even longer-term goal. If you set milestones along your medium- and long-term goal journey, you may find these are great points to celebrate a little.

The reward itself doesn't need to be over the top, so aim to keep it proportionate to the goal. But it does need to be a treat—an item or event that brings you pleasure.

I sometimes think we've lost the concept of a treat. Young people in particular don't want to have to wait for anything: it's all about instant gratification. It's a dangerous habit to get into and doesn't often support the achievement of medium- and long-term goals.

But what form should a reward take? Well, in part it depends on the goal you're working to achieve. Here are some ideas:

- Dinner at your favourite restaurant
- A new pair of runners
- Gold-class movie tickets
- A remedial massage
- A weekend away on the coast
- Something as simple as ordering in your favourite take-out and opening a bottle of wine.

Why is rewarding yourself important?

Rewarding yourself is important to help you maintain your motivation and achieve your 'why'.

I've seen too many people set their 'why' and go too hard to achieve it. Unfortunately, they forget they still need to be able to live today, and so their long-term goal achievement sacrifices their short-term goals altogether, leaving no joy in their lives in the near term. The goal then becomes too hard to achieve.

Often when this happens, people have what I can only describe as a 'blow out'. They stop heading in the right direction and do a 180-degree turn, and they go backwards faster than even they thought possible. It's only once they pause that they realise the damage that they've done to all the good work they'd achieved so far.

Achievement points or milestones along the way mark your medium- to long-term success to date, and you get a reward. Perhaps it's a quarterly or six-monthly treat. With these in place, you're more likely to achieve your longer-term vision. These intermittent rewards provide you with acknowledgement of what you've achieved to date, as well as motivation to keep going towards your medium- or long-term goals (your 'why').

Things to be mindful of

Remember to keep the concept of a treat as a treat—it's not something you have every day. Also, make sure the treat is something that really brings you happiness. We most often associate treats with food, but it doesn't have to be a food reward—instead, it might be an experience you can enjoy.

If you find yourself slipping, re-assess your achievement points or milestones. Talk about them with your partner (if you have one, or find someone to talk about them with if you don't). Having a financial planner as an accountability buddy also works.

If you do manage to blow yourself up, then try to learn from that experience. The worst thing you can do is give up on your 'why' after a blow out. That would be a real tragedy. It reminds me of a good quote I once heard: 'I never lose, I only win and learn.'

* * *

I cannot stress enough how important it is to set good financial foundations. Without solid foundations, you are not giving yourself the best chance to succeed with the strategies you stack on top of them. Hopefully by now you have started to understand your own 'why' and are able to commit to setting some strong foundations in your own financial life.

In Part II, I explore how stacking financial strategies works.

PART II
STRATEGY STACKING

Strategy stacking is a personalised approach I take to creating financial plans for my clients. In this part, I explain the strategy stacking philosophy I use with my clients—what strategy stacking is, why you do it and how it can help you achieve your 'why'. As you might expect, there are some rules around strategy stacking—it starts with the Basic Stack and your 'why'.

It's important to note that the strategy stacks you build for yourself will change over time and be influenced by key life events. Everyone's needs change over time, so it's important to acknowledge that. Therefore, I also share with you the importance of understanding your financial starting position and factoring time into your plan, which is where the Strategy Stacking Calendar comes in.

Finally, before I talk you through the strategies in detail in Part III, I offer some common scenarios of how strategy stacking can help you achieve your 'why' over a lifetime, from saving to buy a house to putting up your feet and enjoying the rewards of your efforts at retirement.

CHAPTER 4

Understanding the Strategy Stacking Philosophy

The concept for strategy stacking came about as a result of a conversation with one of my colleagues. We were talking about how I could explain what I do to new and potential clients. He liked my approach of stacking financial planning strategies, so it became the name we used to describe how I help clients reach their goals. The objective of strategy stacking is to put together different financial planning strategies to help my clients stack the odds in their favour and give them the greatest probability of achieving their goals.

In its simplest form, a philosophy is an attitude or theory that acts as a guide and provides wisdom. To help you make sense of my strategy stacking philosophy, let's consider a few essential questions:

- **What is strategy stacking?** Strategy stacking is the process of putting together different financial planning strategies to create a financial plan. The strategies you stack (or don't stack) will have an impact on your financial life. Strategy stacking is designed to help you maximise the probability of reaching your financial goals.

- **Who is strategy stacking for?** Strategy stacking is for people who want to improve their financial position. Most of my clients are singles or couples. But sometimes they can be joint business owners too. If people aren't engaged with their financial life, I'd argue strategy stacking is not for them.

- **When should you strategy stack?** As soon as you're old enough to earn superannuation, strategy stacking is something you should give thought to. Superannuation of course is a long-term savings vehicle for your retirement and only one component of your financial life. Starting early often means you reach your goals sooner.

- **How do you strategy stack?** How you strategy stack is fundamentally determined by your 'why'—your short-, medium- and long-term goals. As a result, everyone's strategy stack will be different as we all start from a different set of financial circumstances and we all have different financial goals.

This also means that how you strategy stack will change as your life changes. A single person will have different circumstances and goals from a couple or a parent. Of course, some long-term goals (like owning a home or retiring early) may remain the same. It's important to change your approach to strategy stacking to reflect the best stacking approach for you at a given point in time. As a result, strategy stacking is not a set-and-forget process. Chapter 8 shows some strategy stacking scenarios at different life stages.

Like building a tower out of children's building blocks, there are some rules around how to stack strategies. However, unlike a child's building blocks, there's a real danger to your financial health if you get your financial strategy stack wrong and the stack comes tumbling down—which is why I recommend that you use this book alongside advice from a qualified financial planner (Part 4 covers working with a financial planner).

My strategy stacking philosophy is a set of ideas, attitudes and theories that I designed to help me make sense of my clients' personal situations and stack financial planning strategies in their favour. No one strategy can fix or change everything, but using a selection of carefully considered strategies in conjunction with others can make a huge difference over time.

Remember: no financial philosophy can guarantee you results, and anyone who offers guaranteed financial strategy outcomes without explaining the risks should be treated with caution. Understanding risk is an essential part of my stacking philosophy.

Here are the 'rules' of the strategy stacking philosophy I use with my clients.

Understand your 'why'

Without having a clear understanding of your goals or purpose, you can't stack strategies, which is why I spend a great deal of time when I first meet with new clients understanding their 'why'. It perhaps takes an hour or more, depending on how clear they are on the outcomes or goals they're looking to achieve. Often, couples seeking advice realise in the process that they need to have a new conversation about where they want to go.

Without the end in mind, you won't know if you've reached your destination. It would be like getting into the car and starting to drive, without knowing where you're going—or why you're even in the car in the first place. In this case, you should probably head back home and keep off the roads until you get clarity. You'd be a danger to yourself and others!

No one can tell you what your 'why' should be. A good financial planner will offer ideas but their real value is in providing a reality check in terms of what is possible and what isn't and highlighting the options you might not know you have. On my radio show, I say 'you don't know what you don't know' nearly every week, and it remains true to this day. I've lost track of the times a client has said to me 'I wish someone had told me that 10 years ago' after they realise they've had an opportunity sitting right there that could've been helping them reach their 'why'. I can also understand why people don't seek financial advice—you can't value what you don't understand, but that hesitation may be a lot more expensive than you realise.

Understanding your 'why' is the most imperative part of your strategy stack. If you don't have a clear and specific 'why', you'll most certainly build a stack in the wrong place and deliver ambiguous outcomes. (Chapter 2 explores the essentials of understanding your 'why'.)

Remember the five foundations

If you forget about the five foundations of money (refer to Chapter 3), you're sure to build unstable strategy stacks. Let's quickly recap them now:

1. Respect your earnings.

2. Pay attention to your spending.

3. The cost of money is interest.

4. Be realistic.

5. Reward yourself.

All these foundations are important to create a solid strategy stack. Ignoring one or all of these foundations is like getting into a car and actively deciding not to follow some or all of the road rules. For the car buffs out there, it's like not replacing a balding tyre or worn brake pads. If you expect you can continue to drive another 25 000km without increased risk, you're likely to be sorely disappointed when it starts to rain or there are other challenging road conditions. In that context, you can imagine just how dangerous ignoring these foundations might be for your own financial wellbeing.

It's easy to think that some of the foundations are less important than others—for example, that you can build a stack without having to reward yourself along the way—but you need all five foundations in place. You might feel fresh and confident right now, but fatigue and the general (and often unexpected) challenges of life will appear on your journey to derail your progress. We all have those moments that get us down, when we might do something that's not a part of our normal financial behaviour. Genuine short-term rewards are important, not only to celebrate, but to act as milestones that show you're still heading in the right direction towards that bigger goal.

If you're ever in doubt about the importance of these foundations, I encourage you to think about the risk of taking short-cuts on any of them. Even if one of the foundations isn't solid, it can infiltrate how solid your strategy stack is in the short term—and it can have unexpected medium- to long-term effects too that may impact your 'why'. Think of it like this. These foundations are the ground that you stack strategies upon and help achieve your goals. The ground needs to be solid.

Start with the Basic Stack: Budgeting, where earnings meet spending

The time has come to acknowledge the fundamental truth about strategy stacking:

> *Understanding what you earn and what you spend is essential if you want to genuinely stack strategies in your favour.*

I can't tell you the number of times I've sat in financial planning meetings with highly experienced and highly qualified people who work hard and earn good money, yet they're wondering why they feel like they're not getting ahead. They know they're smart and have had success, but they can't seem to get it together. I've had the same experience with plenty of couples and singles too, even retirees. And it always comes down to their budget—their Basic Stack.

Your budget is the floor upon which you build your stack.

Let me repeat that.

Your budget is the floor upon which you build your stack.

This means that creating a budget, managing your money and reviewing your budget isn't up for negotiation if you seriously want to make a difference to the outcomes you're presently achieving in your financial life.

41

Without a budget, you're building your stack on sand—and if there's one guarantee I can make in this strategy book, it's that if you build anything on sand, including your financial house, sooner or later it will fall down.

So if you genuinely want to move forward, regardless of your situation, the budget is your starting point (and a big part of Chapter 6, which helps you assess your starting position).

Over the years, I've seen clients take different approaches to budgeting. Some are very thorough, where they develop a budget within a spreadsheet or on paper and they know what's coming in and going out down to the last cent. Others take a more casual approach—they don't have anything in writing but, broadly, they know what's coming in and out and are able to manage the gaps, often by using a credit card.

Many people think that if they just earned more money, they'd be able to manage better. As a strategy, there's nothing wrong with upskilling yourself and going for job promotions. Experience tells me though that earning more money isn't always the solution. I've met with clients over the years who have been exceptional income earners, but their financial life was probably worse than what yours is right now. Why? Because they've never used a budget. Sometimes the greater the cash flow, the greater the struggle to control where your money goes because you can always justify to yourself that you can afford it or deserve it. Yet without a budget, you'll build an unstable strategy stack.

Typically, the more money people earn, the more money people are willing to spend. Over time, most people upgrade their material life. It might start with a better brand of toaster or new bath towels. Inevitably, it turns into designer clothes and an imported luxury car. And if you don't plan for this spending, there's no budget to keep track of things.

Having a detailed budget helps you keep in control of the five foundations, which is essential if you want to stack other strategies on top and put the odds in your favour. We'll take a closer look at budget management and other fundamental strategies—the Framing Strategies—in Chapter 9. However, there are a couple more points about budgeting that we should consider further here, and they relate to the first two foundations: respect your earnings and pay attention to your spending.

Your income is more than your wage

Most people think that income is just what their boss pays them—and at one point, I used to think this too: I went to work and I earned my income.

I was paid fortnightly when I first started work. I worked harder sometimes than others; however, my income was always the same. Like many people I also did overtime, but I didn't get paid any extra. I did get a bonus or two, but I never really understood how they worked it out—it didn't seem to reflect my performance. I'm not complaining about it though: every bit helped.

I suspect many people reading this book can relate to my experience: you work hard, but there are only ever so many hours in the day. Like all wage-earners, you sell your time for money.

It's important that if you're going to be a wage-earner or time-seller, you sell your time for the best income you can receive. Upskilling yourself, building your career and changing employers when the time is right are very important to increase your earnings.

So, some questions for you:

- Are you being paid reasonably well for the work you're doing?

- If not, can you earn a better income for doing the same work somewhere else?

- What training or qualifications do you need to take the next career step?

- How much can you earn once you take the next step in your career?

- What impact on your budget will increased earnings have?

- How much can you save to make the most of your income?

I challenge you to think about these questions.

I also challenge you to think about generating a second income stream for yourself. You could do this by getting a second job or starting a side hustle (a side hustle or side job is an additional income-making activity you take on in addition to your primary job). Today, so many people have side hustles alongside their full-time jobs. Many of them are internet businesses and involve something that genuinely interests them.

Ideally, however, the second income that I'm really talking about is an income that doesn't involve selling any more of your time for income. I'm guessing many people reading this are busy enough with work, family and life and don't have any more free time they can sell.

What I'm talking about is income from investments. It's money that works for you, without you having to sell your time.

You might read that and think investment income isn't income. But it is, and over time many people replace their job or dial down their full-time role to part-time off the back of their investment income.

Consider the simple examples in table 4.1, showing what your investment income might earn at a few different rates of return.

Table 4.1: Investment rates of return

Amount invested	Rates of return			
	3%	6%	9%	12%
$10 000	$300	$600	$900	$1200
$25 000	$750	$1500	$2250	$3000
$50 000	$1500	$3000	$4500	$6000
$100 000	$3000	$6000	$9000	$12 000
$200 000	$6000	$12 000	$18 000	$24 000
$300 000	$9000	$18 000	$27 000	$36 000
$400 000	$12 000	$24 000	$36 000	$48 000
$500 000	$15 000	$30 000	$45 000	$60 000
$750 000	$22 500	$45 000	$67 500	$90 000
$1 000 000	$30 000	$60 000	$90 000	$120 000

If you had $200 000 invested and received a 6 per cent per annum return, you'd earn another $12 000 after a year. At the time of writing, average weekly earnings are $1604.90 a week, so a $12 000 income from investments is equivalent to an extra two months of work at the average wage—and you haven't had to sell your time to receive it.

I haven't met anyone who'd turn down an extra two months of income, especially when they haven't had to sell their time to do it. How would an extra two months of income affect your budget?

Even if you don't replace all your paid time income with investment earnings, the value provided by an investment income is something you need to get your head around if you want to stack the odds in your favour. That same idea also applies to your superannuation. You're not selling time for the income made on your super. It's going to be an important source of money though when you retire. While it might not be income now, it will become income later so you need to pay attention to it as well! (I consider superannuation strategies in Chapter 11.)

Some of the best conversations I've had with my clients are about generating a second income through investments. Like many, they've been stuck in the idea that the only way to earn money is by selling their time to receive wages, and perhaps even overtime pay and a bonus. Investment and superannuation income aren't the only type of passive, time-free income though—you can also earn extra income from the returns on your savings. The better you understand your options, the more you can maximise your income.

Conversations like this wake up my clients—remember, 'you don't know what you don't know'. Having a second income in my experience inspires many people to get their budgets together. No longer is budgeting a chore that focuses on curbing your spending; instead, it's an activity that can inspire you to save and create that second income.

I'm also not against a second job or side hustle, if you have the time and you want to ramp things up. Go for it, but make sure that you're actively saving your extra income to make the most of your efforts to work harder and earn more.

Spending isn't about denial—it's about choice

For many people, saying the word 'budget' evokes a reaction like the word 'diet'. Suddenly it's all about denial.

For example: 'On a diet, you have to give up everything you love and eat lettuce leaves and other rabbit foods. Goodbye to all the foods I love—watch me suffer through this agony.'

Applied to a budget, it's much the same: 'On a budget, you have to give up everything you love. Goodbye to all the things I like doing—watch me suffer through this agony.'

The reality is that the words 'budget' and 'diet', should never be placed in the same sentence, let alone compared. They're two different things. The number of calories you eat over time will have a physical impact on your body weight, but money can never have a physical impact on your weight. What I am really talking about here is the emotion that's being expressed—it's about feeling like you're going without. Emotions about money can be very triggering for some people. And to be frank, every client I work with, in some aspect of their financial life, muddies the waters with the emotions they attach to money.

We as humans just love to attach emotions to things. Here are some home truths about money and your emotions:

- Your money doesn't care about how you look in the mirror.

- Your money doesn't care if your bum looks big in your new jeans.

- Your money doesn't care about your gym-built six-pack.

- Your money doesn't care about how you look in a photograph.

- Your money doesn't care if you remember a birthday or anniversary.

- Your money doesn't care about your future wellbeing.

- Your money doesn't care about what the bathroom scales tell you.

The more I rationally think about the emotional relationship that we've all had at times with money, the more it makes me laugh. I hope you can think about your own relationship with money and find some home truths and humour that make you laugh too. More importantly, once you've challenged your own emotional connections to money, think about how you can avoid the same behaviours in the future. As a starting point, when it comes to the word 'budget', please don't think about the word 'diet'. A budget is about choice, not denial.

In a financial setting, *choice* really means control and value.

Most of us like to have control over things, but we hate being controlled. Having someone impose their will upon us is not a great place to be. You and you alone have control over your spending. If you don't feel you have control over your spending, then work on your budget. Find out where the money is going.

Two kinds of value impact how we choose to spend our money:

- **Rational value:** The fair value for the good or service we're choosing to pay for, which ensures it delivers what it's meant to.

- **Emotional value:** The price we choose to pay for the good or service above its rational (or fair) value so that it meets an emotional need.

So much of what we pay for in modern life is made up of the more expensive emotional value rather than the more cost-effective rational value.

Consider these examples:

- Do you buy the brand name shirt or the one that's also made of 100 per cent cotton without the brand name?

- Do you buy the brand name shoes advertised by a superstar athlete or the shoes made of the same amount of leather without the brand name?

- Do you buy the high-end luxury car or the car that has the same fuel economy and safety rating?

Businesses create brands they know we'll fall in love with. One of the oldest lessons in advertising (which I was told by one of my clients) is that if they can grab a person's emotions, they're more likely to make the sale. We've all been victims of it. I have too.

Early in my career I worked with senior financial planners who all had really expensive pens they used in front of their clients and gave to their clients to sign their paperwork with. We're not talking $5 pens from the local supermarket, we're talking thousand-dollar designer pens. Yes, you can also buy over-priced pens — who knew, right?

I somehow got it into my head that these people were successful because of the expensive pen they owned, and I made it a goal to get myself one someday when I was a success like them. Well, that someday eventually arrived and I paid a stupid sum of money for a pen. A short time later, reflecting on the purchase, I can't tell you how much I questioned it. As a motivation for the purchase, I had also made it a reward for reaching a goal I had set earlier in the year. The only upside to this story is that it is useful to share it with my clients as it shows that we all need a goal or target to chase and we can reward ourselves when we achieve it.

Earnings and spending: The moral of the story

Sound budget management is the universal starting point if you genuinely want to stack strategies in your favour. Think about that second income as a motivator to help you lift your income, rather than just thinking about selling your time for money. When it comes to spending, it's not about diet and denial—it's about choice, control and value. Learn to tell the difference between rational value and emotional value before you give up your hard-earned dollars.

Your budget is the rock at the base of your own strategy stacks. It allows you to plan and do things over time that directly fund and impact the stacks you use, as you work towards understanding your own 'why'.

Use a Risk Assessment Strategy

Without understanding risk, you're potentially putting your strategy stack in danger. Risk can come in many shapes and forms. It might be market volatility or investment risk (which you can mitigate using strategies involving dollar cost averaging and asset allocation—for more on these, see Chapter 10). It might be more personal risk, like getting an illness and not being able to pay the mortgage (Chapter 13 covers strategies that may help here, such as taking out income protection insurance and trauma insurance).

As a general rule, people who take risk do so because they think the reward achieved by taking that risk is more valuable than the damage the risk will cause. You can think about risk and reward like scales.

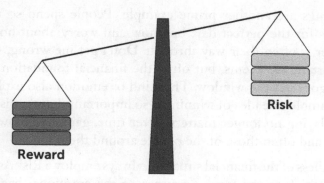

If the reward outweighs the risk, a person is likely to accept the risk to achieve the outcome they're seeking. If you can mitigate the risk using financial strategies, then you can stack the odds more in your favour. For example, income protection insurance enables you to offset the risk of getting ill and not being able to pay the mortgage.

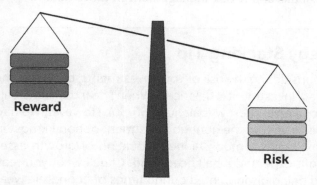

If, however, the risk outweighs the reward (that is, it's riskier), people are unlikely to proceed. Some risks cannot be overcome and no amount of good advice or strategy stacking will mitigate the risk. Sometimes our bodies tell us not to proceed too—in this modern day and age, there's still something to be said for your listening to your gut instinct.

People seem to get themselves into trouble the most when they start thinking about reward and risk and weighing either basket with too much emotion and not enough facts. For example, the desire to buy an amazing new car is so emotional, you can easily forget about the risks associated with taking a loan or lease to purchase it. If you haven't experienced this yourself, you may well have seen it in others—young people often fall into this trap.

Weddings are another prime example. People spend so much on the extras for the perfect day; buy now and worry about how to pay for it later is often their way through. Don't get me wrong, weddings are important life events, but often the financial foundation of being realistic goes out the window. This kind of emotion also explains why people gamble: the idea of winning is so important that the risk and the cost of playing no longer matters. Over time, gamblers blow up their finances, and often those of the people around them too.

Regardless of the financial situation, always employ a Risk Assessment Strategy. Stick to the facts. Be aware of the emotional baggage you might bring to your decision-making. Often, risks can be mitigated. If risks can't be mitigated, then really think about the risk you're willing to accept. A Risk Assessment Strategy will make your stack more certain, and that's why it's an important part of my strategy stacking philosophy (Chapter 9 talks about risk management in more detail).

Strategy Stacking Tip

When considering the risk of your investments, don't assume that a 'balanced' investment is balanced. When I hear the word 'balanced', I think of a level seesaw (balanced 50/50). However, we have seen over the years that the generic investment option in most industry funds maintains a much higher allocation of growth assets than you might expect in a balanced fund. Check what you really hold to avoid being disappointed during times of economic weakness.

Stack your strategies appropriately

The purpose of this book is not to encourage you to build strategy stacks through the rafters of your financial house. It's not the number of strategies that you stack that matters—five well-stacked strategies might be more solid and less complex than 35 precariously stacked strategies.

How you stack the strategies ultimately depends upon your personal situation and your 'why'. There's always been a danger of trying to 'keep up with the Jones's' (or maybe a brother or sister, friends or a work colleague, or someone on social media). There's real danger in using external reference points like these for your own financial life. You never know the full story of what's going on in someone else's world. While the new car they're driving looks great, you don't actually know what kind of debt they've got. Often, you see the material trappings but you never see the debt because it's invisible.

Stacking appropriately also means that you place your strategies in the right order. Getting the sequence wrong could cause you harm; for example, making extra contributions to your superannuation might help your retirement in the future, but it could put you under financial stress right now if you haven't planned how you're going to pay for it.

Stacking appropriately means that you also give consideration to stacking strategies with the assistance of a qualified financial planner who can make sure you're making the most of your stacking options and have an understanding of what it is you're trying to achieve. I know you may have never used a financial planner before, but this book won't have all the advice you need—it can't give out personal financial advice as the advice would be different for every reader. However, arming yourself with knowledge from this book will allow you to have more productive and confident conversations with a financial planner.

Of course, there will be some people who are 'do it yourself' investors, and may never seek professional advice. That's a risk they're prepared to take in their financial life, and everyone is entitled to their decisions—I acknowledge that without judgement. But the danger, as with any action in life, is that you don't know what you don't know. Sometimes the cost of advice can be cheaper than the cost of fixing a mistake.

Assess, execute, review, refine and repeat

Perhaps the most fundamental concept when it comes to stacking strategies is the idea of continuous development and improvement. What happens this year will be different from last year. Seasons change, the economy changes and people's situations change too. Even the rules around money change! Legislation covering taxation, superannuation and retirement also change, which frustrates financial planners like me (and sometimes my clients, if they're affected too). It would make life much easier for us all if the government just decided to make the rules and stick to them. The same can be said for interest rates, which often change too.

If we know that things are going to change, including situations in our own lives, then we need to be disciplined enough to:

- **Assess** a situation or opportunity

- **Execute** (or implement) a strategy (or a stack of strategies)

- **Review** the outcomes and performance (What worked and failed? Why did it work or fail?)

- **Refine** our thinking, using this review, before we make any changes to our strategy stack

- **Repeat** the process again, given the new point in time.

People are rarely disciplined enough to do this by themselves, which is another good reason to use a qualified financial planner—even the best performers across any area of life have help. Superstars like tennis players Serena Williams and Roger Federer follow this same process, with the assistance of a coach. It's hard to do it by yourself, and sometimes it's what you can't see that can hurt you.

You might think that at such an elite level you don't need help, but it's simply not the case. The best singers all have vocal coaches. The best sportspeople often have several kinds of people who help them—coaches, physiotherapists, psychologists and nutritionists. The best businesspeople also hire financial planners, accountants and sometimes consultants to help them with their decision-making and performance. Without a doubt, there will be a few super-humans who can go it alone but it's really the exception rather than the rule.

So, a reviewing and learning component must form a part of your strategy stack. It's the way your strategy stack remains relevant and working in your favour, even after things change.

CHAPTER 5

Strategy Stacking around Significant Life Events

Many life events, especially if they are unexpected and/or traumatising, can have a significant impact on your life and change the course of your 'why'—which may lead you to rethink the goals you have set yourself. In this chapter, I take a look at some of these major life events and some of the key issues you might need to consider.

Remember: it's always best to seek personal financial advice for your own situation.

Redundancy

Whether we're talking downsizing, right-sizing, rationalising, restructuring or simply redundancy, it all means the same thing: the business you work for has decided that your role is no longer needed, and so you find yourself unemployed. There are rules around what happens to employees who have their positions made redundant. You are entitled to an amount of money based on your years of service and your wage or salary, as well as remuneration for any unused annual leave and long service leave.

There are a number of issues to consider, which may include:

- Budgeting and cashflow
- Managing debt, if any is held
- Finding a new job and obtaining government unemployment benefits to help manage the time between jobs
- Considering early retirement (if your age permits)
- Using capital from the redundancy payment to make a non-concessional contribution to your superannuation to maximise your pension value (if you're at retirement age—Chapter 11 covers Superannuation Strategies)
- Utilising transition to retirement legislation (if you do not wish to return to work again on a full-time basis—Chapter 12 covers Retirement Strategies)
- Optimising personal deductible contributions to maximise the tax efficiency of your payment (you may be able to make a personal contribution to your superannuation account and claim a tax deduction for it, which has the benefit of boosting your super and providing a more tax-effective outcome—see Chapter 11)
- Using the carry forward concessional legislation to maximise tax deductions (you can make use of previously unused superannuation contributions limits to make a personal contribution to your superannuation account and claim a tax deduction for it—for more information about personal deductible contributions to super and superannuation contribution limits, see Chapter 11).

If you ever experience a redundancy, it has nothing to do with your value or how well you did your job. Businesses make financial decisions every day, and if reducing their staff headcount is one of them, it's about them—not you. The immediate impact for you is on your income and budget. Ongoing income is the key driver that will help you achieve your 'why'. It's therefore extremely important to make the most of redundancy entitlements and any outplacement or career transition services available to you so that you can find a great new role to turn your income stream on again.

Marriage and divorce

Walking down the aisle or waking up and deciding a marriage is over are both big life events. Most go into marriage with the expectation it will last a lifetime, but sometimes things don't go as planned.

There are a number of issues to consider, which may include:

- Budgeting and cashflow
- Managing debt, if any is held
- Joining or separating your financial lives, depending on the direction you're headed
- Superannuation splitting, which may involve the courts (Chapter 11 covers Super Strategies)
- Assessing the legal issues involved
- Working out your new together 'why' or separate 'whys'
- Getting professional help with your divorce from a family lawyer, which can save you from getting caught up in what other people you know have experienced (which may cause you further frustration and confusion).

Gaining a partner or losing one will have an impact on your financial life. Knowing your rights, what may happen next and the way forward for you to resolve the situation is vital for both your financial and mental wellbeing. Also, when you achieve your 'why' is likely to change—it may also look a little different now as you may be gaining or losing shared short-, medium- and long-term goals. Sometimes we have to compromise or work hard to find a way to make sure both partners' needs are met. Similarly, should you lose a partner, you probably need to spend some time rethinking your 'why' to make sure it fits with your new outlook over the medium to long term.

An unexpected windfall

An unexpected windfall is simply money you didn't expect to receive, and it usually comes as a very welcome surprise in your life. Examples of unexpected windfalls include winning the lottery, receiving a bonus from work or receiving an inheritance from someone who made a bequeath to you in their Will.

Many people lose their minds when this happens. Because they didn't earn the money, they get excited and sometimes blow it all.

There are a number of issues to consider here, which may help you manage the windfall experience:

■ Budgeting and cashflow

■ Managing debt removal

■ Investing outside of superannuation in a trust or other vehicle to provide choice (Chapter 10 covers Investment Strategies)

■ Adjusting your superannuation contributions—deductible or non-deductible (Chapter 11 covers Super Strategies)

■ Exploring your own estate planning issues (Chapter 14 deals with Estate Planning Strategies).

The real benefit of an unexpected windfall is that it can help you jump several steps forward to achieving your 'why'—provided you use the money wisely. It's true that many people who come into unexpected money quickly and without effort often lose it as quickly as they gained it. It can be really hard to resist the temptation to go and splurge on things you'd never before even dreamed about buying. Instead, I'd challenge you to put the money into the bank and continue to live life normally for the next three months. This includes going to work. Give yourself some time and space to think about your 'why' and how the unexpected windfall can help you achieve it rationally, without the emotion or excitement.

Trauma and disability

A serious accident or trauma will have a major impact on your life. If you have a wealth protection stack in place, you may receive a payout from your insurance (see Chapter 13 for more on these strategies). If you become totally and permanently disabled, you're likely to also be able to access your superannuation benefits. And if the events were caused by negligence, you might also receive a compensation payout.

These are all horrible life events but that's why you have a wealth protection stack: to cover the bills and provide you with an income when you can't work, whether temporarily or permanently.

There are a number of issues to consider, which may include:

- Budgeting and cashflow
- Managing debt removal or use of offset accounts (an offset account is an accessible bank account attached to your home loan — any deposits, including wages, that are paid into the offset account will reduce the total balance of your loan)
- Restructuring mortgages to maintain access to the capital
- Factoring in the cost of home refurbishments (if required to make your life easier)
- Making deductible or non-deductible contributions to superannuation (Chapter 11 covers Super Strategies)
- Setting up superannuation disability pensions to access capital
- Establishing trusts or other vehicles to provide income and capital flexibility (where appropriate)
- Exploring your own estate planning issues (Chapter 14 covers Estate Planning Strategies).

Without a doubt, a trauma or disability is one of the most stressful and challenging life events that any of us could personally face. An event like this has the power to completely reshape and challenge your original 'why'. The benefit of a Wealth Protection Strategy payout is that it can help reduce the financial stress while your health becomes your new number-one priority.

Stacking for the next generation

Having kids also delivers a special stacking issue. You not only need to stack for yourself and your partner, but you need to be able to stack to give them the best start you can too.

In Chapter 1, we looked at five truths about money. We acknowledged that our school education doesn't prepare us for our adult financial life. We also acknowledged that our parents, as much as they love us, probably didn't do a great job preparing us for our adult financial lives either in some situations.

So, as a generation, are we destined to repeat the mistakes of our parents (and probably their parents too) or are we going to educate our kids ourselves and show them what good money behaviors look like? Let's aim for the latter!

There are a number of issues to consider here, which might include:

- Starting with the basics: talk to your kids about earning, spending, saving and debt

- Teaching them to respect their earnings through pocket money once they're old enough

- Using technology to connect with them through the use of online saving apps and rounding software for savings plans (phone and app-based tools show them how money works in a language they can understand, given that they will most probably have a phone glued to their hands for years)

- Talking with them as teenagers and young adults about their own 'why' (remember, it's their journey, not yours. How many of us would have been nurtured by a parent who took the time to listen and explore our goals?)

- Incentivising them with help such as matching their savings, adding to their savings and rewarding them for a goal they meet over time.

There is an old story around wealth between the generations: the first generation earns it; the second generation keeps it (because they saw how hard the first generation worked for it); the third generation loses it (because they didn't see what the first generation went through to earn it). When it comes to stacking for the next generation, make sure that family values of waste, opportunity and effort are part of the 'why' you set for yourself and for your children. And if you are concerned about the next generation, you have a responsibility, if you want to achieve your 'why', to equip them with the knowledge they need to thrive financially, or to make sure they seek professional advice.

CHAPTER 6

Getting Started: Assessing Your Starting Position

Every journey has a beginning.

If you're travelling, you need to know where you're starting from, where you're going, and how long you'll be away for. You might also need to redirect the mail, drop the kids off at their grandparents' house, or get someone to come and feed the dog and water the plants. Your end destination will also determine what you need to pack at the start. Will you need summer clothes or winter clothes? Will you be sun-baking with drinks by the pool, or will you be taking skiing lessons in the snow?

Understanding your real financial position is essential for the start of a successful financial journey.

Another way to look at it is through the fable about the man who built his house on the rock and the other man who built his house on the sand. When the bad weather came, only one house was left standing. If you build a strategy stack on sand, you should be prepared for the stack to fail. It might be a really good stack and it might achieve everything you want to achieve. But if it's not built on solid foundations, you're going to have lots of problems.

Some people really need to take a deep breath and clear their head before they get started. I've actually seen clients cry because they've genuinely tried to sort out their financial lives and yet they feel like they've failed. Our financial lives can be really difficult to manage sometimes, so I'd say we've all felt overwhelmed in this way at some time or another. As a financial planner, it's not my place to judge, but in cases like this it's my job to help people clear the rubble and regain focus. Once that's done and we understand the truth of their situation, we can get onto strategy stacking, which allows people to move forward with more confidence and certainty.

The purpose of this chapter is to help you understand your starting position and find your own financial truths. I provide a detailed exercise—the Strategy Stacker's Starting Position exercise—to help you work out your personal starting position before you start strategy stacking.

Know your money truths before you begin

Some of your own truths about money are going to be confronting. They might make you uncomfortable. They might even make you so uncomfortable that you decide to put managing your money in the 'too hard' basket. You probably already know your money truths, and you probably wouldn't go shouting from the rooftops about many of them.

Let's take a look at some typical awkward scenarios around money, where people haven't respected the five strong foundations (from Chapter 3). These are just some of the hypothetical attitudes and behaviours you might recognise in yourself or others, but it's not an exhaustive list:

1. **Not respecting their earnings**
   - They're just coasting at work and haven't done any training or development, but then a redundancy comes along.
   - They use up all their sick leave for fun days, then actually get sick.

- They lose their job because of underperformance.

- They become complacent, thinking that working for a large institution means they will be looked after.

- They assume that if they can't work and they become injured, Centrelink benefits will be enough.

2. **Not paying attention to spending**

- They have a splurge and pay $600 for one pair of shoes.

- They regret losing $1000 at a casino on a boys' weekend.

- They haven't put enough into savings and are disappointed with their position.

3. **Not understanding the cost of money**

- They didn't have enough money to pay the credit card off in full on the due date.

- They have a personal loan from a holiday two years ago.

- They overextend themselves on a new car, but now the loan repayments are painful—with the cost of interest, the car really costs twice as much.

- They didn't get around to reviewing their home loan interest rate when interest rates fell.

- They got to the end of the financial year and didn't have the money for a tax deduction to super to bolster a tax refund.

- They keep multiple credit cards going when they only really need one.

4. **Not being realistic**

- They think they don't have the ability to reach positive goals—yet they did have lots of options, even though they had some debt.

- They thought they could reach the moon, but their real financial position couldn't support that goal.

- They try to do too much, perhaps by having multiple investment properties, and then property prices fall.

- They compare themselves to a previous generation when things were different, rather than dealing with the current financial reality.

- They didn't think they'd have to change any of their current poor financial behaviours to reach their goals.

5. **Not rewarding themselves properly**

- They think rewarding yourself is a stupid foundation and so they ignore it, then later they splurge without thinking.

- They didn't take the time to celebrate when they achieved their goals, even significant ones like paying off a personal loan or long-term credit card debt.

- They over-celebrate the success of a goal, which creates a new financial problem.

- Their long-term goal feels too far away, so they become disheartened and they quit.

So what are your own truths? What is your relationship with the five foundations of money? I often say to my own clients that good financial behaviours are worth as much as the strategy stacks that they use. So, take some time to get the foundations and behaviours right—good financial behaviours help you stack the odds in your favour.

The Strategy Stacker's Starting Position

Now that you have a clear understanding of any financial behaviour weaknesses you might have, it is time to complete the Strategy Stacker's Starting Position exercise. (You can also find this exercise in the form of PDF and Excel worksheets at thestrategystacker.com.au.)

Make sure you have the following resources ready before you start the exercise:

- A pad of paper and a pen
- A lever-arch folder with some dividers
- A hole punch

- A large envelope
- One hour of time each week over the next four weeks (allow an extra hour at the end of the process to assess the outcomes and work out your starting position).

Open the lever-arch folder and write the following on the dividers:

- Bank statements
- Investment statements
- Super fund/pension statements
- Credit card statements
- Loan statements.

Fill up the folder with your last lot of statements. Then, as a matter of habit, throw any future statements into your folder.

If you're more tech savvy, you might turn that pen and paper, lever-arch folder, hole punch, and large envelope into an electronic filing system, where you complete this exercise in Excel and create a series of folders to help you manage your financial life. Your smartphone camera allows you to snap and save. Using something like Evernote or OneDrive/Google Drive can be a simple and easy way for you to create folders and scan documents directly into your phone. For some people, reducing the paperwork means things don't get lost too! You'll achieve the same results—you'll just get there without the paper!

Over the next four weeks, get a receipt for everything you buy and put it in the large envelope. Or, if you're going electronic, buy, snap and save that receipt electronically and track the totals in Excel. Have a receipts folder in your smart phone—you will never lose the receipts in the wash that way.

However you're filing your financial information, when you have your latest statement information filed away, you are ready to start the exercise.

Week 1: Income

Your income can come from a number of sources. To reach your starting point, let's get an overview of your monthly and yearly income. Pull out your pay slips or login to your online bank account to complete the income table (see table 6.1, overleaf).

Table 6.1: Your income

Income	Monthly	Yearly
Salary or wage	$	$
Pension/annuity income	$	$
Centrelink benefit income	$	$
Interest income	$	$
Rental income	$	$
Dividend income	$	$
Child maintenance income	$	$
Business income	$	$
Other (please specify):	$	$
Other (please specify):	$	$
Your Total Income	$	$

Of course, not all of the income sources shown might be applicable to you—just fill in the relevant sections.

Once you've entered all your income details, add up the monthly column and the yearly column to get your total monthly and yearly income.

That's it for Week 1, you're done. Congratulations on that folder too, manual or digital—you're now organised! Just don't forget to keep collecting those receipts...

Week 2: Investments (including superannuation) and personal insurance

It's time to look at your starting point for investments, superannuation and personal insurance. Investments and superannuation are usually set up to achieve medium- and long-term goals. Personal insurance enables you to protect yourself and your lifestyle in the event that something goes wrong.

Many people don't think about superannuation because retirement is too far away. What they don't realise is that they're missing out on many lost opportunities between now and then. They think what they don't understand won't affect the outcome they receive. Sadly, that's not correct. Likewise, many people don't people pay attention to personal insurance. It's these people who are underprepared in the event of an unexpected, health-impacting event.

So, let's not make those mistakes. Let's start by working out your investment, super and personal insurance starting position.

Investment summary

First, take a look at your investments. You might have more than one investment—for example, maybe you have shares, a term deposit or something else.

To reach your starting point, identify the name of your investments in the first column of table 6.2. Add the amount of money you invested (the purchase price), and then add the current value of that investment. You'll also need to add the date you purchased each investment too. Why? It can impact your tax position.

Table 6.2: Your investments

Investments	Date purchased	Purchase price	Current value
	/ /	$	$
	/ /	$	$
	/ /	$	$
	/ /	$	$
	/ /	$	$
	/ /	$	$
	/ /	$	$
	/ /	$	$
Your Total Investments		$	$

Once you've entered all your investment information, add up the purchase price column and the current value column to get your totals.

Superannuation summary

If you've had more than one job in your life, the chances are you'll have more than one super fund (unless you've already used the Consolidation Strategy, which I explain in Chapter 11, to bring your superannuation funds together). In table 6.3, enter the name of each superannuation fund and the current value of that fund. If you don't know, give them a call to find out or login to an online account if they've given you one.

Table 6.3: Your superannuation

Superannuation fund provider name	Current value
	$
	$
	$
	$
	$
	$
	$
	$
Your Total Superannuation	$

Once you've entered all your super fund information, add up the current value column to get your total current superannuation balance value.

Personal insurance summary

If you have a superannuation fund, you might have insurance cover automatically attached to it. You might also hold personal insurance outside of your superannuation. In table 6.4, write the name of your personal insurance provider in the first column and tick if it's held inside or outside your super. Does the insurance cover you for any

Table 6.4: Your personal insurance

Personal insurance	Occupation type premiums	Income protection cover	Total permanent disability (TPD) cover	Trauma cover	Life cover
Provider: ☐ Inside super OR ☐ Outside super	☐ Any occupation ☐ Own occupation	$	$	$	$
Provider: ☐ Inside super OR ☐ Outside super	☐ Any occupation ☐ Own occupation	$	$	$	$
Provider: ☐ Inside super OR ☐ Outside super	☐ Any occupation ☐ Own occupation	$	$	$	$
Provider: ☐ Inside super OR ☐ Outside super	☐ Any occupation ☐ Own occupation	$	$	$	$
Provider: ☐ Inside super OR ☐ Outside super	☐ Any occupation ☐ Own occupation	$	$	$	$

occupation or your own occupation? Note this in the second column. In the final columns, write the value of the insurance held under the different insurance types.

Once completed, table 6.4 is very useful. You'll be able to see what personal insurance you have and don't have. You might add up each of the different types of cover you have to see what your total cover looks like, and consider if it's broadly appropriate for your needs. In assessing cover though, you need to dig deeper. Different providers are likely to have different policy wording, terms and conditions. I cover each of these types of wealth protection insurance in Chapter 13.

That's it for Week 2. Congratulations on finding and documenting your super and insurances! Remember to keep collecting those receipts and putting them into the envelope/your digital filing system.

Week 3: Assets and liabilities

This week's exercise will help you work out your starting position for your assets and your liabilities. Assets are an important part of your financial life too, as we often spend a lot on them. Liabilities also need to be considered. Sometimes, our liabilities include the debts we put ourselves into to buy the assets if we don't save for them.

Assets

When we talk about assets here, we're talking about things that you own or are paying off—in other words, things that don't produce an income for you. Some financial planners call these *lifestyle assets*. They're things that you buy not as an investment, but to use and enjoy as a part of your life.

In the first column in table 6.5, complete the list of assets you own (I include a few commonly held assets to help you get started). In the next two columns, enter the purchase price and the date you purchased the asset. In the final column, write the current value of that asset (which may be very different from what you originally paid for it).

Table 6.5: Your assets

Assets	Date purchased	Purchase price	Current value
Asset 1: Home	/ /	$	$
Asset 2: Home contents	/ /	$	$
Asset 3: Motor vehicle	/ /	$	$
Asset 4: Artwork	/ /	$	$
Asset 5: Collectibles	/ /	$	$
Asset 6:	/ /	$	$
Asset 7:	/ /	$	$
Asset 8:	/ /	$	$
Your Total Assets		$	$

Once you've entered all your asset information, add up the purchase price column and the current value column to get your totals.

Liabilities

When we talk about liabilities here, we're talking about credit cards, personal loans, home loans and other kinds of debt that you're still paying back.

In the first column in table 6.6 (overleaf), write the name of the liabilities you have (I include a few common liabilities to help you get started). In the next two columns, write the name of the lender and the amount you owe them. In the next column, write the interest rate attached to the loan. In the next two columns, identify if the interest rate on the loan is fixed or variable and if the interest is tax deductible or not.

71

Table 6.6: Your liabilities

Liabilities	Lender name	Amount owing	Interest rate	Type	Deductibility
Liability 1: Credit card		$	% per annum	☐ Fixed ☐ Variable	☐ Yes ☐ No
Liability 2: Personal loan		$	% per annum	☐ Fixed ☐ Variable	☐ Yes ☐ No
Liability 3: Home loan		$	% per annum	☐ Fixed ☐ Variable	☐ Yes ☐ No
Liability 4: Investment loan		$	% per annum	☐ Fixed ☐ Variable	☐ Yes ☐ No
Liability 5:		$	% per annum	☐ Fixed ☐ Variable	☐ Yes ☐ No
Liability 6:		$	% per annum	☐ Fixed ☐ Variable	☐ Yes ☐ No
Liability 7:		$	% per annum	☐ Fixed ☐ Variable	☐ Yes ☐ No
Liability 8:		$	% per annum	☐ Fixed ☐ Variable	☐ Yes ☐ No
Your Total Liabilities		$			

Once you've entered all your liability information, add up the amount owing column to get your total.

That's it for Week 3. Congratulations on pulling together your assets and liabilities into one place! The results might have been surprising.

Don't forget to keep collecting the receipts and putting them into the envelope or tracking them in your Excel spreadsheet.

Week 4: Spending

Finally, it's time to look at your spending. You've been collecting all your receipts from everything you've spent over the last four weeks. The purpose of stretching it out over this time was to help you put together a picture of your current spending over a reasonable time frame. How much is in that envelope or listed within that Excel spreadsheet?

You might realise you have some missing expenses that haven't been paid for during the last month, like your car registration or home and contents insurance, but that you do pay over the course of a year. Look up your bank and credit card statements (from your lever-arch folder or online accounts) and add the missing items.

Go through the receipts and complete the monthly, quarterly and yearly expenses in table 6.7.

Table 6.7: Your expenses

Expenses	Month	Quarter	Year
Home and garden			
Rent	$	$	$
Mortgages	$	$	$
Credit card	$	$	$
Land and water rates	$	$	$
House repairs	$	$	$

(continued)

Table 6.7 Your expenses (*cont'd*)

Expenses	Month	Quarter	Year
Strata levies	$	$	$
Council rates	$	$	$
Pool maintenance	$	$	$
Home and contents upgrade	$	$	$
Utilities			
Electricity	$	$	$
Gas	$	$	$
Water	$	$	$
Phone, mobile and internet	$	$	$
Personal items			
Clothing	$	$	$
Shoes	$	$	$
Haircuts	$	$	$
Grooming/cosmetics	$	$	$
Gifts/pocket money (for children)	$	$	$
Cigarettes	$	$	$
Gambling	$	$	$
Laundry/dry cleaning	$	$	$
Donations/other	$	$	$
Postage	$	$	$

Expenses	Month	Quarter	Year
Maintenance			
Children	$	$	$
Insurance			
Home and contents	$	$	$
Car insurance	$	$	$
Boat insurance	$	$	$
Health cover	$	$	$
Life cover, total permanent disability (TPD) cover, trauma cover, income protection insurance (outside super)	$	$	$
Medical			
Doctor fees	$	$	$
Dentist fees	$	$	$
Chemist/prescription costs	$	$	$
Eye care and optometrist fees	$	$	$
Pet and vet	$	$	$
Transport			
Petrol	$	$	$
Servicing and repairs	$	$	$
Licence and registration	$	$	$
Fares/tolls	$	$	$
Public transport fares	$	$	$

(continued)

Table 6.7 Your expenses (*cont'd*)

Expenses	Month	Quarter	Year
Entertainment and leisure			
Concerts/theatre/cinema	$	$	$
Streaming TV	$	$	$
Newspaper/magazines	$	$	$
Sport and fitness memberships	$	$	$
Holidays	$	$	$
Education			
Childcare/school/university fees	$	$	$
Uniforms	$	$	$
Self-education/tools or equipment costs	$	$	$
School excursions	$	$	$
Tutoring/books/printing	$	$	$
Sports/out of school activities	$	$	$
Food			
Groceries	$	$	$
Meat	$	$	$
Fruit/vegetables	$	$	$
Pet food	$	$	$
Takeaways/food deliveries	$	$	$
Restaurants and bars	$	$	$
Alcohol	$	$	$

Expenses	Month	Quarter	Year
Financial services			
Accounting fees	$	$	$
Financial planning fees	$	$	$
Bank or Credit Union account fees	$	$	$
Other items (add as you need to)	$	$	$
Total Expenses	$	$	$

Once completed, add up your total monthly and yearly expenses to find your totals.

That wraps up Week 4! Congratulations on getting across your spending—it's often the hardest point of determining your starting position.

Working out your starting position

So, now you've completed the four-week exercise, what does your starting position look like? Here, I offer some questions to help you think about your starting position and where you might head to next—considering the topics from each week of the exercise. Take an hour (or as long as you need) to consider your answers to these questions:

Week 1: Questions around income:

- Do your earnings reflect your effort?
- Can you upskill or move jobs to earn more?

Week 2: Questions around investments and personal insurance:

- Considering each of your investments (including super), do you know what asset allocations they are invested in?

- Check your risk profile—are you driving too quickly or too slowly?

- Consider the investment menu within your investment and super funds—can you buy the assets you are after (such as exchange-traded funds, managed funds, listed shares)?

- Are you salary sacrificing to superannuation when you could do it later in the year and lower your interest costs on a mortgage?

- Personal insurance—how much is enough for each type of cover? For example, if you have more than one super fund, you might be paying for income protection you'll never use. Alternatively, do you have enough cover? If something happens to you, can you still cover your spending needs and liabilities?

- Is your personal insurance cover in 'any' occupation or your 'own' occupation? (Learn more about this difference in Chapter 13.)

- How will you hold and pay for your personal insurance? Will it be held inside or outside of your superannuation?

Week 3: Questions around assets and liabilities:

- Do you have things around the house you don't use and could sell for some extra cash?

- Do you have the ability to remove or consolidate debt?

- Can credit cards or personal loans be moved to your mortgage for a lower rate?

- Is your home loan rate competitive when compared with others in the marketplace? And is your mortgage debt structured correctly—for example, are you making principal and interest loan repayments, or interest only?

- Can you use an offset account to reduce the balance of your loan? (Remember, an offset account is a savings account linked to your loan. Any money you add to it reduces the balance of your loan.)

- Do you have an offset account over a redraw on your investment property for added flexibility?

Week 4: Questions about spending:

- Earning versus spending—where is it at? What does good behaviour look like? Go back to the foundations in Chapter 3 here if you need to. Are you respecting your earnings? Have you paid attention to your spending? And, most importantly, is there room for improvement in either of those things—and what changes specifically will you make?

- Is there money going to regular locations that you can review, perhaps with cheaper providers?

- Are you directing a portion of your income to your offset account first when you get paid (and perhaps a second offset account for the kids)?

- Have you checked the costs of your expenses (car insurance, mortgage, lease, other packaged items)? Shopping around to make sure you're getting a competitive price is one way to find improvements.

From a financial planning perspective, your starting position is used to determine what kinds of stacks you might create to achieve your 'why'. In order to achieve your 'why', each of the aspects you've explored in the four-week exercise in this chapter play differing parts in your financial life and will ultimately determine the short-, medium- and long-term outcomes you achieve.

Don't be too disheartened if your starting position isn't where you'd like it to be—for example, if you're spending money on things that aren't delivering enough value to you or you've got an annoying credit card debt. By recognising those things, you're actually identifying some short- and medium-term goals. Alternatively, you might be in a better position than you thought you were and might be able to stack some strategies to help you achieve your 'why' even more quickly.

And if you're using the services of a financial planner, they'll be absolutely over the moon if you presented this information to them in a meeting. Rarely are clients this well prepared when they seek advice from a financial planner for the first time!

CHAPTER 7

Making a Plan: The Strategy Stacking Calendar

The reality is that even the best laid plans will only ever hit the road when you implement them. If you don't implement your plans, then they just become like all the other ideas that never see the light of day—and you never move forward. The same can be said for your own financial planning strategy stacks. You should set yourself a time frame. Exact dates aren't necessary, but monthly or yearly time frames certainly provide good direction to help you achieve your short-, medium- and long-term goals—your 'why'.

I'm sure we all have things in the past that we've either missed or skipped. Some of them might have been things related to your financial life. It's not a great feeling and it might lead to regret. I've seen this kind of regret a lot in my line of work. So many times I've heard the words, 'I wish I had done that sooner.'

We often don't give ourselves the best chance of success because we're too busy working or worrying about other people. I see this with clients all the time. They prioritise the needs of their employer or their career over the need to pause and take stock of their own financial life. Other clients do it with family or other important people in their life, prioritising others first before they look after themselves. If you're one of those people on the career ladder, or you're putting others before yourself, I genuinely encourage you to take some time out. Your personal goals and your 'why' matters. If you don't look after yourself in the medium to long term, you'll probably start to resent the time and effort you've expended—or worse still, become burned out and feel like you have nothing to show for it.

I also often meet with clients who have not sought help with their financial lives as a resulting of fearing the cost of financial planning. However, the actual cost of not seeking advice may be a lot more expensive than you realise. Let's say you're a person with six months until you retire. You've got limited time to make personal contributions to super and get a tax deduction. If you had sought advice, you might have realised 20 years ago that you could make contributions to super and get tax deductions along the way, which makes a significant difference to your super balance.

I also appreciate that people are reluctant to pay for something when they don't understand its value. If you think this, I'd say a few things to you. Firstly, you don't know what you don't know. We're not all car mechanics, but we'll certainly pay for a mechanic when there's something wrong with our vehicle rather than trying to guess what might be the problem. Secondly, ignorance might be bliss, but it's risky to take financial actions on things you don't understand. Finally, I'd say if you do decide to go and seek a financial planner, use your starting position and your goals to help you determine how much value they can add. Chapter 16 talks about the financial planning process, and I hope it takes the mystery out of what financial planners do.

From my own experience, I know that the kitchen is the heart of the family home and a good place to keep calendars and lists. I've come up with a one-page calendar that you can use as a strategy stacking reminder. You can stick it on the fridge. It's called the Strategy Stacking Calendar and you can write your own goals on it as a reminder too. Chapter 2 talks about the importance of understanding your own 'why', it guides you to set short-, medium- and long-term goals.

The calendar includes a couple of pre-filled activities:

- At the start of the year, create a new budget—it's a great time to plan your spending needs and wants.

- Each month, review your budget to make sure you're staying on track.

- Towards the end of the financial year, pull your tax information together and get it to the accountant.

You can find a template for the Strategy Stacking Calendar at thestrategystacker.com.au.

Of course, there are other activities you might add depending on your own 'why', such as:

- Move your savings to a high-interest account or investment.

- Pay off that pesky credit card debt.

- Make contributions to superannuation leading into the end of the financial year to maximise your tax deductions.

- Make extra mortgage payments, or fill up your offset account with a windfall or bonus, which brings you another step closer to full home ownership.

- Review your Will.

- Put a binding nomination onto a super fund or pension account.

- Have a review with your financial planner.

- Recognise your progress towards a goal (or the achievement of one) with a celebration/reward. You have to reward yourself for hitting goals so you can stay engaged with the process and the journey.

I'm not asking you to live in a tent on a diet of beans to send money in the direction of your goals—just don't go crazy and live on all of your income.

Whatever the activity is that's helping you move forward, add it to your Strategy Stacking Calendar and stick it on the fridge. It's a simple idea, but one that I hope will help you turn your strategy stack ideas into actions and outcomes.

The Strategy Stacking Calendar

Short-term goals		
_____	_____	_____

Medium-term goals		
_____	_____	_____

Long-term goals		
_____	_____	_____

January	February	March
Create budget.	Review last month's budget performance.	Review last month's budget performance. Check quarterly savings goal. Reward yourself for your three-month target.

April	May	June
Review last month's budget performance.	Review last month's budget performance.	Review last month's budget performance. Check quarterly savings goal. Reward yourself for your three-month target.

July	August	September
Review last month's budget performance. Organise information for tax return.	Review last month's budget performance. Complete tax return.	Review last month's budget performance. Check quarterly savings goal. Reward yourself for your three-month target.

October	November	December
Review last month's budget performance.	Review last month's budget performance.	Review last month's budget performance. Check quarterly savings goal. Reward yourself for your three-month target.

CHAPTER 8
Strategy Stacking Scenarios

Strategy stacking is the process of putting together different financial planning strategies to create a financial plan. The strategies you decide to stack (or don't stack) will have an impact on your financial life. It might be tempting to think that you need to use every strategy in the stack at every point in your life. If you're thinking that, I'd like to temper those thoughts somewhat, as not every financial planning strategy will be useful and productive for you, all of the time. It's great though that you're thinking about strategies that can help you achieve your own 'why' and that you have the motivation to stack the odds in your favour.

Before I look at any of the financial planning strategies in detail and how they might be useful for your stack, I want to share with you some strategy stacking scenarios. I think these examples will be useful as they are practical and are based on typical life events that many people share in their own lives. But before we start, let me summarise the key takeaway messages to keep in mind when it comes to strategy stacking:

- How you strategy stack is determined by your 'why'—your short-, medium- and long-term goals.

- How you strategy stack will change as your life changes.

■ There are some rules around how to strategy stack, including set strong foundations, start with the Basic Stack (Chapter 4) and use the Framing Strategies (Chapter 9) for all the stacks you build. The Basic Stack (budgeting) is your floor, and the Framing Strategies will guide you on what kind of strategy stack you build. The Framing Strategies are the Budget Management Strategy, the Cash Flow Management Strategy, the Debt Reduction Strategy and the Risk Assessment Strategy.

■ Consider using a financial planner to help you strategy stack.

With those points in mind, let's take a look at four common strategy stacking scenarios:

1. I want to save more and buy a house one day.

2. We want to reduce the mortgage and raise our family.

3. We want to retire comfortable and debt-free.

4. We want to retire, but how do we actually do it?

I've chosen these four scenarios as they appear to be the most common ones I see with my own financial planning clients. One or more of these scenarios may apply to you. It's also important to note that the scenarios here focus specifically on achieving a somewhat narrow outcome. In reality, you're likely to want to look more widely and more long term at your own 'why'—at your short-, medium- and long-term goals. If that's the case, then by all means stack appropriately and more widely than the examples shown in the scenarios here. (If I were to provide fuller scenarios here, I'd need to write a whole financial plan for each of them, which could be another book!)

Remember, if you need help strategy stacking, use this book to have a more educated and productive conversation with a financial planner about your specific situation. I look at the reasons to speak to a financial planner in Chapter 15 and how the financial planning process works in Chapter 16.

Strategy stack: 'I want to save more and buy a house one day'

Let's meet James, who is 31:

- James is single and doesn't have any kids.

- He spends a lot of time with friends.

- He has a full-time job that pays him $60 000 before tax.

- In winter, when he's on holiday, you might find him on the slopes snowboarding.

- He owns his car after paying back a personal loan.

- He has credit card debt of $4000, which is a hangover of an overseas snowboarding trip plus some everyday spending.

- He's got $6000 in a high-interest savings account.

- He rents with a friend but one day wants to buy a place of his own.

Strategy stacks start with 'why'. For James, his 'why' is: 'I want to save more and buy a house one day.'

The strategy stack

All strategy stacks start with the Basic Stack (Chapter 4). Earnings and spending will determine how quickly James can achieve his goal to buy his first home. The Framing Strategies and Investment Strategies are good places for James to start his strategy stacking journey.

The Framing Strategies (Chapter 9) James might consider:

- The Budget Management Strategy
- The Cash Flow Management Strategy
- The Debt Reduction Strategy
- The Risk Assessment Strategy.

The Investment Strategies (Chapter 10) James might consider:

- The Dollar Cost Averaging Strategy
- The Investment Structure Strategy
- The Asset Selection Strategy
- The Investment Selection Strategy.

James hasn't paid much attention to his earning and spending (the Basic Stack). He has considered the Framing Strategies (Chapter 9). He's started a budget and knows when key bills are due. He's decided to get rid of the credit card debt after realising how much interest he's paying. He's also thought about the kind of investor he is and he's really quite conservative, even though he wants to buy a home as soon as he can. Table 8.1 shows his earnings information so we can work out his take-home pay.

Table 8.1: Calculating James's take-home pay

Earnings information	James
Gross income[1]	$60 000
Income tax payable	$9967
Medicare levy payable	$1200
Total tax and levy payable[2]	$11 167
Take-home pay	$48 833
Employer super contributions[3]	$6300

1. For simplicity, this assumes only their wages, not any investment or other income and after superannuation is paid by his employer. This includes the Medicare levy at the full rate. In this example, we assume gross income is simply made of their wages; income from investments however would also apply.

2. Based on the tax rates at the time of writing, although these can change.

3. Based on 10.5% of gross income.

James can see he's paying a lot of money in tax, which he hadn't realised. Welcome to adulthood, James! He works out that his monthly take-home pay is $4069.42 ($48 833/12).

After considering his budget (the Budget Management Strategy), he realises he's probably wasting some money too. He's spending way too much on eating out—it's actually more than his groceries! After reviewing his budget, he believes he can save $260 a month. He's not really been committed to saving since he paid off his car loan.

James also hasn't paid much attention to when the bills are due. He occasionally gets a late fee on a credit card payment, phone bill or electricity bill. Using the Cash Flow Management Strategy, he plots out when things are due and sets up direct debits. This gives him a saving of at least $250 a year without any extra effort. He puts this $250 over a year into his savings account instead. Using an account not linked to his online banking also protects his savings from nights out with his mates, who may talk him into buying things online!

James loves his credit card as it allows him to buy stuff when he's running short. Taking a look at the Debt Reduction Strategy, he realises he's paying a huge 19 per cent per annum interest on his $4000 credit card debt. He's got money in a high-interest savings account, but it's only paying 2.5 per cent per annum. James pays off the credit card debt using money within his high-interest account. James saves himself $760 (0.19 × $4000) a year in interest costs. He commits himself to paying off his credit card every month to avoid interest. He also places the $760 into his savings account.

James also has the option of linking his credit card to a savings account so it's cleared automatically, just in case he forgets at the end of the billing cycle. Automation is your friend at times.

Tables 8.2 and 8.3 (overleaf) show the situation for James, with and without strategy stacking.

Without the stack, after 12 months James would have had not saved anything from his budget and would still have credit card debt.

With strategy stacking, James:

- Has saved an additional $4130 from his budget

- Uses money he already had in his high-interest savings account to pay off his credit card, as it's paying a low rate of return and the interest rate on his debt is much higher

- Is in a better financial position after 12 months.

Table 8.2: Savings comparison

Issue	Without the stack after 12 months	With the stack after 12 months
Savings from budget	$0	$260 per month ($3120 a year)
Late fees	Cost of $250 a year	Nil. $250 extra a year to savings
Credit card interest	Cost of $760 a year	Nil. $760 extra a year to savings
Total Savings	$0	$4130

Table 8.3: Debt comparison

Issue	Without the stack after 12 months	With the stack after 12 months
Credit card	$4000 plus $760 interest (19% pa)	$0
Total Debt	$4760	$0

James has a goal to save, buy and own a house one day. His current high-interest savings account isn't really helping him get ahead (especially as he's wisely used $4000 to clear his credit card debt). So he decides to use the Dollar Cost Averaging Strategy to turn part of his remaining $2000 in savings into an investment that can one day be used to fund the deposit of his home.

James has a fairly simple objective and wants to keep the paperwork to a minimum, so by using the Investment Structure Strategy he decides that individual ownership is best as home ownership is his personal goal.

James wants growth for his investment, so by using the Asset Selection Strategy he decides he's attracted to shares. He's not sure what shares to buy and doesn't seek advice. Using the Investment Selection Strategy, he finds and chooses an exchange-traded fund (ETF) that includes Australian shares, which gives him diversification and is very cost-effective, maximising the amount of money invested (when compared to a managed fund in the same sector). James can also have income distributions reinvested into additional EFT shares to further compound the value of his investment over time. Using $1000 from his savings account and his ongoing monthly savings of $260 ($3120 a year), James uses the Dollar Cost Averaging Strategy to save into the ETF and he regularly buys new shares in the ETF. It has a return of 8 per cent per annum.

In looking at his strategy stack, the biggest risk to James is losing his income if he becomes sick or injured for an extended period of time. James considers the Wealth Protection Strategies (Chapter 13). James has income protection insurance as a part of the default cover in his superannuation that will pay him 75 per cent of his income after a 30-day waiting period. He's comfortable he can still afford to live for 30 days using his sick days and annual leave if he needs to, as well as taking on a short-term loan from his parents or using the credit card if he really needs extra funds. There's no extra personal cost to James for this insurance as it's funded by the contributions his employer already makes to his superannuation account, but because he doesn't hold it in his own name, he won't get a tax deduction for the income protection component. He may wish to move the policy to his own name when his savings have grown, which could let him maintain a contract with better definitions and allow him to claim the cost of cover as a tax deduction each year, but for the time being the default cover in his superannuation seems to be sufficient.

Table 8.4 shows the progress James can make towards his goal in one year by strategy stacking.

Table 8.4: Saving for a home deposit

Issue	Without the stack after 12 months	With the stack after 12 months
High-interest savings account	Total value $6000 plus $150 in interest (2.5% pa), total of $6150	Remaining value $1000 plus $25 in interest (2.5% pa), total of $1025
Exchange-traded fund (ETF)	$0	$1000 initial investment plus $3120 ($260 a month in savings) plus earnings $80 (8% pa), total of $4200
Total Home Deposit	$6150, but with a credit card debt of $4000	$5225 plus interest, but without any credit card debt

By taking some time to create a strategy stack, James is well on his way to a $30 000 home deposit—and best of all, he's finally debt-free. After the first year, he has $24 775 left to save ($30 000 – $5225). If James continues with his stack, he might expect to reach that goal in five years—or perhaps even sooner if he works harder with his budget and savings. A pay rise or new job could accelerate what James can achieve. Remember, it's not the *amount* of money that makes your strategy work, it's consistent behaviour and having a plan. The numbers change as your situation evolves or you earn more.

Additional strategies James might consider

It might seem like a lifetime away—35 years or more—but what James does now with his super can make a big difference to his future. James might consider these Superannuation Strategies (Chapter 11):

- The Consolidation Strategy
- The Super Investment Strategies.

Although James can expect to have a long life ahead of him, it's still important that his affairs are in order in case something unexpected were to happen. James might consider these Estate Planning Strategies (Chapter 14):

- The Last Will and Testament Strategy
- The Power of Attorney Strategy
- The Superannuation Nomination Strategy.

On the next page you can see James' Strategy Stacking Calendar for the goal: 'I want to save more and buy a house one day'.

Short-term goals	Budget better	Pay off credit card debt	
Medium-term goals	Save a deposit for my first home	Buy my first home	
Long-term goals	Build super for a comfortable retirement		

January	February	March
Create budget. Pay off credit card. Opens EFT investment with $1000. Save $260 to ETF. Bank savings resulting from credit card interest and late fees, which he no longer pays.	Review last month's budget performance. Save $260 to ETF. Bank savings resulting from credit card interest and late fees, which he no longer pays.	Review last month's budget performance. Save $260 to ETF. Bank savings resulting from credit card interest and late fees, which he no longer pays.

April	May	June
Review last month's budget performance. Save $260 to ETF. Bank savings resulting from credit card interest and late fees, which he no longer pays.	Review last month's budget performance. Save $260 to ETF. Bank savings resulting from credit card interest and late fees, which he no longer pays.	Review last month's budget performance. Save $260 to ETF. Bank savings resulting from credit card interest and late fees, which he no longer pays.

July	August	September
Review last month's budget performance. Save $260 to ETF. Organise information for tax return. Bank savings resulting from credit card interest and late fees, which he no longer pays.	Review last month's budget performance. Save $260 to ETF. Complete tax return. Bank savings resulting from credit card interest and late fees, which he no longer pays.	Review last month's budget performance. Save $260 to ETF. Bank savings resulting from credit card interest and late fees, which he no longer pays.

October	November	December
Review last month's budget performance. Save $260 to ETF. Bank savings resulting from credit card interest and late fees, which he no longer pays.	Review last month's budget performance. Save $260 to ETF. Bank savings resulting from credit card interest and late fees, which he no longer pays.	Review last month's budget performance. Save $260 to ETF. Bank savings resulting from credit card interest and late fees, which he no longer pays.

Strategy stack: 'We want to reduce the mortgage and raise our family'

A lot can happen in 10 years. Sometimes it can feel as quick as the turn of a page. For James, who is now 41, more than a few things have changed:

- He's now married to Trish (aged 37) and they've got two kids aged five and seven.

- James has a full-time job that pays him $110 000 a year before tax, plus super.

- Trish also works, but only part-time. It pays her $35 000 a year before tax, plus super.

- James and Trish have bought a home together. They have a mortgage of $650 000 and 26 years left on a 30-year mortgage. The interest rate is 3 per cent (per annum) and they pay $10 a month in fees.

- James and Trish have no lingering credit card debt and no other loans.

- James has $35 000 in an investment portfolio, which he saves $300 a month into. Trish has $8000 in a high-interest savings account and saves $2000 every year to it.

- Together, they have $15 000 in a joint everyday account.

- Their super balances are growing, although neither is contributing anything above what their employer does.

- James and Trish know their biggest financial hurdle is their mortgage.

Strategy stacks start with 'why'. For James and Trish, their 'why' is: 'We want to reduce the mortgage and raise our family.'

The strategy stack

All strategy stacks start with the Basic Stack (Chapter 4). Earnings and spending will determine how quickly James and Trish can achieve their goals of paying down the mortgage and raising their family. The Framing Strategies, Investment Strategies and Superannuation Strategies are good places for James and Trish to start their strategy stacking journey. And now they have growing assets, kids and a mortgage, it's important they also think about the Wealth Protection and Estate Planning Strategies as part of their strategy stack.

The Framing Strategies (Chapter 9) James and Trish might consider:

- The Budget Management Strategy
- The Cash Flow Management Strategy
- The Debt Reduction Strategy
- The Risk Assessment Strategy.

The Investment Strategies (Chapter 10) James and Trish might consider:

- The Dollar Cost Averaging Strategy
- The Investment Structure Strategy
- The Asset Selection Strategy
- The Investment Selection Strategy.

The Superannuation Strategies (Chapter 11) James and Trish might consider:

- The Contribution Strategies
- The Government Co-contribution Strategy
- The Super Splitting Strategy.

The Wealth Protection Strategies (Chapter 13) James and Trish might consider:

- The Income Protection Strategy
- The Trauma Protection Strategy
- The Total and Permanent Disability Protection Strategy
- The Life Protection Strategy.

The Estate Planning Strategies (Chapter 14) James and Trish might consider:

- The Last Will and Testament Strategy
- The Power of Attorney Strategy
- The Superannuation Nomination Strategy.

James and Trish pay attention to their budget and both bring something into the household. With a mortgage and two kids, there never seems to be a shortage of expenses. They do wonder if they can do better. James and Trish consider the Framing Strategies (Chapter 9). They both manage their budget but haven't reviewed it in a couple of years. They know when their key bills are due, so they're also managing their cash flow. Debt is limited to the home loan, but it feels like a big debt. They have also thought about the kind of investors they are. They are comfortable with more growth assets, as over the medium and long term they've seen how much better they perform than term deposits. They're comfortable with the risk given their investment time frame.

Table 8.5 looks at the current earnings situation for James and Trish, including their take-home pay and employer contributions to super.

Table 8.5: Calculating James and Trish's take-home pay

Earnings information	James	Trish
Gross income[1]	$110000	$35000
Income tax payable	$26217	$3192
Medicare levy	$2200	$700
Total tax and levies paid[2]	$28417	$3892
Take-home pay	$81583	$31108
Employer super contributions[3]	$11550	$3675

1. For simplicity, this assumes only their wages, not any investment or other income and after superannuation is paid by each of their employers. This includes the Medicare levy at the full rate. In this example, we assume gross income is simply made of their wages; income from investments however would also apply.

2. Based on the tax rates at the time of writing, although these can change.

3. Based on 10.5% of gross income.

Combined James and Trish have a take-home pay of $112 691 ($81 583 + $31 108). This translates into a monthly income of $9390.92 ($112 691/12).

The biggest expense in their monthly budget is the mortgage. It takes up $3360 of their monthly income. However, a review of their budget means they can afford to pay off the loan faster—paying $4000 a month instead of $3360. Their financial planner crunches some numbers and refers them to a mortgage broker in their network to find a better deal on their interest rate—it pays to review your fixed costs on a regular basis, as rates change over time and the more you save the more you own. Table 8.6 shows the difference this makes.

Table 8.6: Debt comparison

Issue	Without the stack	With the stack
Home loan balance	$650000	$650000
Monthly repayments	$3360	$4000
Interest rate	4% (pa)	4% (pa)
Monthly loan fees	$10	$10
Length of the loan	26 years, 1 month	19 years, 8 months

With advice, they realise they can save $107 550 in interest and fees, as well as own their home outright seven years earlier than anticipated. By doing some work on their budget and using a Debt Reduction Strategy, James and Trish are suddenly a lot further along the road than they thought they would be.

James continues to save $300 a month into his investment portfolio, and Trish saves $2000 a year into a high-interest savings account. But they're probably not making the most of their options here. Trish should be saving to her offset account as the home loan interest rate can be more than what banks are offering at times (especially now). A good home loan may allow up to 10 offset accounts depending on your lender. (An offset account is a savings account that you can deposit and withdraw from. The benefit of an offset account is that anything you save to it offsets your home loan when interest is calculated by the bank—without you losing access to the funds.)

James has the ability to save to his super *and* earn a tax deduction by making a personal concessional contribution to his superannuation. He does this by considering the Contribution Strategies (Chapter 11). When making personal concessional contributions to super, it's important not to forget the limits that apply. Table 8.7 shows the difference between James saving his $3600 ($300 × 12) to investments and saving it to super.

Table 8.7: Savings comparison (James)

Investment saving	Without strategy stacking	Superannuation saving	With strategy stacking
Yearly savings into investments	$3600	Yearly savings into super	$3600 (contribution tax of 15% applies, if James wants to claim a personal tax deduction)
Tax deduction of saving to investments	$0	Tax deduction of saving to superannuation	$3060

Rather than saving to super every month, James decides to put his money into the home loan offset account each month to reduce the interest on his home loan even more—after all, their goal is to pay down that mortgage. In mid-June however, he then withdraws the money to make his personal concessional contribution to super to get his tax deduction. That's a stack on a stack!

A look at Trish's situation reveals she's eligible for the government super co-contribution, which helps boost her retirement savings too using the Government Co-contribution Strategy (Chapter 11). Table 8.8 shows the difference this strategy makes to Trish's super account, when compared to saving into a savings account.

Table 8.8: Savings comparison (Trish)

Investment	Without strategy stacking	Superannuation	With strategy stacking
Yearly savings into fixed interest account	$1000	Yearly savings into super	$1000
Government super co-contribution	$0	Government super co-contribution	$500

Using a Super Splitting Strategy, they would also be able to move funds from Trish's super to James's super, given their age difference. They could move up to 85 per cent of her concessional contributions to James. As he will reach his Commonwealth preservation age first, they could access capital for Trish to then reduce her work hours or possibly retire fully when James is 65. While their combined super value won't change, they could have access to additional funds earlier.

The other part of their 'why', and the most important to James and Trish, is raising their kids. They've got a lot of expenses ahead of them, and the cost of high school and eventually university education is their biggest concern. They haven't started saving anything specifically for their kids' education, but they can use some of their existing funds, plus additional savings, to kick off that objective. One approach could be to rename one of their offset accounts, so they are still paying off the home while allocating money for their kids.

The savings accounts for the kids (and any surplus income) may be held in this offset account, which could allow the kids to build their own accounts but also offset Mum and Dad's mortgage over time, helping them save on the interest incurred. You should check with your mortgage lender about their offset account policy and use it to your advantage. Table 8.9 (overleaf) shows the comparison between a simple saving strategy and the Debt Reduction Strategy.

Table 8.9: Savings and debt reduction comparison

Issue	Without the stack after 12 months	With the stack after 12 months
Savings for the kids' education	$0	$5000
Home loan 3% interest saved	$0	$150 (3% x $5000)

While the $150 might not look like much of a saving, year on year and the more they save to their offset account for their kids' education, the saving will be worth thousands of dollars.

Giving their kids and family the opportunities they deserve relies very heavily on both their incomes. If something were to happen to James, Trish would find it difficult to make ends meet as well as manage the household. Equally, if something were to happen to Trish, James would need day-to-day support to keep the household going: Trish does so much at home to keep the wheels turning. Sitting down with their financial planner, they talk about the cover that they need not only to pay off the mortgage but also to cover the living expenses they have. They create a Wealth Protection Strategy (Chapter 13 covers the Wealth Protection Strategies). Both James and Trish make their household function; therefore, they both stack the following Wealth Protection Strategies for themselves and their family: the Income Protection Strategy, the Trauma Protection Strategy, the Total and Permanent Disability Protection Strategy and the Life Protection Strategy. Table 8.10 shows the comparison with and without the Wealth Protection Strategies.

Table 8.10: Wealth protection comparison

Issue	Without the stack	With the stack
Income protection	Some cover in their super, but not very good	80% of income covered plus a tax deduction (if held outside of super)
Trauma protection	No cover held	A fixed dollar amount covered

Issue	Without the stack	With the stack
Total and per-manent disability protection	Some default cover in their super with an 'any occupation' definition	A fixed dollar amount cov-ered using a super linking strategy for 'own occupa-tion' cover
Life cover protection	Some default cover in their super	A fixed dollar amount covered
Outcome	Not very clear on cover	Very clear on cover

When James was single, he was really carefree. Although he knew he needed a Will, an Enduring Power of Attorney and a nomination on his super fund, he only ever got around to adding a nomination to his super fund (which is now out of date). With advice, his financial planner assisted both James and Trish with the binding nominations on their super funds and referred them to a solicitor for the rest of their Estate Planning Strategies (Chapter 14). The conversation with the solicitor was quite confronting as they realised what would happen to the kids if anything happened to them both. The solicitor pointed out the benefits of a Testamentary Trust to protect their assets and pass them to the kids, which would also allow them to benefit from adult marginal tax rates while they are still minors. They realised the importance of both of them having their Estate Planning Strategies in order, so they both implemented the Last Will and Testament Strategy and the Power of Attorney Strategy with the solicitor. Table 8.11 shows the comparison without and with the Estate Planning Strategies.

Table 8.11: Estate planning comparison

Issue	Without the stack	With the stack
Binding nominations	James's nomination is out of date. Trish has never had one.	Complete and current
Last Will and Testament	James has never had a Will. Trish's Will is out of date	Complete and current
Enduring Power of Attorney	Neither has an Enduring Power of Attorney	Complete and current
Outcome	Large estate planning risks	Very clear on estate planning outcomes

Additional strategies James and Trish might consider

It might still seem like a lifetime away, but what James and Trish do now with their super may make a big difference over time.

They might also consider additional Superannuation Strategies (Chapter 11):

- The Consolidation Strategy
- The Super Investment Strategies.

On the next page you can see James and Trish's Strategy Stacking Calendar for the goal: 'We want to reduce the mortgage and raise our family'.

Short-term goals	Create and review their budget	Consider and implement Wealth Protection Strategies	
Medium-term goals	Contribute more to home loan repayment, to pay the loan off sooner	Set up kids' education savings account to give them a kick-start to life	
Long-term goals	Contribute to super to help achieve a more comfortable retirement one day		

January
Create budget.
Pay $4000 to home loan.
Set up kids' education savings account.

February
Review last month's budget performance.
Pay $4000 to home loan.
Implement Wealth Protection Strategies.

March
Review last month's budget performance.
Pay $4000 to home loan.
Implement Estate Planning Strategies.

April
Review last month's budget performance.
Pay $4000 to home loan.

May
Review last month's budget performance.
Pay $4000 to home loan.

June
Review last month's budget performance.
Pay $4000 to home loan.
James makes his super contribution and claims a deduction.
Trish makes a personal contribution of $1000 to super for the $500 government co-contribution.

July
Review last month's budget performance.
Pay $4000 to home loan.
Organise information for tax return.

August
Review last month's budget performance.
Pay $4000 to home loan.
Complete tax return.

September
Review last month's budget performance.
Pay $4000 to home loan.

October
Review last month's budget performance.
Pay $4000 to home loan.

November
Review last month's budget performance.
Pay $4000 to home loan.

December
Review last month's budget performance.
Pay $4000 to home loan.

Strategy stack: 'We want to retire comfortable and debt-free'

And just like that, another 10 years pass. James is now 51 and Trish is 47, and the kids are growing up:

- Their kids are now teenagers, aged 15 and 17.

- James has a full-time job that pays him $135 000 a year before tax, plus super.

- Trish now works full-time. It pays her $100 000 a year before tax, plus super.

- James and Trish have made good inroads into their mortgage. They've got $405 000 left to pay, but interest rates have risen from 3 per cent to 5 per cent.

- James and Trish still have no lingering credit card, but James has a $15 000 outstanding personal loan after upgrading the family car. The interest rate on that loan is 12 per cent (per annum).

- James has $75 000 in an investment portfolio. Trish has $25 000 in a high-interest savings account.

- Together, they have $10 000 in a joint everyday account.

- Their super balances are growing too, although neither is contributing anything above what their employer does.

- James and Trish are looking forward to paying off the home and they're confident about funding the kids' education. The next challenge they see is in regard to their retirement. They're not sure how much they need to retire on, but James would like to retire before his 65th birthday.

Strategy stacks start with 'why'. For James and Trish, their 'why' is now: 'We want to retire comfortable and debt-free.'

The strategy stack

All strategy stacks start with the Basic Stack (Chapter 4). Earnings and spending will determine how quickly James and Trish can achieve their goals of retiring comfortably and debt-free. The Framing Strategies, Investment Strategies and Superannuation Strategies are good places for James and Trish to start their strategy stacking journey. And now the kids are older and more independent, it's really time to focus on getting rid of that mortgage and making the most of their superannuation to fund those retirement goals.

The Framing Strategies (Chapter 9) James and Trish might consider:

- The Budget Management Strategy
- The Cash Flow Management Strategy
- The Debt Reduction Strategy
- The Risk Assessment Strategy.

The Superannuation Strategies (Chapter 11) James and Trish might consider:

- The Contribution Strategies
- The Super Splitting Strategy
- The Appropriate Super Fees Strategy
- The Super Investment Strategies.

James and Trish consider the Framing Strategies (Chapter 9). They both manage their budget well. They know when their key bills are due, so they're also managing their cash flow. Debt is limited to the home loan and personal loan, but it's manageable for them. They have thought about the kind of investors they are with the help of a financial planner, but James wonders if he should be more conservative given his wish to retire. However, they have continued to be comfortable with more growth assets, as over the medium and long term they've seen how better they perform than term deposits.

James and Trish still pay attention to their spending too and both continue to bring something into the household (see table 8.12, overleaf).

Table 8.12: Calculating James and Trish's take-home pay

Earnings information	James	Trish
Gross income[1]	$135000	$100000
Income tax payable[2]	$35017	$22967
Medicare levy	$2700	$2000
Total tax and levy payable[3]	$37717	$24967
Take-home pay	$97283	$75033
Employer super contributions[4]	$14175	$10500

1. For simplicity, this assumes only their wages, not any investment or other income and after superannuation is paid by their employers. We assume gross income is simply made of their wages; income from investments however would also apply.

2. Based on the tax rates at the time of writing, although these can change.

3. This includes the Medicare levy at the full rate, although this can change.

4. Based on 10.5% of gross income.

Combined, James and Trish have a take-home pay of $172316 ($97283 + $75033). This translates into a monthly income of $14359.66 ($172316/12).

The biggest expense in their monthly budget continues to be the mortgage. It takes up $4000 of their income. With a recent rise in interest rates, it means paying off the home will take longer, and as a result, they will pay more interest too. A review of their budget and current savings finds that they can make further inroads into the mortgage. James takes $40000 from his investments and Trish takes $5000 from hers to make a $45000 contribution to their offset account. This means they can re-draw the money if there's an emergency or other expense. James would also have the option to take the money out of the offset account if he wished to buy back his existing investments, which may allow him to convert non-deductible home loan debt into deductible investment debt. If he thought his investments could grow faster than the interest rate on the home loan, James could maintain his portfolio over the longer term also. They can also afford to pay $4500 a month from their budget—an extra $500 per month (see table 8.13).

By making this change, they save $71385 ($185945 – $114560) in bank interest and fees. It also means they'll own their own home outright by the time James reaches his 60th birthday. Now there's a reason to celebrate!

Table 8.13: Debt comparison

Issue	Without the stack	With the stack
Home loan balance	$405 000	$360 000
Monthly repayments	$4000	$4500
Interest rate	6.5% (pa)	6.5% (pa)
Monthly loan fees	$10	$10
Length of the loan	12 years, 4 months	8 years, 10 months
Interest and fees paid	$185 945	$114 560

Given their current focus is also around retiring comfortably, attention returns to their retirement savings. Superannuation offers a tax-effective vehicle to save for retirement.

At the present time, James has $400 000 in his super and Trish has $90 000 in her account. In retirement, they estimate they'll need $55 000 a year to live.

With advice, their financial planner works out what their current retirement situation might look like to see if their current savings are enough to meet their retirement lifestyle needs. Both James and Trish haven't thought about when they'd like to retire, so their financial planner starts by looking at their situation if James retires at age 65 (see table 8.14). Trish is happy to retire when James does.

Table 8.14: Projection (estimate) of future superannuation

Issue	James	Trish
Years to retirement	14 years	14 years
Retirement age	65 years	60 years
Current superannuation balance	$400 000	$90 000
Forecasted super balance[1]	$603 191	$181 979

1. Assumptions 5% return, $50 (pa) administration fee, Indirect Cost Ratio (ICR) 0.6%.

In 14 years' time (when James turns 65), their combined estimated super is worth $785 170 ($603 191 + $181 979).

If they want $55 000 a year from their retirement savings, they'll only be able afford to do this for around 14 years ($785 170/$55 000)

That's not a problem if both of them were only going to live for another 14 years after retirement, but it's likely they'll live into their 80s or more. This means that, like many people, James and Trish have a gap of perhaps 15–20 years they'll need to fill. That's an extra $1 100 000 ($55 000 × 20) they'll need—which is more than the $785 170 they'll have.

With advice from their financial planner, they decide it's time to get pre-retirement stacking. James has confirmed that they need $50 000 of after-tax income to meet their day-to-day living costs after making their mortgage payments. With their financial planner, they consider the Contribution Strategies (Chapter 11).

James should increase his contributions to super, and Trish should consider making additional contributions up to their concessional limit of $27 500, cash flow permitting (remember employer contributions count also). He currently has cap space of approximately $14 000, with Trish able to direct up to $17,500 to super due to her pay rise. Assuming she directs $15 000 to super each year, this could see a further $29 000 of pre-tax contributions added to the fund each financial year—or $406 000 (excluding earnings) going towards their retirement asset base in superannuation by the time James hits 65.

To continue funding the Retirement Strategy, with the home loan paid off in approximately nine years, this would free up a further $54 000 per annum ($4500 × 12) for a period of five years through to James's anticipated retirement at age 65. The cash flow saving achieved by paying off the house may be directed to superannuation for James as a non-concessional contribution each year, as it would be below the annual limit of $110 000 and would not impact his ability to continue claiming a personal tax deduction for the concessional contribution made by himself and his employer through to retirement.

Using a Super Splitting Strategy, they would be able to move funds from Trish's super to James's given their age difference. They could move up to 85 per cent of her concessional contributions to James. As he will reach his Commonwealth preservation age first, they could access capital for Trish to reduce her work hours or possibly retire totally when James is 65. Should she love her job and wish to continue working part-time, she could do so and further bolster their total income position.

Their financial planner also talks to them about the Appropriate Super Fees Strategy. James and Trish had never thought about shopping around for a better super fund deal. Moreover, they never really thought about the fees they were paying either. On a combined balance of the $490 000 they have invested (they both use the same super fund), they pay a 1.8 per cent ICR with their current super account (let's call it Super Fund A). This equates to $8820 in fees a year.

Their financial planner believes this is too costly. Over 14 years (the number of years to retirement), they'd pay $123 480 on their current super balances (14 × $8820). Super Fund A has returned about 5 per cent a year and charges a $50 administration fee too.

As a result, their financial planner recommends switching to Super Fund B, which has a 0.6 per cent ICR. On a combined balance of $490 000, this equates to $2940 in fees a year. Super Fund B has returned about 5 per cent a year and charges a $50 administration fee too.

Table 8.15 shows the impact of making additional contributions and using a better super fund.

Table 8.15: Pre-retirement comparison

Strategy	Without strategy stacking	With strategy stacking
Personal deductible contributions	$0	James $14 000 Trish $15 500
Personal non-deductible contributions	$0	Mortgage payment from when home loan paid off with new contributions and income $54 000 (pa) for five years
Appropriate Super Fees Strategy	Super Fund A: 1.8% ICR[1] Total Cost: $8870 each year (ICR and admin fee)	Super Fund B: 0.60% ICR[2] Total cost $2990 each year (ICR and admin fee)

1. Super Fund A: 5% return, $50 pa administration fee, ICR 1.8%—without the strategy.
2. Super Fund B: 5% return, $50 pa administration fee, ICR 0.6%—with strategy.

The value of James's super fund over a five-year period could increase from $768 836 to $800 876 by considering the ICR costs of his underlying investments as part of his Appropriate Super Fees Strategy. Over time this could make a significant difference to the value of his retirement income stream when he reaches age 65.

The value of Trish's super fund may be increased from \$199 414 to \$207 323, a difference of \$7909 over the same five-year period. This illustrates the value of looking at your underlying investment costs within your fund to avoid unnecessary waste.

The new fund (Super Fund B) also provides them with a range of assets and investments that can help them achieve their goals. Their financial planner was able to provide them with professional investment advice as well by considering the Asset Alllocation Strategy and the Super Investment Strategies. They'd never been engaged enough with their super over the years to see how well it was going. They see the benefit of doing that now.

Additional stacks James and Trish might consider

Superannuation is a great vehicle for saving for retirement; however, it doesn't mean that you should forget about your non-super investments (the investments you have outside of super). These are really important investments as, unlike super, you can access the money at any age.

James and Trish may wish to add these Investment Strategies (Chapter 10) to their strategy stack:

- The Diversification Strategy
- The Dollar Cost Averaging Strategy
- The Investment Structure Strategy
- The Asset Allocation Strategy
- The Asset Selection Strategy
- The Investment Selection Strategy
- The Franking Credit Strategy
- The Fee Reduction Strategy
- The Appropriate Tax Strategy.

On the next page you can see James and Trish's Strategy Stacking Calendar for the goal: 'We want to retire comfortable and debt-free'

Short-term goals	Create and review their budget to make the most of their money	Pay off the personal car loan
Medium-term goals	Increase payments to pay off the house	Contribute more to super, make smarter use of super
Long-term goals	Retire comfortably and debt-free	

January	February	March
Create budget. Move $45 000 from investments to offset account. Use the Appropriate Super Fees Strategy to improve outcomes.	Review last month's budget performance. Save any surplus to the offset account tied to the mortgage.	Review last month's budget performance. Save any surplus to the offset account tied to the mortgage. Review home loan interest rates to ensure they are as low as possible.

April	May	June
Review last month's budget performance. Save any surplus to the offset account tied to the mortgage.	Review last month's budget performance. Save any surplus to the offset account tied to the mortgage. Check last year's fund value cap space and consider the Contribution Catch-up Strategy to bolster super.	Review last month's budget performance. Save any surplus to the offset account tied to the mortgage. Make personal deductible contributions up to concessional limits.

July	August	September
Review last month's budget performance. Save any surplus to the offset account tied to the mortgage. Super split contributions to superannuation from Trish to James once deduction notice has been actioned. Organise information for tax returns.	Review last month's budget performance. Save any surplus to the offset account tied to the mortgage. Complete personal tax returns.	Review last month's budget performance. Save any surplus to the offset account tied to the mortgage. Review home loan interest rates.

October	November	December
Review last month's budget performance. Save any surplus to the offset account tied to the mortgage	Review last month's budget performance. Save any surplus to the offset account tied to the mortgage	Review last month's budget performance. Save any surplus to the offset account tied to the mortgage

Strategy stack: 'We want to retire, but how do we actually do it?'

James is ready to retire at 65, but Trish, aged 61, has a great opportunity to work part-time with a girlfriend through to 65. Their lives look different yet again:

- Their kids are now adults, aged 25 and 27. Their first grandchild has just arrived too, and they're excited to be grandparents.

- James will access his superannuation at 5 per cent as a tax-free income stream from an account-based pension.

- Trish continues to work part-time. It pays her $60000 a year before tax, plus super.

- Before starting her new role, Trish starts an account-based pension in her own name to ensure her superannuation is tax-free as well. She draws the legislated minimum of 4 per cent for her age.

- The home is paid off and is now worth $1.2 million, almost twice as much as what they paid for it 30 years ago

- James and Trish still have no lingering credit card debt or personal loans.

- James is looking forward to saying goodbye to the week-day commute, and Trish can start late and finish early as well.

Strategy stacks start with 'why'. For James and Trish, their 'why' is now: 'We want to retire, but how do we actually do it?'

The strategy stack

All strategy stacks start with the Basic Stack (Chapter 4). Earnings and spending will help determine how James and Trish can achieve their goal of giving up work and retiring. Although James won't be going to work to earn an income, there's still household and other expenses to pay. The Framing Strategies, Superannuation Strategies and Retirement Strategies are good places for James and Trish to start their strategy stacking journey. And now they have a grandchild, they might also think about how they will keep their grandchild entertained (but perhaps that's the topic of other books!).

The Framing Strategies (Chapter 9) James and Trish might consider:

- The Budget Management Strategy
- The Cash Flow Management Strategy
- The Debt Reduction Strategy
- The Risk Assessment Strategy.

The Superannuation Strategies (Chapter 11) Trish might consider:

- The Contribution Strategies.

The Retirement Strategies (Chapter 12) James and Trish might consider:

- The Retirement Readiness Strategy
- The Retirement Income Vehicles Strategy
- The Transition to Retirement Strategy.

James and Trish consider the Framing Strategies (Chapter 9). They continue to manage their budget well, although with the arrival of their first grandchild, Trish and James probably did go a little over the top in helping with the costs around setting up a nursery. They know when their key bills are due and continue to pay them on time, so they're also managing their cash flow. Debt is a memory for them. They own their home. They have considered the kind of investors they are with their financial planner in this new phase of retirement.

Trish is still working. This means the Contribution Strategy is still important for her. James has retired from work and he gave real thought to the Retirement Readiness Strategy. During his working life, his work was his life—and that's typical for many people who see their professional careers as more than just a job. He spent time thinking about this strategy for himself and with Trish. He realised he still has things he wants to achieve, as does Trish. That includes doing a lap of Australia.

With their financial planner, they also considered the Retirement Income Vehicles Strategy, which would help them turn their super and investments into a retirement income stream. As James enters retirement and Trish continues to receive super, they will have a new income position (see table 8.16).

Table 8.16: James and Trish's income when James reaches retirement age

Earnings information	James	Trish
Gross wage income[1]	$0	$60000
Pension income[2]	$53459	$15679
Income tax payable[3]	$0	$9967
Medicare levy payable	$0	$1200
Total tax and levy payable	$0	$11167
Take-home pay	$53459	$64512
Employer super contributions[4]	$0	$6300

1. For simplicity, this assumes only their wages, not any investment or other income and after superannuation is paid by the employer. This includes the Medicare levy at the full rate. In this example, we assume gross income is simply made of their wages; income from investments however would also apply. Based on the tax rates at the time of writing, although these can change.

2. James takes a 5% pension drawing from his super fund (which is valued at $1069180).

3. As both James and Trish are over 60, income from each of their account-based pension accounts is tax-free. Trish only pays tax on her gross wage income. Based on the tax rates at the time of writing, although these can change.

4. Based on 10.5% of gross income for Trish (employer contribution rate is likely to change over time).

On the advice of their financial planner, James uses the Retirement Income Vehicles Strategy and selects an account-based pension to turn his superannuation into a retirement income stream. As James is over 65, any income he takes from this pension or interest that it earns inside the pension account is tax-free.

Trish also considers and uses the Transition to Retirement Strategy to supplement her part-time wages shown in table 8.16. Although drawing this amount is above their personal income requirements, Trish and James decide to gift some money to their adult kids, so the money is put to good use.

Combined, James and Trish have a take-home pay of $117971 ($53459 + $64512). This is a lot more than their intended $55000, which is nearly met with James's pension alone. With Trish working on a part-time basis, she may wish to consider the following strategic options:

- Not taking a transition to retirement pension and preserving her capital base in super

- Adding back to superannuation with personal funds to lower her tax position (where it's worthwhile)

- Adding surplus income back to superannuation as a non-concessional contribution to further bolster her superannuation for when she finally retires.

Strategy Stacking Tip

James could take a small capital sum from his pension ($10000), once he's retired, as a pension and they could live on Trish's after-tax income. This could give James the ability to grow his superannuation balance over time while Trish is working part-time. He could draw the rest of his pension at the end of the financial year and then recontribute it back to super using the Contribution Strategies (Chapter 11).

James and Trish have benefited from long-term active advice and have been able to meet their living costs easily with surplus income that they can use for travel or lifestyle.

The use of strategies doesn't stop when you retire. Depending on your cash flow position, you should always think about how to best use the funds you have available. If you can live on a salary and take a part pension, then consider restructuring your early pension payout accordingly; if you don't need the pension income, take it at the end of the year. A pension is the action of taking money out, it doesn't mean you have to default to a fortnightly payment. Accessing your pension funds as needed offers flexibility when it comes to funding your lifestyle in retirement. You can generally take it as you wish, within the guidelines set by your pension provider.

Working on a part-time basis still means you have retired in a sense, because you have the ability to quit and maintain the same lifestyle. Where you can do this, I believe that you are actually retired—you're just working because you enjoy your job or want to keep learning and growing.

Additional stacks James and Trish might consider

At different points in our lives we might consider Estate Planning Strategies. Retirement is often a good time re-visit these plans, especially if you've acquired new assets since you last updated your Will or you have new family members arrive (like grandchildren). James and Trish may want to consider the following Estate Planning Strategies (Chapter 14):

- The Last Will and Testament Strategy (perhaps also with a gift to their grandchild)

- The Power of Attorney Strategy

- The Superannuation Nomination Strategy or the Reversionary Pension Strategy.

The Power of Attorney Strategy is also important. Although James and Trish aren't yet in their golden years, in another turn of the page they might be and they may need someone to act for them.

The Superannuation Nomination Strategy/Reversionary Pension Strategy is something they should both consider if they end up with account-based pensions. Like superannuation, your Will doesn't determine what happens to your account-based pension when you pass. Generally you have two options here: your pension payment can revert to your partner or you can request your partner (or others) receive the balance of your account-based pension as a lump sum (less any tax payable). For more information about these options, see the Superannuation Nomination Strategy and the Reversionary Pension Strategy in Chapter 14.

James's and Trish's Strategy Stacking Calendar is much simpler now too. Each month they just need to keep an eye on their budget and ensure they have the funds available when they are ready to start their journey around the country.

A final note on these scenarios

These scenarios are designed to show how strategy stacking can help stack the odds in your favour. Let the stacks you build be guided by your own 'why'.

For example:

- There's nothing wrong with a 20-year-old having a retirement goal.

- There's nothing wrong with a 40-year-old who's been locked out of the housing market to have the goal of buying their first home.

- There's nothing wrong with a 60-year-old saving for a motorbike or trip to Bali.

How you strategy stack is determined by your 'why'—your short-, medium- and long-term goals. It will change as your life changes—and working with a financial planner may be a useful approach at any stage of your life.

Part 3 is where I look in detail at the financial planning strategies that financial planners use with their clients. Which ones might you use to build your own strategy stack?

PART III
THE STRATEGIES

You've made it. This section of *Smart Money Strategy* outlines the financial planning strategies that I use with my financial planning clients. As a financial planner, one of the best parts of my job is looking at a client's starting position and seeing which of these strategies I can stack to help them achieve their goals.

In the following chapters, I break the strategies down into different categories that will help you understand how they work. Specifically, we will look at:

- The Framing Strategies
- The Investment Strategies
- The Superannuation Strategies
- The Retirement Strategies
- The Wealth Protection Strategies
- The Estate Planning Strategies.

Within each of these chapters are lots of financial strategies you might use to stack the odds in your favour, as well as some strategy stacking tips for you to keep in mind when considering what might work for you and your situation. Seek the assistance of a financial planner if you need help to make sense of the strategies for your own stack.

CHAPTER 9

The Framing Strategies

Budgeting, what you spend and earn, sits at the centre of your strategy stack—this is the Basic Stack, which I introduced in Chapter 4 (think of it as the floor on which you build your strategy stack). But to build a stack you need a set of strategies that *frame* your stack, in much the same way as a house frame structures the walls and rooms when you're building a house.

There are four Framing Strategies that shape how you build your strategy stack:

- The Budget Management Strategy—this strategy takes a closer look at how you use your income and expenditure. Are you saving anything?

- The Cash Flow Management Strategy—this strategy looks at the flows of income and expenditure. Have you got enough money to pay the bills when they arrive?

- The Debt Reduction Strategy—this strategy considers your options for reducing debt and, as a result, the amount of interest you pay (which could be going to other things). Many people have a plan to spend, but do you have a plan to pay back your debt?

- The Risk Assessment Strategy—this strategy evaluates your appetite for risk. Are you conservative or aggressive in how you approach your financial life?

This chapter covers these Framing Strategies in detail and just like the Basic Stack (where spending meets earnings), these collection of four strategies should be used at the start of every strategy stacking journey you take.

The Budget Management Strategy

The Budget Management Strategy is probably the most important financial planning strategy and it combines two of the foundations about money: your earnings and your spending (refer to Chapter 3). In order to give yourself the best chance to reach your 'why', budget management has to be considered. Quite simply, budget management involves understanding your earnings and your expenses over time, then deciding how to best make use of your earnings and your spending with your 'why' in mind.

Regardless of how much you earn, you can't ignore the Budget Management Strategy.

How does it work?

At a simple level, budget management starts with listing your sources of earning and spending (which the Strategy Stacker's Starting Position exercise in Chapter 6 helps you do).

Here's some common earnings and expenses to help you get started.

Total earnings are made up of:

- Your take-home pay
- Your partner's take-home pay
- Bonuses and overtime
- Saving and investment income
- Government benefits
- Other income.

Total spending is made up of:

- Home expenses:
  - Rent (if a non-homeowner)
  - Home maintenance and renovations
  - Rates
  - Gardening/pool expenses
  - Home services (cleaning)
  - Pest control
  - Phone, mobile and internet
  - Electricity and gas
  - Other
- Living expenses:
  - Groceries
  - Clothes and shoes
  - Household purchases
  - Medical/chemist purchases
  - Doctor, dentist, physiotherapist and other specialist medical expenses
  - Pet care
  - Laundry and dry cleaning
  - Education expenses
  - Other
- Children:
  - Baby products
  - Childcare
  - School fees
  - Sport and activities

- o Excursions
- o School uniforms
- o Pocket money
- o Other
- ■ Vehicle and transport:
  - o Licence and registration fees
  - o Maintenance and repairs
  - o Fuel costs
  - o Transport (bus, train, taxi, Uber)
  - o Parking
  - o Other
- ■ Mortgage and debt repayments (also note the interest rate for each of these, if applicable):
  - o Mortgage
  - o Car loan
  - o Credit cards
  - o Personal loans
  - o Store cards
  - o Afterpay
  - o Laybuys
- ■ Leisure and entertainment:
  - o Take-aways and restaurants
  - o Holidays
  - o Music and TV streaming subscriptions
  - o Sports, hobbies and club memberships
  - o Newspapers, magazines and books
  - o Gifts (Christmas, birthdays)

- ○ Alcohol, cigarettes and gambling
- ○ Other
- ■ Financial services and superannuation:
  - ○ Life, disablement, income protection and trauma cover
  - ○ Private healthcare cover, Medicare levy
  - ○ Home and contents insurance
  - ○ Car, boat, caravan and trailer insurance
  - ○ Key person premiums, workers' compensation and public liability insurance (if you're in business)
  - ○ Superannuation contributions
  - ○ Savings contributions
  - ○ Accounting costs
  - ○ Financial advice fees
  - ○ Other.

Once you've identified your list, work out the amounts over a month. You might also multiply it out over a quarter (your monthly expenses × 3) and a year (your monthly expenses × 12). You can then work out if you're spending more or less than what you earn. This is great information! In my experience, people get a real surprise about their spending—it's not always what you think it is.

When you have this information, you've got some decisions to make:

- ■ Are you earning enough?
- ■ What do you need to do to earn more, if needed?
- ■ Are you getting value from all of your spending?
- ■ What spending can you change or get even more value from?

It's common for people to realise how much value they're missing from the income they earn, which can leave them feeling deflated or angry. Those feelings are good feelings for making helpful changes, however. You work hard for your money—if you give it to anyone (such as a bank, an investment or a retailer), you should get good value in return. As an income earner and spender, work hard to get the best value you can.

You don't have to be a technological whizz to work out a budget—a pen and a piece of paper will do. Use the calculator on your smartphone if you have to. If you're good with technology, turn your budget into a spreadsheet. Tools like this help you track your spending over time too. Also consider adding a receipt-catcher app to your smartphone. Instead of having to keep physical receipts, you simply take a photo on your phone and enter a few details, then download this information at home later.

Regardless of how busy you are, receipt-catching apps make keeping track of your spending easy. Some good apps include ReceiptJar and Receipt Catcher. Your phone's app store will have plenty of other options too. Some banking apps also offer spending tracking features. If you don't like apps, you can also take a photo of all your receipts and save them in a receipts file or track them using an Excel spreadsheet (Chapter 6 talks you through keeping an accurate record of your spending in more detail).

Once you've got the numbers in your budget period, it's easy to see if you're saving some of your income or if you are spending more than you earn. Look at ways you can get more value from what you spend by shopping around. Equally is there any spending that's just wasteful and can be cut? This kind of thinking will help you to live more comfortably within your means rather than feel under financial pressure. Keeping track of your budget keeps you informed of where your money is coming from and going.

The greater purpose for doing this is really about setting up your next Framing Strategy for your strategy stack. If you have the ability to save, you'll be able to build a different kind of stack to someone who doesn't have the ability to save. The stack you build of course, as I've said previously, relates back to your 'why' or your personal goals.

When to do it?

A Budget Management Strategy should be the first strategy you implement. It's not a set-and-forget strategy though—it requires regular attention from you. Monthly reviews are a great way to start learning about your spending habits, where your money is actually going, and what you might like to do to help you get to your goals (you can schedule a monthly review of your budget on your Strategy Stacking Calendar—refer to Chapter 7).

Do

Do consider a Budget Management Strategy:

- When you first make a commitment to improving your financial life

- When you're concerned about not saving enough

- Before you take out any debt or to help you pay back debt

- When you're working towards achieving your 'why', and review it regularly

- Any time your earnings or fixed costs change.

Don't

Don't fall into these traps:

- Making decisions about budget management that you can't keep—always be realistic

- Letting that thing that stops you from doing a budget hold you back (such as fear, procrastination or apathy, which are common feelings when we think about something we want to avoid). You do have the ability to make change. It's time to break through that barrier!

- Being too shocked by what you're spending on some things when you complete your budget; it's normal to be surprised by your spending, and by setting out your earnings and spending you're giving yourself the ability to make better decisions.

It will never matter how much you earn or spend, if you don't take steps to understand what you're doing

You might think someone (or a household) earning six figures would have more money than they know what to do with, but the reality is most people don't—and it's usually because of one or more of the money truths that I outlined in Chapter 1. Your ability to earn an income has nothing to do with your ability to manage money.

I recently had a chat with a client of mine who asked me, as their financial planner, if I thought they were smart. This client is an experienced and qualified doctor. I paused before replying to give me time to think. My eventual reply was, 'Yes, I think you are smart but only in the areas that interest you. There are a lot of things you probably don't know, just like all of us.'

The doctor laughed and replied, 'Yes, you're right!'

Achieving anything in life requires effort. The same goes with your financial life. The Budget Management Strategy is one I ask you to take up right now. Put down the book. It will still be here once you've finished, waiting for you patiently. If you haven't completed the exercise in Chapter 6, now's a great time to do it.

The Budget Management Strategy is a very important Framing Strategy for your strategy stack and achieving your 'why'. Your ability to manage your resources well and save a little more will impact how quickly you reach your goals.

The Cash Flow Management Strategy

The Cash Flow Management Strategy, like the Budget Management Strategy, combines two of the foundations about money: your earnings and your spending (Chapter 3 covers all five foundations in detail). Rather than looking at what you're earning and spending specifically, cash flow management looks at the relationship between earnings and spending, and time.

If you spend less than you earn in a month, your position is *cash flow positive* over that month. Over time, this outcome means you have money to use for other things, including the savings and investments you need to help you reach your 'why'. Surplus cash flow also means you're in a better place to deal with unexpected events that might otherwise cause you financial stress.

However, if you spend more than you earn in a month, your position is considered *cash flow negative*. This means you've had to rely on some kind of debt to help you pay the bills (or you haven't paid the bills). In this case, you don't have anything spare and you're probably incurring interest (or risking your credit rating). It also means you may struggle to deal with unexpected financial events, should they occur, and over time it becomes increasingly difficult to benefit from compounding interest (refer to Chapter 3).

How does it work?

In order to understand your cash flow, you need to understand your earnings and spending—and the Budget Management Strategy is a great place to start. You specifically need to understand when your earnings are going to be paid and when your spending is likely to happen.

Table 9.1 offers a way for you to plan out when your spending needs to happen. It's easy to start with your bigger expenses first. The examples in table 9.1 show some of your likely spending, which you can use as a starting point (as you build up your table, add the relevant amounts for each of your expenses). Then you can work out what you need to save before they're due.

Table 9.1: Planning your spending

January	February	March	April	May	June
School fees	Electricity bill Council rates	Home and contents insurance	Easter holiday	Car service and registration Electricity bill	Personal tax-deductible super contribution
July	**August**	**September**	**October**	**November**	**December**
New lounge furniture	Electricity bill	Boat and trailer insurance	New TV	Electricity bill	Christmas gifts Christmas holiday

Having money available to pay for your spending, without the use of debt or credit cards, is the key here. For example, let's say you know that during the month ahead you've got phone, internet, grocery, entertainment, fuel and loan costs—which sounds like a usual month. By knowing when these expenses are due to occur, you can plan your spending to pay them when you need to with the income you earn. However, if you know you've got a big expense headed your way in the next three months, like school fees, getting the car serviced/registered or paying for that holiday, you can start putting some money aside each week for these expenses so you can pay for them when they arrive. With time on your side, you can avoid using debt for these irregular expenses.

It's not by any means a hard concept, but most people fail at it. Why? It requires you to do two things: first, you have to understand at what points you will need money; second, you have to save something along the way from your earnings before that big expense arrives. People fail at this not because they don't have the ability to save, but because they haven't planned for the arrival of this irregular expense. So, they fail because of a gap in their knowledge and not sitting down and planning.

Creating a situation where you are in a position of being cash flow positive enables you to really move forward. The free cash flow—that is, the money you haven't allocated spending to—enables you to save and invest. Free cash flow can also be put aside for those irregular bills and help you avoid ridiculous credit card fees. For me, cash flow will *always* be King!

To implement your Cash Flow Management Strategy, spend some time thinking about when those irregular bills are due and keep something aside for them over each week so you know you've got it covered. No one likes that 'bill shock' feeling. An example is your car's registration and insurance. Depending on the age of your car, insurance costs and government registration fees can really add up. And if you're more than a one-car family, it costs even more. If you know the overall cost is about $1200 a year, for example, then it's easier to save $100 a month than find $1200 in the month the bills arrive.

The other thing you're likely to discover by looking at when your bills are due is the order you need to pay them in. It might sound like a small thing, but if money is tight, ordering your bills by the due date makes a lot of sense. There's no point in paying a bill that's due in a month if you've got one due this week.

When to do it?

A Cash Flow Management Strategy should be the second Framing Strategy you implement. Like budget management, it's not a set-and-forget strategy, as bills often go up and down and you're likely to revise your spending plans. It's a good strategy to look at though if you plan your spending quarterly, half-yearly or yearly—it ensures you know what's coming up so you can be prepared. Taking a longer-term view gives you more options too, as you've got the benefit of time on your side. Another option is to set up a regular payment of a smaller amount so that when the bill does come, it's not going to have the same impact if you have chipped away at it during the year with spare cash flow.

Do

Do consider a Cash Flow Management Strategy:

- When you first make a commitment to improving your financial life

- When you're not saving enough, and want to be in a cash flow positive position

- When you don't know what bills are due when

- When you need to smooth your spending due to larger bills you receive from time to time:

  ○ Use separate accounts if it provides you with piece of mind or motivation. It won't change the outcome but your money will have a specific purpose that you can tie to the spending or saving behaviour.

  ○ Consider setting up direct debits to pay your bills automatically. Automation is a great way to stay in control, without the day-to-day hassles.

- You're working towards achieving your 'why', and you review it regularly

- When you want to reward milestones and plan the related spending through your savings accounts or via buffers in other accounts. It's a marathon not a sprint, and it still has to be fun!

Don't

Don't fall into these traps:

- Forgetting to pay your bills on time—and if you need an extension, talk to the provider involved

- Being afraid to switch things up if you need to (perhaps that holiday can be pushed back or the car service pushed forward)

- Forgetting to pay off your credit card by the due date if you've spent on credit. When interest rates are so high on these cards, it pays not to forget about it.

Even if you're earning more than you're spending, without cash flow management you can still find yourself in financial stress

I've met people earning great incomes for the work they do, yet they still find themselves in unhappy money places. Often the reason is because they haven't managed their cash flow. They don't know when the bills arrive, and suddenly they're facing school fees, home and contents insurance, and the car registration—and on top of that, the hot water system fails. Sometimes when it rains, it pours.

All these bills hit in the same month, but making regular, small payments towards bills throughout the year makes the pain of one-off bills less of an issue. Setting aside $50 a week is money you may not miss, but $600 a quarter hurts. Making regular payments also allows you to manage what you have to spend week to week.

When things get financially tough, many people turn to a credit card. And over time, they might keep turning to the credit card, and perhaps even add a second and third credit card. They don't have a solid plan to pay them back, while they're paying all that interest to banks. It's heart-breaking to me because they're not giving themselves a chance to achieve their 'why'.

The solution to their problems isn't that hard. They just need to figure out when the bills are due and keep a little something as back-up for that rainy-day event. Being ready for the spending events before they arrive requires a little bit of planning, but it's worth it for your financial peace of mind.

The Debt Reduction Strategy

The Debt Reduction Strategy is as it sounds: it's all about paying off debt. *Debt* occurs when you borrow money for spending today. You pay back the borrowed amount in instalments over an agreed time frame and with interest at a set rate, depending on how you borrowed the money. The repayments include interest repayments too until the owed amount has been fully repaid to the lender. Most debts also charge account and loan fees.

There are many debt products in the marketplace. Examples include payday loans, credit cards, buy-now-pay-later products, personal loans, home loans and business loans. It's important you understand the terms of any debt before you enter into debt, as well as any fees charged in addition to interest.

> I gave the credit card a workout while I was on holidays overseas.

> You'll need another holiday by the time you pay it off!

All debt needs to be paid back at some point. Some loans require you to make principal and interest repayments, while other loans offer interest-only repayments, where the outstanding loan does not reduce over time. Depending on your cash flow, you may wish to consider either option to meet your goals.

For investment loans, where you want to reduce the minimum interest payment while being able to pay off the loan as needed, you could use interest-only repayments alongside an offset account. This way you have the best of both worlds: reduced payments to the bank and the ability to pay off the loan with savings or other assets in the future. Additionally, some loans (such as home loans) can offer offset accounts and redraw facilities. An offset account allows you to put your pay into an account and, as the name suggests, the value of that account is offset against the value of the outstanding loan and the interest you pay. You can still use your offset account like a savings account to withdraw money from as you need to. Other loan features might include a redraw facility; in this case, you can withdraw some of the equity you've built up from the repayments you have made. However, withdrawing this money will keep you in debt longer if it's not used for investment purposes. You need to keep in mind that re-drawing on a loan that is intended for investment but using the re-drawn funds for non-investment purposes can result in a change in the tax deductibility of your loan.

Debt is attractive to many people and should not be viewed as negative as it allows you to buy what you want today and pay it back later, without having to save. Used correctly, debt is a powerful tool but it MUST be controlled. You have to pay that debt back with interest—and interest is a tax on your patience, where the borrowing is not growing an investment asset (such as a car).

How does it work?

The Debt Reduction Strategy works through understanding your budget and your cash flow.

Debt adds an ongoing expense to your budget that you need to be prepared to pay. It's important to also understand your cash flow to ensure you have the money available to repay the debt when repayments are due.

Reducing your debt quickly reduces the amount of interest you have to repay. This interest is really lost money. Paying interest to someone stops you spending or saving this money in other areas.

Let's consider two examples: a smaller purchase like a new TV on a credit card and a larger purchase of a house through a home loan.

The TV

You've shopped around and found a good deal on a new TV that costs $2600. You purchase it using a credit card, which has 18 per cent per annum interest. The minimum monthly repayment is either 2 per cent of the balance at the end of the month or $25—whichever is the greatest. For ease, I assume there's no additional monthly fee.

Take a look at the interest amounts for different levels of repayment of this $2600 debt (see table 9.2).

Table 9.2: Repayment options for a TV bought using a credit card

Repayment amount per month	Time to pay back	Total amount paid back	Total interest paid
$60	5 years and 9 months	$4112	$1552
$80	3 years and 8 months	$3517	$917
$100	2 years and 9 months	$3257	$657
$120	2 years and 2 months	$3111	$511

If you want to calculate repayment options for a debt, Moneysmart has a debt calculator you may find helpful: moneysmart.gov.au/credit-cards/credit-card-calculator.

When you look at the interest you're paying, suddenly that new television doesn't look like a good deal. Even if you're repaying the debt at $120 per month, the $511 dollars in interest you have to pay might have paid for three or four weeks of groceries or paid for part of a holiday. Or it might have even been used to put towards an investment that could earn you some money.

The house

If the interest you pay on buying a TV using debt doesn't excite you, let's take a look at debt on a bigger purchase—a house.

FRAMING

You've done your homework and decided to buy a house that's a 40-minute commute from work. The cost of the house is $590000. You've saved a $40000 deposit, so you borrow $550000 through a home loan. It's a fixed rate home loan at a 4 per cent per annum interest rate. This means that over the term of your loan, the interest rate will remain the same. There's $10 a month in loan fees too.

Let's take a look at different levels of repayments (see table 9.3).

Table 9.3: Repayment options for a house

Repayment amount per month	Time to pay back	Total amount paid back	Total interest paid (including fees)
$2000	63 years and 8 months	$1527601	$977602
$2500	33 years and 5 months	$1001311	$451311
$3000	23 years and 10 months	$856182	$306182
$3500	18 years and 8 months	$783652	$233652

If you want to calculate repayment options for a mortgage, Moneysmart also has a mortgage calculator you may find helpful: moneysmart.gov. au/home-loans/mortgage-calculator.

If you were worried about interest costs on the TV, then the interest paid on a home loan should really give you something to think about. Let's say you pay back $2500 a month. In the above example, you'll end up paying $451311 in interest. That's over half of what you borrowed! I'm sure you could find something better to do with $451311 than pay it to a bank.

As both of these real-life examples highlight, there's benefit in looking at your budget and cash flow and paying back the debt with higher repayments. This means you'll pay off the debt quicker and pay less interest. Of course there's also financial benefit in shopping around for a better interest rate. Even a 0.5 per cent reduction in your home loan interest rate can save you tens of thousands of dollars over the life of a typical home loan.

When to do it?

A Debt Reduction Strategy should ideally be considered before you enter into a debt. The ideal situation is that you go into a debt with your eyes wide open. There should be no surprises. For many though, the strategy only comes to light after the debt has been acquired. At this stage, there's still good gains to be made. Making debt repayments more quickly means you have saving and spending opportunities in other areas as future cash flows change, and you can save quickly when you have repaid your mortgage(s).

Do

Do consider a Debt Reduction Strategy:

- Before you take out any debt, so you know what you're in for
- When you're concerned about the debt you have
- When your debt is rising
- When interest rates rise or fees and charges rise (always factor in a 1 per cent or more interest rate to your cash flow so you have a buffer if interest rates rise over time).

Don't

Don't fall into these traps:

- Making decisions about debt repayments that you can't keep—always be realistic
- Going into debt without understanding the interest, the costs, the repayments and the term of the loan
- Going into debt without shopping around for the best deal. It's important you get the best interest rate and terms you can. Like any expense, you owe it to yourself to get the best value. Do this regularly as your bank will not tell you if other lenders are cheaper. Get yourself a broker if you need assistance with this.
- Assuming the rate will stay the same—allow for an increased interest rate before you start to build in a buffer over the medium term.

The instant gratification gene can cause a spending itch

I don't know that scientists have found it yet but as the generations go on, I think the instant gratification gene is becoming stronger and stronger. Younger people today want it all now; they're not prepared to wait, and when it comes to their financial lives it means they will easily acquire debt without thinking about the consequences to their budget or cash flow.

However, there's something special about delayed gratification, like saving for something and owning it outright. While this might not be possible or realistic for a house (most of us will need a home loan for that), it's more likely or possible for a new car, a holiday or a new TV. Best of all, if you save into a savings account that pays interest, you can achieve your goal sooner.

Beware of the need for instant gratification and consider how it fits with your 'why'. If it means paying hundreds or thousands of dollars in interest, surely it pays to stop and think before you spend using debt.

If you have to buy something, consider using an 'interest free' option and then make additional payments to repay the debt over a selected time frame—don't just make the minimum repayment. Divide the total debt by the number of months and set up a direct debit to manage your payments.

Using interest free debt is great when it's controlled. Left uncontrolled, however, it will destroy you, your credit rating and your confidence.

The Risk Assessment Strategy

The Risk Assessment Strategy seeks to assess your thoughts about risk and return before you make any decision to invest. By understanding your attitudes and feelings about risk and its impact on the likelihood of making or losing money, you can make investment decisions that keep you feeling comfortable.

How does it work?

The Risk Assessment Strategy works by questioning your approach to risk-taking when compared with return. If you've been stressed out at night over the rise or fall in the value of the shares you've bought, you might be a more conservative investor. However, if share prices don't keep you awake at night, you've probably got more appetite to accept risk and potentially receive a higher return.

There's no right or wrong answer when it comes to the Risk Assessment Strategy, but your attitude to risk will determine how you frame your stack. And that's exactly what you want. You should never build a stack that keeps you awake at night. Ultimately, your stack needs to work for you and no one else.

Let's explore your attitudes to risk through the analogy of driving a car—something many of us do every day. If you're driving down the freeway and the speed limit is 100km/hour, and you decide to drive at 40km/hour, a few people driving behind you might get emotional. You're also probably going to be late to wherever you're going. When it comes to investing risk, this more cautious approach to the road would be comparable to investing in cash and fixed interest investments, such as term deposits. These are called *defensive* assets. Over time, they're not going to provide growth because that's not what they're designed to do. Capital growth may be an objective, however, if you wish to maintain the purchasing power of your capital.

Similarly, imagine you're driving down the freeway at 160km/hour. There's a fair chance you won't be able to talk your way out of a speeding ticket. There's also a chance you might not walk away from an accident at all, and if you did get caught driving at that speed you would lose your licence. This high-risk approach to the road is comparable to higher-risk investments, such as Australian and international shares, and property. These are called *growth* assets. And while high growth can be the important return from investments like this, could you handle the impact of up and down movements in the rate of return over time and still sleep well at night?

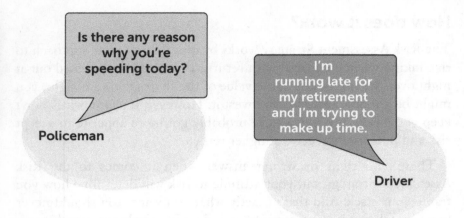

However, if you drive the car down the freeway between 90 and 110km/hour, you can limit the impacts of extreme events at either end of the spectrum.

Both extremes (investing your money in only defensive assets or only growth assets) are as dangerous as each other in isolation. Your overall risk profile should align with your 'why' at the end of the day because sleeping at night is more important than taking on too much risk. A balanced approach is to have 50 per cent of your assets as defensive assets and 50 per cent as growth assets.

Taking too little risk can also be dangerous, because over time the rising costs of living means you're left short—especially if you're retired and need to fund your lifestyle. Likewise, if you have too much risk you can see lots of volatility in your investments that may cause you emotional and financial stress at times when the value of your investment is falling.

So, spend some time thinking about your attitude to risk and what you need to achieve your goal—your 'why'. If the foundational principles in this book are the foundations of your financial house, then the Risk Assessment Strategy is the floor of that house, sitting on top of those foundations. Everything else must stack on top of it.

When to do it?

A Risk Assessment Strategy should be considered after you have set your goals but before you make any decision to invest your money. This is why it's a Framing Strategy. By understanding your attitude towards risk (how fast you're prepared to drive your car), you'll make decisions that you're emotionally comfortable with, while also understanding the likely risks and returns.

Do

Do consider a Risk Assessment Strategy:

- When you set new financial goals

- Before you make any decision to invest

- When large events occur that impact your time frame or capital base

- When you review your investments.

Don't

Don't fall into these traps:

- Thinking that risk doesn't apply to you—it applies to everyone

- Investing in anything if you don't understand the risks

- Investing in anything that has too much risk for your appetite

- Forgetting to think about risk as you move through life—like many things in life, your attitude to risk may change as you become older

- Buying an investment just because your friends have.

That time I took too much risk

Recently, I started mountain bike riding—a good excuse to build up some fitness, get out of the office and enjoy some fresh air. Like many first-time mountain bike riders, I took the advice of my friends about what kind of bike to get and what safety gear I needed. Things were going well until one day I confused ambition with ability.

I had picked up too much speed coming down a hill so I went a lot further off a jump than planned, and unfortunately hit a tree on landing. I even thought to myself while in mid-air, 'Oh no, this is going to be an income protection claim.' That's the problem with being a

FRAMING

financial planner, you're always thinking about the consequences of actions! I landed hard and was battered and bruised with a dislocated shoulder. I couldn't move for a few days and it took me six months to recover. If that had been a financial fall instead of a physical one, it could have been equally painful for my financial future.

Don't put yourself in harm's way. Always assess risk.

CHAPTER 10

The Investment Strategies

Investing is different from saving. *Saving* is the act of putting aside some money from your income every week or month and letting it grow over time through this repeated behaviour. *Investing* seeks to put your savings to work to generate more income to help you achieve your 'why'.

Investors typically have one or more of three expectations:

- That they'll receive a return (for example interest, dividends, distributions or rent) from the money invested (*income*)

- That their initial money invested will be returned (*capital*)

- At the point of sale of the investment, they will sell their investment for more than they paid for it (*growth*).

Income, capital and growth are the fundamental components of any investment.

Another way to look at these components of investment is through the life of an apple farmer using different Investment Strategies.

On the Strategy Stacker's Apple Farm, the apples that grow on the trees generate the **income** that the farm receives.

In order to grow the apples, the farm needs apple trees and other farming equipment. The farm uses **capital** to buy the trees. This capital is like the money you make an investment with.

Over time, the farmer decides to plant more apple trees. The value of your initial investment in the farm will show **growth**, because now the farm has the ability to produce more apples to sell. This makes the farm more valuable.

The apple farm is a good metaphor for thinking about investing and how it links back to what you want, or your 'why'. Do you want more apples (income)? Do you want more apple trees (growth)? Or do you want both? And do you want to sell your share in the farm at some point to get your money back (capital)?

The management of the apple farm also plays an important part in how the farm performs. Does the farmer water and fertilise the apple trees at the right time? Does the farmer protect the crop against pests? Are the apples picked at the right time and in the right way so they're not damaged? How well an investment performs is also the direct outcome of the people or company managing the apple farm—or in this case, your investment.

The apple farm concept is also useful for looking at risk. The apple crop might be impacted by a bad weather event like flood or hail. The apple crop might benefit from perfect growing conditions. The apple farm might also be impacted by government regulations or a customer's willingness to keep buying apples. There might be new competitors entering the market that make selling apples more competitive. These factors are called *business environment risks*. All investments have them and it pays to be aware of them.

This chapter provides you with some ideas on how to look at your apple farm—wait, I mean investment portfolio! Specifically, I explore these strategies:

- The Diversification Strategy
- The Dollar Cost Averaging Strategy
- The Investment Structure Strategy
- The Asset Allocation Strategy
- The Asset Selection Strategy
- The Investment Selection Strategy
- The Franking Credit Strategy
- The Fee Reduction Strategy
- The Appropriate Tax Strategy
- The Gearing Strategy.

In addition to personal investments, many of these strategies can be used with your super too. Remember that superannuation is a 'structure'. In a lot of cases, what you invest in personally you can also hold within super, provided you have the correct fund. (Chapter 11 explores specific superannuation strategies—super is a special kind of investment that has a bunch of other strategies you can use to help you achieve your 'why'.)

Strategy Stacking Tip

People often say they don't like super as it went down during the Global Financial Crisis (GFC) and during COVID-19 in 2020. However, it was the asset allocation and the subsequent investments held that went down. It didn't have anything to do with using a super account as an investment structure.

The Diversification Strategy

The Diversification Strategy seeks to protect you from a drop in the value of your money through the performance of a single investment provider. By spreading your money across multiple investments, you reduce your risk—in other words, 'you don't have all your eggs in one basket'.

How does it work?

Let's take a look at how it works. Imagine you hold two different investments. Both investments are of the same amount of money. Within scenario A, you only have one investment provider. Within scenario B, you hold nine smaller investments.

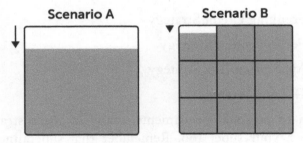

Let's imagine that the value of one of your investments in each scenario falls by a quarter. That's a big drop in the value of your money and means that for every $1 you have invested, the value has fallen by $0.25.

If you hold all your money in one investment (scenario A), you've taken a bigger risk than diversifying your investments (scenario B). In scenario B you can see how diversification reduces your overall risk.

Different investments will perform differently over time. Some investments may rise and some may fall. A Diversification Strategy provides you with the ability to protect your money and obtain a better financial outcome over time, rather than by placing your money in a single investment.

You can diversify your investments by investing:

■ In different market sectors (such as fixed interest, Australian shares or property)

- In different locations, local and international
- In different types of industries
- In different managed funds (most funds are already diversified)
- With different investment providers or managers.

When to do it?

The Diversification Strategy becomes more important for medium- and long-term goals, and where your investments carry more risk. For example, a short-term investment might be held in a term deposit in a bank or in a cash account. There's very little risk of you losing any money, so diversification is less important here. However, if you have a longer-term goal you might decide to invest in shares; if so, you should consider using a diversification strategy to minimise risk.

You should also review your diversification strategy over time, as different investments will perform differently. The diversification strategy is not a set-and-forget issue.

Do

Do consider a diversification strategy:

- When you're investing for an extended period of time
- When you're adding more money to an investment over time
- When you're thinking about how fast you want to go; in other words, your time frame
- When you're planning to place new money into investments.

Don't

Don't fall into these traps:

- Risking putting all your money in one type of investment where there is unknown or added risk and uncertainty
- Stopping diversifying (even if returns on one investment have been great), as past performance doesn't guarantee future performance

- Investing at someone else's speed limit—invest for you in line with your 'why'
- Following the pack—as they can be wrong too!

Where did the saying 'don't put all your eggs in one basket' come from?

In 1605, a Spanish novelist by the name of Miguel de Cervantes is thought to have originated the saying: 'Tis the part of a wise man to keep himself today for tomorrow, and not venture all his eggs in one basket.' Other writers since that time have borrowed and built upon that idea.

It's a practical idea for all aspects of life—to reduce the risk regardless of what it is you're doing. It's especially important for those with families and others relying on them too. Within your financial life, a diversification strategy is perhaps one of the oldest financial planning strategies that still holds true.

The Dollar Cost Averaging Strategy

The Dollar Cost Averaging Strategy is designed to help reduce market volatility when you start investing. The purchase prices for investments, such as shares and managed fund units, go up and down. It's impossible to time your share purchase for the lowest price because no one knows what the future holds.

Typically, most people buy an investment in one go—but that's not the case with this strategy. Using the Dollar Cost Averaging Strategy, you would invest over six or 12 months, or perhaps even longer, using smaller equal amounts. Dollar cost averaging also helps take the emotion out of investing as it stops you looking at the share price every day and having a negative or positive emotional reaction to it.

How does it work?

Imagine you plan to buy $6000 of shares at a share price of $72.70. At that price, $6000 would buy you 82.53 shares (6000/72.60).

INVESTMENT

Let's compare that approach with the Dollar Cost Averaging Strategy. Instead of investing $6000 all at once, you instead invest $1000 a month, over six months, in shares in a company listed on the Australian Stock Exchange (see table 10.1). You purchase each batch of shares on the first day of the month when the market is open (the sharemarkets are closed on weekends, so it won't always be the first day of the month).

Table 10.1: The changing share price over six months

Purchase month	Share price	Amount invested	Number of shares purchased
July	$72.70	$1000	13.76
August	$73.71	$1000	13.57
September	$71.21	$1000	14.04
October	$70.42	$1000	14.20
November	$68.94	$1000	14.51
December	$71.55	$1000	13.98
Total amount invested			$6000
Total shares purchased			84.06
Average share price			$71.38

In this example, you see how you can average the share price over time. You didn't pay the highest price, which was in August, and you were able to enjoy the advantage when the shares were at their lowest price, in November. As a result of this strategy, you end up with more shares at an overall lower price than if you bought them all on day one.

Of course, share prices do go up and down, and it's important to remember this strategy goes both ways. I've also resisted the urge here to use an actual share for the example as I'm not endorsing particular shares or investments in this book. It's a book about strategies. If you need advice, talk to a qualified and experienced financial planner.

When to do it?

Dollar cost averaging can be especially useful in times of market volatility. It works by allowing you to buy into an investment over time, at an average price over many price points, rather than just buying in at the price on one day.

Do

Do consider a Dollar Cost Averaging Strategy:

■ If you're looking to remove the emotion of starting your investment journey

■ If you want to take an investment holding and are concerned about market volatility over time, or in a specific sector, to build a bigger position with a savings plan as a part of your cash flow management

■ To smooth your entry price into an investment.

Don't

Don't fall into these traps:

■ Confusing dollar cost averaging for guaranteed returns. That's not why you do it. It's a strategy designed to reduce volatility and it does not guarantee returns.

■ Expecting that dollar cost averaging will always give you more shares than buying at one time. If there's a price correction, you can still end up with fewer shares.

■ Forgetting to include the costs of transactions into your decision-making. Fees and charges for buying shares can add up.

■ Letting one individual asset impact your diversification over time. Your overall portfolio should still hold a diversity of assets rather than skew towards an increased holding of one asset over time.

The emotional investor also lives an emotional financial life

Stefan made decisions through feelings and, more often than not, if Stefan felt good about something he did it. Stefan made the decision to invest in some bank shares. He didn't really have a goal in mind and didn't take the time to think about the associated risk.

Stefan's emotional life carried right over onto the newly bought shares. One day they fell by 25 cents. Stefan felt sad. The next day they rose by 16 cents, and Stefan was happier. The day after that they fell by 4 cents, so Stefan was unhappy. The day after that they went up by 13 cents, and Stefan was happy again.

Stefan also forgot about the dividends (income) paid by the shares. He was only thinking about the money he'd invested (capital). The shares were returning a cash dividend of about 6 per cent year on year. The share price only becomes more important at the time you want to sell. Just like a property investment, you hope the price is as high as it can be (growth), but the rent (income) keeps coming in week after week.

What's the moral of the story? Emotions and investing don't mix. When people are stressed or more emotional than usual, they don't generally make good decisions. Don't ever let emotions make an investment decision for you. You'll forever be a victim of your decisions, both good and bad. Before you make investment decisions, understand what happens to your capital, how your income is generated, and how you can expect your capital to be returned, along with any associated risks. The cautionary tale here also highlights the importance of the Framing Strategies, and in particular the Risk Management Strategy (Chapter 9).

The Investment Structure Strategy

An Investment Structure Strategy investigates and determines the best way to own or hold an investment. Different investment structures have different features, and different benefits and considerations. But chances are you have a couple of different investment structures already in place. Individual ownership—that is, holding investments in your own name—is the most common one, and the second most common is probably a trust. 'But I don't have a trust working for my investments,' I hear you say. Well, if you have a super account then let me tell you that you do. Super is held in a trust structure.

How does it work?

Let's take a look at how it works. To select the right investment structure (such as a company or trust), you need to consider each of the items below to make sure they're the right fit for you and for the other people within the structure (if there are other people involved):

- Know who controls the structure
- Understand what the structure is and why it has been chosen over other structures
- Determine who controls the structure
- Understand how the structure distributes income and capital
- Consider how well they protect investments
- Review how the structure is taxed
- Determine what happens when a person dies.

You might think this is a complex area—and you'd be right. Seeking professional advice is always a good idea when investments become more complex. As I keep saying, 'you don't know what you don't know'. It's often hard to fix a 'wrong structure' situation too if an incorrect decision about a structure is made and implemented—you want to get this right the first time if at all possible. You need to think about the structures with the end in mind: Why are you using them, and what are the long-term benefits of the option you've selected?

Let's take a look at four typical investment structures.

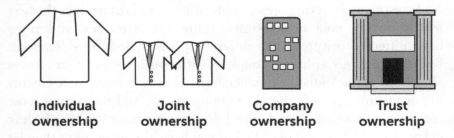

| Individual ownership | Joint ownership | Company ownership | Trust ownership |

Features of **individual ownership** include:

- The investment is owned by the individual only.
- It's up to the individual to determine what they do.
- The individual is only responsible to themselves.

- The structure offers little protection of assets.

- Tax is paid by the individual.

Features of **joint ownership** include:

- The investment is owned by the individuals.

- The individuals are responsible to each other.

- The structure offers little protection of assets.

- Tax is paid by the individuals.

- Ownership passes to the surviving individual on death.

Features of **company ownership** include:

- The investment is owned by the company, and the directors of the company make the decisions.

- There's usually a company constitution, which outlines how the company will be run.

- The company is responsible to the shareholders of the company.

- The structure offers asset protection and the ability to control where your income is paid in the future. It allows you to control assets in a structure that is not in your own name, which is handy as a company has a different tax rate compared to your own, different protections from litigation and a different way of distributing income.

- Tax is paid by the company at the prevailing company tax rate.

Features of **trust ownership** include:

- The investment is owned by the trust, and the trustees of the trust control the entity.

- There's usually a trust deed, which outlines how the trust will be run.

- The trust is ultimately responsible to the members or unit holders of the trust.

INVESTMENT

- Trusts offer asset protection, depending on the trust's underlying structure.

- Tax is paid by the beneficiaries of the trust.

The Investment Structure Strategy is one of the most complex strategies within this book and it's impossible to provide a comprehensive guide—it's really a book all by itself. However, if you're looking for more information, I suggest you talk to a financial planner about what you're trying to achieve. Your financial planner can work with a solicitor to set up any legal structure if necessary.

When to do it?

The Investment Structure Strategy can be considered before you decide to invest; however, it is possible to switch investment structures in some cases after you've started. For example, an individual can put money into a super trust, which will invest for their retirement. A super trust, however, cannot provide the individual with that money until they reach retirement age.

For a non-super investment, a family trust, unit trust or company are all viable options. The right structure for you will be driven by who is involved and the outcome you're aiming for (your 'why'). Obtaining tax advice is always recommended as tax implications (and limitations) can impact the suitability of each option. It's also best to speak with an accountant before you make any decisions. I've never found anyone who likes surprises when it comes to tax matters.

Remember, don't set a structure up just because your friends have. They may differ from you in ways you don't know—and they may have a different 'why'.

Do

Do consider an Investment Structure Strategy:

- When you're making investments by yourself or with others

- If you're concerned about protecting your assets

- If you want to maximise control and flexibility

- If you're concerned about taxation, income distribution or income splitting

- If you're ready to seek advice from a professional about which investment structure is best for your 'why'

- If you have a specific objective or outcome that you're after

- If you have common goals with others and there's more than one person involved.

Don't

Don't fall into these traps:

- Rushing into an Investment Structure Strategy

- Entering into agreements or arrangements without understanding the implications to you personally

- Relying on handshake agreements—always put everything in writing, have everything reviewed by a legal professional and ensure documentation is signed by all parties

- Setting up a structure without an exit plan.

Follow the KISS theory—Keep It Simple, Stupid

A good rule of thumb when thinking about what kind of investment structure you need is to keep it simple. It's easy to over-engineer what you need, and I've seen people make their lives really complicated by having multiple structures that they don't really need or understand. For many people, having individual asset ownership along with a super fund (a trust) for their retirement savings is enough. You need a reason to set up a trust rather than having one for no reason.

Thinking about the investment structure you need is like designing plans for a house. Just like the rooms of a house, every investment structure needs to have a purpose. While you might need three bedrooms in a house, you probably don't need three different superannuation funds or three different companies. And just like house plans, the more complexity you have, the more expensive it becomes. Think long term, as there are generally no short-term structures.

Keeping it simple helps you stay focused on why you're selecting an investment structure. It also keeps the management and the costs associated with that structure under control.

The Asset Allocation Strategy

The Asset Allocation Strategy seeks to guide what you invest in — and the overall asset-sector-based holdings within your portfolio — taking into account your agreed risk profile (from your Risk Assessment Strategy, refer to Chapter 9). By considering your goals and attitude to risk, you increase the probability of achieving your goals if you use an appropriate Asset Allocation Strategy. Thinking back to the car and speed analogy from Chapter 9 for a moment, asset allocation is what you use to control the speed at which your portfolio drives at. It's like the acceleration and the brakes.

How does it work?

Some investments we hold are designed to provide us with income (just like apples from a tree).

Other investments, however, are designed to provide us with income *and* growth (apples from a tree, plus more trees that can produce more apples).

I outline some examples of each of these types of assets in table 10.2.

Table 10.2: Example asset types

Income-producing assets (income assets)	Income and growth-producing assets (growth assets)
Cash	Property
Bonds	Infrastructure
Fixed interest	Australian shares
	International shares

For a cash investment, you receive income in the form of interest as your return. Bonds and fixed interest assets will provide you with a cash payment reflected as the rate of return, depending on the type of underlying investment used.

Property and infrastructure can provide dividends or rent as a return, depending on the type of investment structure used. The value of the property or infrastructure asset itself can also rise to provide growth too. Australian shares typically will provide you with income in the form of a dividend, as well as growth through a rise in the share price. The same could be said for international shares, which tend to have a slightly lower average income rate.

Different asset class sectors have different return characteristics, so it's important that these align with your goals and needs.

You might have already seen an asset allocation in the details of your superannuation fund. The same kind of asset allocation will also apply to an investment portfolio. You often see them presented as pie charts breaking down the percentage of each sector (see figure 10.1).

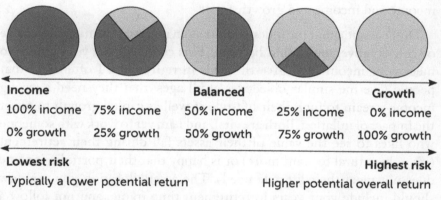

Income		Balanced		Growth
100% income	75% income	50% income	25% income	0% income
0% growth	25% growth	50% growth	75% growth	100% growth
Lowest risk				Highest risk
Typically a lower potential return				Higher potential overall return

Figure 10.1: Example asset allocations for investment portfolios (including super)

Each option in figure 10.1 offers a different rate of return and level of risk (in this case showing different asset mix weightings). Your weighting to either end of the risk scale should take into account the time frame over which you will hold the asset. Regardless of your risk allocation, you must consider what the investment is doing in line with your 'why' and how long you will hold it for.

Which one do you choose?

INVESTMENT

Well, that depends on your answers to a range of questions that a financial planner would work through with you. However, here are some key issues to factor into your decision:

- What is your 'why'?

- What's your time horizon?

- What does your risk assessment (refer to Chapter 9 for the Risk Assessment Strategy) tell you about how you should invest?

- Do you need to match investments to an investment structure?

- Is there anything you are against or wish to avoid? Examples might include investment types such as fossil fuels, weapons, alcohol and tobacco.

The Asset Allocation Strategy that you use needs to consider all these questions and more. Sometimes the right answer will be a mix of both income and income and growth assets.

Don't assume that the older you get as an investor, the more defensive or conservative you should become. This could impact your ability to meet your income and growth needs in retirement. I often find that people give me similar objectives at all ages: that they need a strong income stream to fund their lifestyle as well as capital growth to offset the impact of inflation. Both are vital, and I am yet to work with someone who likes to see the value of their assets fall during their retirement (it's only natural to want more) or is happy that their portfolio income does not meet their lifestyle needs. The asset allocation you use now should include your years in retirement time frame, and not follow a time frame until retirement and then change to a different strategy. In the current environment, with cash paying so little, the annual income from a portfolio of cash may be well below your living costs, therefore you may need to buy more growth-based assets to maximise the opportunities available. Currently, cash may not meet your living costs, which could put your capital at risk as you have to draw from it to fund your living expenses.

It's also important to remember that sometimes your goal might not be achievable in your time frame. At that point you have an important decision to make. Can you push back your time frame, or do you need to take more risk?

Time is the biggest asset we have, but it's limited. If you've got time on your side, however, you may not have to take high risks. If your risk assessment does not allow for a suitable exposure to growth assets, it will impact your ability to generate income or benefit from capital growth. Your risk assessment and understanding 'how you feel' is vital to ensuring a suitable asset allocation.

When to do it?

The Asset Allocation Strategy applies to every investment you make, regardless of whether you proactively consider it or not. If you have more than one investment, which most people do, you need to consider the whole picture every time you make a new investment, sell your investments or change your investments. Fundamentally, asset allocation is really about how much risk you're willing to take and the return you're hoping to see across your whole investment portfolio.

Do

Do consider an Asset Allocation Strategy:

- Before you make any decision to invest
- When you invest new capital
- If your income needs change
- When you review your investments
- If your 'why' changes or your appetite for risk changes
- If you need to decide what will make up your asset allocation—for example, shares, exchange-traded funds and/or managed funds.

Don't

Don't fall into these traps:

- Chasing easy money—if someone is offering something too good to be true in relation to the return, it probably is

- Underestimating the power of time—although we live in a short-term society, don't make the mistake of forgetting about your long-term goals like your retirement and final superannuation balance. It's about time in the market, not trying to time the market.

- Confusing income and growth—make sure your asset allocation allows you to control your exposure to income-based assets if it's income you need

- Assuming that you need to be more defensive/conservative just because you're getting older. Remember that driving at 40km/hour in a 100km/hour zone is just as dangerous!

The name of an asset allocation might be fake news, so be careful

Unfortunately, you can't compare different returns across different asset allocations with the same name. There aren't any laws to define what an income, balanced or growth portfolio should contain in terms of income and growth assets. You really need to dig deeper to discover what the mix is for yourself as the label (for example, 'balanced' or 'growth') of the risk profile won't necessarily tell you what you're holding when it comes to percentages and weightings.

The titles of some asset allocations are so misleading right now that if you were to make a decision based on the title alone, you might be taking on an unacceptable level of risk. One example of an award-winning balanced fund wasn't actually balanced at all. It had 80 per cent growth assets and 20 per cent income assets. That's actually closer to a 100 per cent growth portfolio than a balanced portfolio of 50 per cent growth-based and 50 per cent income-based assets. So, dig a little deeper and make sure you're comparing like asset allocations with like asset allocations, and not just comparing names.

The Asset Selection Strategy

The Asset Selection Strategy seeks to help you decide what types of investments you should invest in within the different types of asset classes. Specific investments can take many forms, but here I limit it to the most common types of investments you can expect to invest in. Some of the more exotic investment options could fall under alternative options (like collectibles, art or venture capital) and have their place—provided your risk profile can tolerate them.

How does it work?

The strategy works by considering the types of investments within an asset class, and how much of each asset class you need within your asset allocation.

Let's take a look at a range of different asset classes. Before you can create your investment portfolio, you need to understand the range of options available to you.

Fixed income investments

Fixed income investments can include terms deposits, offered by banks and other large institutions, and are defensive, conservative investments. You earn interest on your investment, at a fixed rate and over a fixed period, with a term deposit. As these kinds of investments carry little to no capital risk, the return on offer is usually less than other types of investments. Once you've purchased your investment, your money is usually locked away for the term agreed. Interest on term deposits is usually paid monthly or at maturity. If you break the term, there's usually a penalty, such as lost interest, for doing so and there may be a specific time frame within which you can access your capital.

Other fixed income investments, such as actively managed defensive funds, exchange-traded funds and specialist products (for example, converting preference shares or hybrids), can also be of a defensive nature, but keep in mind that nothing is risk-free. The value of fixed interest funds and products can change over time, such as when interest rates rise. They tend to offer a stronger income stream than something like a term deposit as they can benefit from a positive change in interest rates over time.

Strategy Stacking Tip

Just because you see the word 'fixed', don't take this to mean risk-free! It means the return could be at a fixed or floating rate, depending on the type of investment used. It doesn't mean that the capital is risk-free. Remember to seek advice if you don't understand something. Lack of knowledge is a big risk—'you don't know what you don't know', as I often say to my clients.

Bonds

Bonds are like fixed income investments, but instead of being offered by banks, they're offered by governments or an individual company. You still earn interest on your investment, although with a bond it's called a 'coupon amount' that's returned to you, along with your initial investment amount, after a fixed period. As these kinds of investments carry little to no risk, the return on offer is usually less than with other types of investments.

Bonds can have fixed rate returns or floating rate returns, depending on the type of bond you purchase. Fixed rate bonds show a fixed interest rate for the life of the investment. Floating rate bonds have a variable return over the life of the investment. Earnings on bonds are generally made quarterly or half-yearly. If you want to get out of the investment but the bond hasn't reached its maturity date, you can trade it on the Australian Securities Exchange (ASX). You can also access bonds through a specialised managed fund.

Australian shares

Australian shares are units of ownership within a company listed on the ASX. It's very hard for an individual to buy a share of a company themselves; however, the ASX offers companies the opportunity to raise the money they need in return for providing individual investors with shares in that company.

You can earn two kinds of return from Australian shares:

- Growth in the share price (or a fall in the share price, which is also a return, it's just a negative return rather than a positive return!)

- A portion of the company's profits that gets paid back to shareholders, known as a dividend. In some ways it's like interest as it provides an income for you.

As these kinds of investments carry more risk, they usually have higher returns than fixed interest investments or bonds. Dividends on shares are usually paid twice a year (usually called the interim dividend and the final dividend). If you want to get out of the investment, you can sell your shares on the ASX at a price set by the market on any given trading day. You can also access shares through a specialised managed fund or Separately Managed Account (SMA). (An SMA is a type of structured investment that allows investors to hold cash, managed funds, and shares in one place through professionally constructed portfolios, taking into account a range of risk profiles. SMAs allow investors to see all their assets in one place and receive consolidated reporting, including tax reporting. The underlying assets are changed by the provider of the SMA so the investor doesn't have to do it themselves.)

International shares

International shares are units of ownership within a company listed on an overseas stock exchange. The principles are very much as they are as shares on the ASX. There's an additional point to note here, however. In addition to the share price and dividends paid, your return is also influenced by currency exchange rates, as different currencies aren't worth the same in value.

Let's look at a simple example. You invest $1000 in international shares—let's say, shares in the United States.

On the day you buy the international shares, $1 Australian is worth $0.75 US. This means your investment in the shares is $750 in US dollars ($1000 × 0.75). Over time, the exchange rate changes.

If the Australian exchange rate falls (meaning the US rate rises), what happens to your investments? Let's say the value of $1 Australian changes to $0.70 US and the share price of your international shares doesn't change. Your $750 in US dollars investment is now worth $700 ($1000 × 0.70).

If the Australian exchange rate rises (meaning the US rate falls), what happens to your investments? Let's say $1 Australian is worth $0.80 US and the share price of your international shares doesn't change. Your $750 in US dollars investment is now worth $800 ($1000 × 0.80).

Three factors can contribute to your return on international shares: share price movements, dividends and exchange rates. You can also access shares through a specialised managed fund or SMA.

Property

Property, as the name suggests, refers to a physical asset. For most investors, it's a direct investment in a property, home or business premises that they rent out. It could also be an indirect investment in a collection of property assets offering an exposure to a range of property sectors, such as industrial, office, commercial and so on. They are known as real estate investment trusts (REITs).

You get two kinds of returns on property: rent (the income earned on the property) and growth in the value of the property (or a fall in the value of the property, which is also a return—it's just a negative return, not a positive return). Property can also form the basis of a managed fund or an exchange-traded fund (see the next two sections).

Direct ownership of property isn't as liquid as other types of investments, however, and it can be hard to sell if you need to get your money back quickly. Listed property (a managed fund or ETF that invests in a portfolio of property assets) is a little more flexible as you can sell units in an investment trust.

Managed funds

Managed funds offer investors the opportunity to invest in a range of investments, such as Australian shares, international shares, different industry types or sectors (such as resources or healthcare), or investments in different countries. Managed funds are offered by investment managers. Like a group of shares, they provide individual investors with the ability to have ownership in a broad collection of assets in a single investment.

You don't actually buy shares; instead, you buy units in the overall investment that reflect a measure of the value of the total portfolio of assets. Where companies have shareholders, managed funds have unit holders.

You can earn two kinds of return from managed funds:

- Growth in the unit price (or a fall in the unit price, which is also a return—it's just a negative movement, not a positive movement)

- A share in the fund's returns that gets paid back to shareholders, known as a distribution.

As with shares, these kinds of investments can carry more risk. Depending on the underlying assets, they usually have higher returns than term deposits or bonds. Distributions on your managed fund investment can be paid monthly, quarterly, half-yearly or yearly, depending on the rules of the fund. You can buy and sell units of a fund through the provider of the fund.

Exchange-traded funds (ETFs)

Like managed funds, exchange-traded funds (ETFs) offer investors the opportunity to invest in a specific sector of the market, such as Australian shares, international shares, industry types or sectors, or investments in different countries. ETFs are offered by investment managers. Like managed funds, they provide individual investors with the ability to have ownership in a specific sector, and they are generally extremely cost-effective. They provide investors with the ability to gain good diversification and may be used to diversity a portfolio. ETFs can also provide dividends, depending on the sector targeted.

ETFs have grown in popularity since the GFC as investors review investment costs and access to broader investment markets. Generally, ETFs replicate a specific share index, such as the ASX 200 index (the top 200 Australian shares), the S&P 500 index (the top 500 shares in the US) or a property index. An ETF is normally a passive exposure, so the investment manager may not actively trade the underlying portfolio. This is an ever growing and evolving market, with new product offerings coming to the market all the time.

Shares in an ETF are traded like Australian shares on the ASX. You can earn two kinds of returns from ETFs:

- Growth in the unit price (or a fall in the unit price, which is also a return—it's just a negative return, not a positive return)

- A return on the investment paid back to shareholders, known as a dividend.

Depending on the underlying assets of the ETF, you may also benefit from the use of franking credits as part of your annual dividend (I discuss the Franking Credit Strategy later in this chapter). If the ETF holds offshore assets (that is, outside of Australia), your return will also be impacted by movements in the exchange rate, so you may wish to consider currency hedging to limit changes in its value (depending on your view of currency). As these kinds of investments carry more risk, they usually have higher returns than fixed-interest investments or bonds. If you want to get out of the investment, you can sell your units through the ASX.

Infrastructure

Infrastructure is the things we need for our society to function. It includes things like electricity, water, roads, airports and railways. These tend to be big and expensive items, and often there's not much competition among infrastructure assets as a result of their cost. Certainly an individual investor would never be able to own an infrastructure asset by themselves (unless they were ridiculously wealthy!). Even then they probably wouldn't hold it all by themselves because they'd know the importance of diversification.

Infrastructure investments offer investors the ability to invest in a piece of social infrastructure that is located domestically or overseas. Infrastructure can typically be invested in through a managed fund or an ETF, and the fund itself will hold different types of infrastructure assets.

Income from infrastructure is determined by the type of asset. For example, roads produce tolls as income, while electricity and gas earn fees charged by the providers to their consumers.

As with shares, these kinds of investment can carry more risk. At the same time, they usually have higher returns than term deposits or bonds. Distributions on your infrastructure managed fund investment may be paid to you monthly, quarterly, half-yearly or yearly, depending on the rules of the fund. You can buy and sell units of a fund through the provider of the fund.

When to do it?

An Asset Selection Strategy is best considered after you have completed the Risk Assessment Strategy (refer to Chapter 9). Having a clear understanding of your 'why' and your risk profile will ensure the potential return is in line with your needs.

Do

Do consider an Asset Selection Strategy:

- Before you invest
- When you're exploring your 'why' and your investment objectives
- When you're reviewing your assets over time, taking into account economic events
- If you're adding capital or withdrawing money
- To help you purchase assets that you understand—it's important you hold investments for the right reasons
- If you're updating your risk profile for a specific reason
- When you're evaluating your assets. Take a long-term view and make short-term changes. Make sure you understand why you hold the investment and what it does in your portfolio. Each asset and each sector has a different role to play.

Don't

Don't fall into these traps:

- Jumping in and buy the first managed fund or stock that you see. Just like shopping for a car, you've got to do your research. Not all investments deliver the same results.

■ Forgetting to look at the fees associated with investments as they will impact on your overall return. Remember to look at the fees on property, too. There's a range of fees property investors often forget about—stamp duty, property listing and management fees, property maintenance and repair costs, property insurance, bank interest if there's a loan attached to the property, and the costs of selling if you ever want to get out of the investment.

I'm not biased...I just have favourites

Playing favourites is a human condition, and many people have favourite asset classes. Some people love property. Some love shares. Some lean more towards fixed interest because it's lower risk. It's important to remember, though, that all asset classes have strengths and weaknesses, and at different points in the economic cycle they will perform differently.

It's fair to say that over the medium to long term we can see what the typical (but not guaranteed) returns of different asset classes are. Being focused on too many growth assets might carry too much risk; being too focused on defensive income assets might mean your money is eroded over time against inflation. Both extremes bring their own set of problems.

Be aware of your own biases when it comes to looking at different asset classes, and explore them in terms of the risk and return you need from them. There's no point in getting upset that your international ETF hasn't made the same dividend as an Australian share. Maybe it won't, but perhaps it's doing a different job in your portfolio.

Asset allocation also helps you control the speed you drive your 'risk assessment' car at. Driving 40km/hour in a 100km/hour zone can cause problems, as could driving 170km/hour.

The next strategy (the Investment Selection Strategy) explores the roles and responsibilities of specific investments in a portfolio, so you can get a better understanding of what to expect from each asset class when you have your broader allocation in place.

The Investment Selection Strategy

The Investment Selection Strategy helps you decide which specific investments you should use to achieve your 'why' in line with your broader asset allocation and investment objectives.

Typically, investments have up to three key parts: capital, income and growth. Income is determined by the interest, dividend or distribution you get from the capital you have invested. Growth is determined by the rise in the value of your capital, such as a rise in a share price. Investments like term deposits though have no growth component; you just get your capital returned to you at the end of the investment period, along with any income in the form of interest.

How does it work?

The purpose of this book is not to recommend specific investments. If you need personal advice, talking with a financial planner who offers investment advice is a great place to start (Part 4 may also provide initial guidance on seeking professional advice). Financial planners have access to investment research across all the investment types outlined for this strategy.

However, we can take an overview of some of the things you might consider when selecting a specific investment.

Fixed income investments

Things to look out for include:

- Who is providing the fixed income investment?
- The return on offer
- The term on offer
- The fees charged
- When interest is paid, either monthly or at the end of the term
- Liquidity—can you access the capital when it is needed or is it locked away?
- Withdrawal costs or limitations.

INVESTMENT

Fixed income investments just provide income. There's no growth component to a fixed income investment.

Bonds

Things to look out for include:

- Who is providing the bond—the quality of the issuer could impact the return
- The coupon amount (return) and if it's fixed or floating
- The term on offer—the period of time over which your money is invested
- The fees charged
- When the coupon amount is paid—quarterly or half-yearly
- What happens if you need to sell the bond—how liquid is it?

Bonds just provide income. There's generally no growth component to a bond.

Australian shares

Things to look out for include:

- Which company is the share for?
- The earnings profile of the company
- The franking credits rate—some are fully franked, while others are not
- What the share price has been like in recent times
- Brokerage costs
- The quality of the product and its market share
- The business environment outlook for the industry in which the company operates
- The share's distribution history and the consistency of income paid.

Not all shares are the same. Some shares are very good at producing income and franking credits, while other shares are better at growth, which is growing their share price—in other words, it is growing the capital you invest when you buy the shares. Some shares also offer a mix of both income and growth.

Your investment objective will impact what shares you hold and you should invest within your risk tolerance. When deciding on the shares to hold, you should also consider the time frame of your investment. Some shares may be held for short-term capital uplift; others may be held for income and capital growth over the longer term. Again, you can come back to the analogy of driving the car—too many high-risk shares may see you driving at 180km/hour in a 100km/hour zone, which is definitely dangerous!

International shares

Things to look out for include:

- Which company is the share for?
- What have the most current dividends been?
- What has the share price been like in recent times?
- The fees charged to buy and sell the shares
- The outlook for that specific company
- The business environment outlook for the industry in which the company operates
- The impact of the exchange rate on income or total return.

Like Australian shares, international shares offer income, growth or a mix of both.

Property

Things to look out for in listed property include:

- The quality of the underlying assets
- The fees charged, including any Indirect Cost Ratio (ICR) (an ICR identifies the total costs of managing the investment and can include performance fees, accounting and legal fees, and other operational costs. This fee is deducted from the assets of the investments rather than charged directly to you as an

investor. As a result, it can appear to be hidden, but you should take the time to find out if an ICR is being charged, as some of these types of fees can be high)

- The yield of the assets held in the fund
- The quality of the underlying management of the property fund
- The weighting of specific companies in the fund
- Performance relative to the index
- Where geographically the assets are held (domestically or overseas).

Things to look out for in physical property include:

- Location
- Expected yield
- The depreciation available
- The tax deductibility of costs
- Any borrowing expenses (including interest rates)
- The time frame of property ownership.

Not all property investments are the same. Units, houses and commercial properties have different characteristics and will behave differently in different market cycles. Property tends to have a mix of income and growth over time. Despite what some people may think, property prices, like share prices, can rise and fall.

Managed funds

Things to look out for include:

- Who is the underlying manager?
- What industry sector(s) does the managed fund operate in?
- The fund's top 10 holdings (if available)
- Performance relative to its selected benchmark
- What the unit price has been like in recent times

- The fees charged to invest in the managed fund, including any ICR and performance fees
- The outlook for the underlying assets of the managed fund
- The business environment outlook for the industry sector(s) in which the company operates
- The exchange rate strategy—hedged or unhedged (if applicable).

Managed funds can offer investors income, growth or a mix of both depending on what they invest in.

Exchange-traded funds (ETFs)

Things to look out for include:

- Who is offering the ETF?
- What industry sector(s) does the ETF operate in?
- The ETF's top 10 sectors (if available)
- What have the most current investment returns been?
- What has the share price been like in recent times?
- The fees charged to invest in the ETF
- The outlook for that specific ETF
- The business environment outlook for the industry sector(s) in which the fund operates
- The impact of the exchange rate income or total return.

ETFs are designed to deliver both income and growth depending on the underlying assets of the structure. They tend to follow the index rather than provide growth in your capital.

Infrastructure

Things to look out for include:

- Who is offering the infrastructure investment?
- What form does the investment take—is it a managed fund or ETF?

- What kinds of infrastructure does the investment hold?
- What have the most current investment returns been?
- Where are the assets held (domestic or international)—are there any political risks in the countries where the assets are located?
- The fees charged to invest in the managed fund, including any ICR and performance fees
- The outlook for the underlying infrastructure held within the investment
- The business environment outlook
- The exchange rate strategy—hedged or unhedged (if applicable).

Infrastructure investments are designed to deliver income and capital growth.

When to do it?

An Investment Selection Strategy is best considered after you've completed a Risk Assessment Strategy (refer to Chapter 9) and an Asset Allocation Strategy (covered earlier in this chapter).

Do

Do consider an Investment Selection Strategy:

- When you know your investment objectives
- When you have agreed upon your underlying asset allocation
- When you have defined your income and growth needs
- When you know your liquidity needs
- When you have defined your cash flow requirements
- When you have agreed your time frame
- Before you invest
- When you're adding additional capital to your portfolio

Don't

Don't fall into these traps:

- Buying without doing your research, or paying someone like a financial adviser to do the research for you

- Being influenced by your emotions—buying an investment should not be an emotional decision

- Investing more than you're prepared to lose

- Chasing this year's winner—every asset has its day.

Forget brother Bob, sister Sue and your best friend Fred

I often have conversations with first-time financial advice clients about some of their investments, and in particular why they chose an investment over an alternative option. I've lost count of the times clients have said they decided to invest because a relative or friend invested in the same product.

There's a real social danger in following others' investment journeys. You don't know what research, if any, they've done; you don't know what the risks are; and you don't necessarily know why they chose that investment or what their goal is. If the investment heads south, who are you going blame? Brother Bob, sister Sue—or perhaps it was your best friend, Fred?

It's easy to think, 'How could they tell me about an investment that was going to go bad, knowing I might invest in it? What's wrong with them? Couldn't they see the future?'

Of course they couldn't see the future. No one can.

In this case, like all investment decisions, you need to take responsibility and own the outcomes that you get, both good and bad. Do your own homework or seek financial planning advice from a licensed adviser who has an investment research capability. They will be able to provide assistance with selecting sound investments. Also remember that if you have a long-term investment horizon, long term means exactly that. Don't turn 10 years into 10 months because of a short-term need for cash.

INVESTMENT

The Franking Credit Strategy

The Franking Credit Strategy seeks to make use of franking credits through the ownership of Australian shares as part of your investment strategy. A *franking credit* (also called an *imputation credit*) is a tax credit that provides you with the opportunity to reduce your personal income tax (or potentially receive a tax refund).

How does it work?

Imagine you own shares in a company on the ASX and the company makes a profit of $1 million. The company has to pay tax on that profit (at the time of writing, the tax rate for companies is 30 per cent—so let's go with that).

The company has to pay $300000 (30% × $1000000) in tax to the government. Ouch, that's a lot of biscuits! Now you know why companies want the company tax rate lowered.

This means the company has $700000 ($1000000—$300000) left over. The company directors might use some of the money to reinvest within the business, but they might also decide to pay their shareholders a dividend on the shares they own.

Let's say in this case they decide to pay the $700000 as dividends to all their shareholders. There are 350000 shares, so the dividend amount is $2 per share ($700000/350000).

If you own 1000 shares, you'll receive a total dividend payment of $2000 ($2 × 1000).

But that's not all you get. You'll also get some franking credits because the company has already paid tax on the money they've earned.

So, why are you entitled to some franking credits? You have invested in the company and are therefore entitled to the tax benefits offered by each company. The tax paid by the company offering full franked income results in you getting a tax credit for the tax they have paid when their dividends are paid out.

The benefit of this tax credit depends on your personal tax situation. Many retirees on low or tax-free incomes enjoy franking credits as they provide them with a tax refund when their tax returns are completed. A pension is a tax-free structure so surplus franking credits are returned as a cash payment from the Australian Taxation Office (ATO). Superannuation funds benefit from franking credits as they can reduce the amount of tax paid within the fund each year. Individuals can also benefit from the credits in their personal tax returns.

When to do it?

The Franking Credit Strategy needs to be considered as a part of your overall tax position. It might not be suitable for everyone.

Do

Do consider the Franking Credit Strategy:

- Before you invest
- When you're considering the structure in which you hold the assets to maximise the opportunity
- When you're reviewing your tax planning
- If you have a medium- to long-term investment time frame
- When you're concerned about the amount of tax you're paying.

Don't

Don't fall into these traps:

- Employing a Franking Credit Strategy (or in fact any strategy) as an end within itself. Most people plan for a tax deduction (one of the five truths about money from Chapter 1), not their 'why'—and that's a big mistake to make.
- Don't forget about the risk of investing in shares by falling in love with the idea of tax credits. There's always risk!

Self-funded retirees often use franking credits to help provide their income

In Australia, one of the largest groups to use the Franking Credit Strategy is self-funded retirees. These are people who might not be eligible for full Centrelink pension benefits, so they need to generate

INVESTMENT

income from the money they have. Typically, they have Australian share portfolios with shares that have a strong income (dividend) profile and shares that typically deliver strong franking credits.

This kind of share portfolio seeks to generate ongoing investment income, and it relies on the franking credits to supplement the dividends received from the shares. This kind of strategy has a higher risk than a term deposit, and as a result typically has a higher return. Also, if someone is over the age of 60, they have the ability to start a tax-free income stream, such as a pension resulting in tax-free income. Even if you're under the age of 60, you can benefit from franking credits as they may offset the tax payable within the fund while they're in the accumulation phase (that is, their pension payments have not started yet).

In recent times, there's been talk around whether federal governments should remove franking credits for people who don't pay tax. This change therefore also affects self-funded retirees who've worked to build assets. Should they lose out because they've chosen to try and be self-sufficient? It's a complicated issue and, like all federal government decisions, there are usually winners and losers.

Generating additional income within your portfolio by using franking credits in an account-based pension or other tax-effective structure can help generate cash flow that can be used to supplement ongoing pension payments. As a pension is a tax-free structure (legislation permitting), surplus franking credits from the companies you invest in is returned in the tax return of the pension account. The use of franking credits can be used to fund lifestyle objectives and protect retirees from the need to draw down on capital or to top up the shortfall between lifestyle costs and the total income earned from the portfolio.

The Fee Reduction Strategy

The Fee Reduction Strategy involves looking at the fees you pay for your superannuation and investments. Fees aren't often as straightforward as you'd like them to be, and some investments even have hidden fees (like the ICR) that you need to know about. A Fee Reduction Strategy really employs the 'pay attention to your spending' foundation (Chapter 3), which seeks to ensure you're value-checking what you have. Sometimes higher fees mean more value or flexibility in a financial product; therefore, it pays to understand what you're paying for.

How does it work?

Let's take a look at the most common types of fees you might see on investment, superannuation or retirement pension products (see table 10.3). Fees are charged by providers to cover their operating costs and profit margins.

Table 10.3: Investment fees

Fee name	What is it for?
Account fee or administration fees	These are fees charged to cover the costs associated with running your account.
Managed Expense Ratio (MER)	This fee is commonly charged on some investments and can include management fees (charged for the cost of managing the investment), performance fees (a payment made to the investment manager for generating positive returns) and brokerage fees (a fee or commission to a broker).
Transaction fees	These fees are charged when you transact on your account. Within a banking environment, it might be a withdrawal fee from taking money out of an automatic teller machine (ATM). Within a superannuation environment, it might be a switching fee for changing the investment option within your fund. A buy-sell spread is also an example of a transaction fee, often found in older super products. These are often activity fees based on a kind of transaction you undertake. In some cases, you can even be charged a fee for making a contribution to your super.
Investment fee or investment choice fee	These fees are often charged in superannuation and managed fund investments for managing your investments. These are separate to transaction fees and are usually charged for the investments used.

(continued)

Table 10.3: Investment fees (*cont'd*)

Fee name	What is it for?
Indirect Cost Ratio (ICR)	This is also a fee you should consider. It's not one that's taken directly out of your superannuation or investment. Instead it's paid to an investment manager (or a number of investment managers) before the provider pays you a return/distribution. I've seen ICRs as high as 2.5 per cent. This means that 2.5 per cent of the investment return gets paid to an investment manager instead of being returned to you.
Contribution fee	Some managed funds and super funds charge you a fee when you deposit new money for an investment. These fees can really add up over time and might be avoided with a different provider.

There are a lot of fees and the names for them often change depending on the product type and provider you're looking at. But on something as significant as superannuation, even a 1 per cent reduction in fees on a balance of $100 000 saves you $1000 a year, or $20 000 over 20 years of your working life. I'm sure we'd all like a little more retirement money once the paycheck stops.

I think it's also important to point out that high fees aren't always bad fees. If you require a certain product feature, then you're probably going to have to pay a little more to get it. Needless to say, it pays to shop around or seek the advice of a qualified and licensed financial planner. Considering your overall position is important; considering things in isolation can be dangerous.

When to do it?

Ideally, you'd consider a Fee Reduction Strategy at the time you start your investment or superannuation fund. But I know from experience that many people don't engage until they've got enough of a balance to worry about. In most cases it's about $40 000 to $50 000. However, this strategy can be implemented at any time and should be something people consider each year.

Do

Do consider a Fee Reduction Strategy:

- Before you buy any investment, super or retirement product

- At any time during the ownership of an investment, super or retirement product

- As part of an investment review or portfolio review when considering your overall asset allocation

- If you have an older style of investment, super or retirement product.

Don't

Don't fall into these traps:

- Going for the cheapest option just because it's cheap. While a short-term goal might be to spend less, you've got to think about your 'why' and the medium- and long-term goals you're trying to achieve, considering your asset allocation and your income and growth needs.

- Forgetting about the risks of investing. Cheaper fees are only one aspect you should consider of the overall features being offered. There's always risk.

Those old-style super products can be nasty

Some of the fees for old-style superannuation products are just plain nasty. Imagine paying a fee every time you or your employer makes a contribution to your super. Then, imagine paying an ICR as high as 2.5 per cent along with that! The ICR alone on a balance of $100000 is $2500 ($100000 × 0.025) a year. Over 20 years of your working life that's $50000 (20 × $2500) you won't have, not to mention the lost interest on that money.

It pays to check fees and costs on all your investments and even your day-to-day bank accounts. Knowing horror stories like this hopefully makes you feel uncomfortable enough to engage with your super and where it's going, rather than just leaving it and hoping for the best.

The Appropriate Tax Strategy

If we don't like fees, then we certainly don't like taxes. The Appropriate Tax Strategy involves looking at the tax you pay and ensuring you meet your obligations effectively.

Like them or not, taxes are an important part of our social structure. They pay for the hospitals, schools, roads and other services we some-times take for granted. This strategy isn't about tax avoidance—that's illegal. Everyone needs to pay their fair share. This strategy is about ensuring you're not paying more than you need to.

In my experience as a financial planner, everyone loves a tax deduction and often reducing tax is the only strategy that many people pay proactive attention to. When you look at the Appropriate Tax Strategy, you're not just looking for a tax deduction or franking credit (tax credit) here and there. It's something that's got to be considered across your all your income and your assets. By doing this, the strategy is more useful to helping you achieve your 'why'. It's also something you think proactively about with your accountant too, not just as an afterthought when doing your tax return.

How does it work?

Tax planning takes the time to look at the tax you're paying and make sure you're using all your options to ensure you're not paying too much. Table 10.4 outlines some of the frequently used strategies.

There's limit to the information I can provide in this book given the complexity of this topic, but the two certainties in life still hold true—you can't avoid death or taxes. I hope this information has provided you with a sound introduction to this strategy.

Table 10.4: Tax planning strategies

Strategy	What is it?
Eat more of the good stuff	On goods and services in Australia, we pay 10 per cent GST on almost everything we buy. But did you know that fresh fruit and vegetables, cheese, bread, flour, cooking oils, meats, spreads, spices and sauces are among the exempt items? Tea and coffee are also exempt. So homemade pizza is GST exempt, but you'd pay tax on a shop-bought one.
Claim your tax deductions	Your occupation could typically determine the kinds of tax deductions you can claim. Work-related expenses can usually be claimed as a deduction off your tax.
Select the right investment structure	This is an investment strategy from earlier in this chapter (the Investment Structure Strategy). Different structures sometimes have different tax implications, which will impact on the amount of tax you pay.
Make use of franking credits	Franking credits is the basis for another strategy from earlier in this chapter (the Franking Credit Strategy). Franking credits might provide you with the opportunity to achieve more appropriate outcomes for you, depending on your situation.
Claim your income protection premiums	Did you know that the premiums you pay for income protection insurance are tax deductible? I don't think most people realise this. It might be better to protect your income in the event of illness and accident and get a tax deduction in the process.
Seek specialist tax planning advice regularly over time	Clearly tax is a very complicated area of your financial life and the strategies you implement need to be personal to your specific income and investment situation. Seek proactive specialist tax planning advice over time as your needs and lifestyle change.

INVESTMENT

When to do it?

Ideally, you'd consider an Appropriate Tax Strategy at the time you first start paying tax. But, given the complexity of the tax system, it's something more people rely on their accountant to deal with rather than learn more about. It is worthwhile having a conversation with your accountant or financial planner about. You can implement this strategy at any time, but it's always good to have a look before the end of the financial year.

Do

Do consider an Appropriate Tax Strategy:

- As part of your overall investment strategy from the outset
- As part of an investment review
- At the time you do your tax return, and plan forward
- As part of who you vote for.

Don't

Don't fall into these traps:

- Becoming a tax avoider. The penalties are high and the stress isn't worth the effort.

- Expecting that you can live a tax-free life. As part of living in a developed country, taxes are inevitable. Be prepared to pay what you're required to under the law. It's part of the responsibility of being a citizen of a country. And if you think it's really all unfair, then spend your next holiday in a developing nation and live among the challenges those countries have for a while. You'll be glad you live in a developed country with high-quality schools, hospitals, roads, services and so on.

Not a penny more, not a penny less

I don't think you're allowed to write a book about money in Australia without including at least one reference to the late Kerry Packer. Packer was Australia's wealthiest man during his life, with significant shares in media businesses. In 1991 he was called to appear before a federal government print media enquiry, and he had an exchange with the parliamentarians that will go down in history.

When asked if he paid tax, Packer replied, 'I've already given you the answer on this subject, I have told you that I pay whatever tax I am required to pay under the law, not a penny more, not a penny less, and the suggestion that I am trying to evade tax, which is what you're putting forward, I find highly offensive and I don't intend to cooperate with you in the blackening of my character.'

Packer also told the parliamentarians he didn't think the government was spending it that well. I bet we've all had the same thought at some time too.

The Gearing Strategy

The Gearing Strategy is an investment strategy where you take out a loan to invest, in addition to using your own money. It might sound like an odd thing to do. 'Why wouldn't I just invest my own money?' you might wonder. Well, it can be useful if you're unable to buy the investment you want on your own, such as a house or a share portfolio.

The benefit to investors of taking on such a debt is that the interest you pay and the expenses you incur relating to the investment are tax deductible. Additionally, the type of asset you invest in is likely to have both income and growth components, for example rent (income) and a rise in the value of the property over time (growth).

How does it work?

Gearing works because interest from the investment debt and expenses related to the investment may be claimed as a tax deduction. By claiming these deductions, you pay less tax. Remember the truth about most people planning for a tax deduction not a lifestyle in Chapter 1? Most people forget their 'why' and just focus on the tax deduction, which is why gearing gets them excited.

An asset can be negatively geared or positively geared, and it's important to understand the difference.

Negative gearing occurs when the income (for example, rent or dividends) from the investment you buy is less than the interest from the debt and other expenses that result from the investment. Essentially, it means you're making a loss.

Positive gearing occurs when the income from the investment you buy is more than the interest and other expenses that result from the investment. In this case, you're making money from the start, from a cash flow perspective, even though you still hold debt. In this case you're also likely to be paying tax on the additional income.

Let's take a look at a share portfolio without gearing, and with positively and negatively geared investments, belonging to Chris, who has $100 000 invested in shares (see table 10.5).

Table 10.5: Chris's share portfolio with different gearing options

	Example 1. Without gearing	Example 2. With negative gearing	Example 3. With positive gearing
Annual income	$75 000	$75 000	$75 000
Plus investment earnings	$6000	$24 000	$12 000
Less interest	$0	$24 000	$8000
Less expenses	$0	$1000	$1000
Taxable income	$81 000	$74 000	$78 000
Tax + Medicare levy	$19 492	$17 077	$18 457
Net income after tax	$61 508	$56 923	$59 543

Example 1: Investing without gearing

Let's say Chris earns $75 000. In the 'without gearing' case, Chris is able to earn 6 per cent of his investment of $100 000 in a share portfolio, which is $6000 (0.06 × $100 000). There are no tax-deductible expenses as there no debt is attached to the investment. So Chris has a taxable income of $81 000 ($75 000 + $6000). On that taxable income, he pays $19 492 in income tax and the Medicare levy and has $61 508 left.

Example 2: Investing with negative gearing

In this case, all the same factors apply but Chris decides to borrow $300 000 to invest with the $100 000 he already has. He now earns an investment income of 6 per cent on $400 000, which is $24 000 (0.06 × $400 000). Chris is able to claim back the interest and expenses on the investment loan. If the investment loan has interest of 8 per cent on the $300 000 he borrowed, it comes to $24 000 (0.08 × $300 000). Chris is also able to claim expenses on the investment—say, account fees, loan fees and investment management fees of $1000. As a result,

Chris has a taxable income of $74 000. Chris pays $17 077 in tax and the Medicare levy and has $56 923 left. In this case, Chris is negatively geared because his earnings from the investment are less than his interest and expenses.

Example 3: Investing with positive gearing

In the final case, all the same factors apply but Chris decides to borrow $100 000 to invest with the $100 000 he already has. He now earns income of 6 per cent on $200 000, which is $12 000 (0.06 × $200 000). Chris is able to claim back the interest and expenses on the investment loan. If the investment loan has interest of 8 per cent on the $100 000 he borrowed, it comes to $8000 (0.08 × $100 000). Chris is also able to claim expenses on the investment—say, account fees, loan fees and investment management fees of $1000. As a result, Chris has a taxable income of $78 000. Chris pays $18 457 in taxes and the Medicare levy and has $59 543 left. In this case, Chris is positively geared because his earnings from the investment are more than his interest and expenses.

As you can see from the examples, the benefits of gearing are derived from claiming the interest from the debt and the expenses of the investment over a year. This really excites people who love tax deductions. What you can't forget though are some very important things. Firstly, you still need to pay back the money you borrow—only the interest is tax deductible. Your budget and cash flow need to be able to afford the repayments when they arrive. Secondly, you also can't forget about the risks associated with all investments and the impact this might have on the long-term value of your investment, be it positive or negative.

Remember: gearing your assets can accelerate both positive and negative returns over time.

When to do it?

A Gearing Strategy should only be considered as a long-term investment strategy. The ideal situation is that you have money to service the debt of the life of the investment loan without causing stress in other areas of your spending plan. Also, aim to seek professional taxation advice relevant to your personal situation before embarking on this strategy.

Do

Do consider a Gearing Strategy:

- When you complete a Risk Assessment Strategy (refer to Chapter 9) and if it's appropriate for your long-term needs

- Before you take out any debt

- When you understand what happens if interest rates rise and have factored the interest rate rise into your cash flow

- When you understand what happens if the value of your investment falls, you have capital available or you have surplus capital to protect your overall position

- When you have a long-term investment need.

Don't

Don't fall into these traps:

- Following this strategy just because you want more tax deductions!

- Going into investment-related debt without understanding the interest, the costs, the repayments and the term of the loan, as well as factoring in change over time

- Going into interest-related debt without shopping around for the best deal. It's important you get the best interest rate and terms you can. Like any expense, you owe it to yourself to get the best value.

- Assuming your loan-to-debt structure is the same as everyone else's. Review and understand where and how your assets are held.

'She said she owns eight investment properties'

From time to time in the media, you'll hear about the person who pops up claiming to be a multi-millionaire because of all the investment properties they own, yet they look like Mr or Mrs Average. They might also talk about how anyone can do it and you should follow their advice. But people like this may not be telling you the whole story because they never tell you about the serious amount of debt they hold. I suspect they tell their story because they want to make money off people (by selling a 'how to do it' program) or they want to make themselves seem more important than they are.

In such cases, I suspect that the bank owns more of the properties than they do. I suspect they also forget that interest rates on their loans, just like property prices themselves, can rise and fall. What happens when interest rates rise and they can no longer afford the repayments on all that debt? Do you think the bank is going to forgive that debt? Hell no! They'll probably be forced to sell their investment properties in a market that has falling prices in some situations. Property prices are likely to be falling because people just like them were counting on low interest rates and high property prices forever. It's just not reality.

If you're going to borrow to invest, do it sensibly and armed with the best information you can get. Stress test what happens under different interest rates. How would you feel if the investment went down in price? Also consider what happens if you lose your job—will you still be able to afford to pay back the debt? There's a lot to consider here beyond chasing another tax deduction. So, do your homework and seek professional advice first.

INVESTMENT

— CHAPTER 11 —

The Superannuation Strategies

Superannuation (or super) is an investment structure, but it's a special kind of investment structure and that's why it deserves a special focus. *Superannuation* is money put aside while you're working for your retirement that you can't access until you reach a legislated age. Your employer takes a portion of your total remuneration and places it into a superannuation account. Regardless of how much you earn, your employer is required by law to pay at least 10.5 per cent of the total wages you earn to your super. In today's superannuation system, you can also make additional contributions to your superannuation account.

Outside of the family home, superannuation is generally the largest asset people will accumulate over their working lives. It's therefore a very important part of your strategy stack.

Just like any other kind of investment, superannuation members typically have one or more of three expectations:

1. That they'll receive interest from the money invested (income).
2. That they'll have their initial money returned or see it go up or down (capital).
3. At the point of sale of the investment, they'll sell for more than they paid for it (growth).

This chapter provides you with some additional Investment Strategies that may be used in conjunction with the underlying investment of superannuation. Specifically, I explore these strategies:

- The Super Vehicle Strategy
- The Consolidation Strategy
- The Contribution Strategies
- The Contribution Catch-Up Strategy
- The Super Splitting Strategy
- The Spouse Contribution Strategy
- The Government Co-contribution Strategy
- The Re-contribution Strategy
- The Appropriate Super Fees Strategy
- The Appropriate Tax in Super Strategy
- The Downsizing Contribution Strategy
- The Super Investment Strategies.

SUPER

The Super Vehicle Strategy

The Super Vehicle Strategy investigates and determines the best way to hold and use superannuation. In Chapter 10, I explored different kinds of investment structures; superannuation is a special kind of trust structure. Many people don't realise this, thinking trusts don't apply to them. Think again! All superannuation funds are trusts (and there are specific rules set by the government about how they must be managed). There are however different superannuation vehicles you can use to hold your superannuation (*vehicle* simply means the type of superannuation fund you wish to use to meet your objectives).

The vehicles have different features and different benefits. All the vehicles have one thing in common though — a trust deed. The trust deed outlines how the superannuation fund will be run.

There are six kinds of superannuation vehicles people tend to use to accumulate money for their retirement:

1. Industry super funds
2. Retail super funds
3. MySuper funds
4. Corporate or public sector funds
5. Self-managed superannuation funds
6. Legacy funds.

Let's take a look at each of these vehicles:

- **Industry super funds:** Industry super funds were originally started to provide retirement savings for workers of a specific industry. Many of them were trade union based. Industry funds typically operate on a profit-to-members basis, which means they don't have shareholders. Traditionally they had limited investment choices, although this has changed over time. Most didn't offer financial planning advice to members either. Now, most industry funds are open to the public, not just members of the original industry. Their options and investment flexibilities continue to improve.

- **Retail super funds:** Retail super funds were originally started to provide retirement savings for workers regardless of which industry they worked in. Unlike their industry super fund cousins, they were started by financial institutions, fund managers and banks rather than trade unions. Retail funds operate on a more commercial basis, which means they have shareholders. Financial advice has often been provided to retail super fund holders as it's been easier to get fund information from retail super fund providers compared to industry super fund providers, which weren't set up with advice in mind. A retail super fund will have an approved product list from which a member can select investment options.

SUPER

- **MySuper funds:** MySuper was a style of superannuation introduced by the government to make superannuation easy for people to understand and operate. These funds have low fees, simple features and a single diversified investment option that may change as you get older. Many industry and retail super funds turned to MySuper as a default option. These are very basic superannuation offerings and have limited strategic uses, other than holding small account balances.

- **Corporate or public sector funds:** Corporate or public sector funds were started by employers, either corporations or governments, to look after the retirement funds of their employees. Traditionally, and in many cases today, you have to be an employee of the business or public sector organisation to be a member of the fund. However, some public sector funds are opening to the public. Depending on the company or sector, they might have also paid more than the legislated amount of employer superannuation contributions, usually as part of a wage agreement.

- **Self-managed superannuation funds:** In all the preceding cases, superannuation is 'outsourced' to someone else to manage on your behalf. Self-managed superannuation funds, however, offer an individual or group of individuals the ability to take on the responsibilities of being a super trustee and actively manage their own superannuation. This means they are responsible for all aspects of running the fund, including meeting the legal requirements. In many cases, people who choose to operate their own self-managed superannuation funds (or SMSFs) hire in external financial planners, accountants and auditing functions to help them meet their obligations. 'Self-managed' is rather misleading as in the majority of situations members choose to have the day-to-day operations of the fund handled by a professional. This is because people are either time-poor or don't have the skills to effectively manage it themselves.

- **Legacy funds:** Today, most super funds are considered to be accumulation funds; that is, the superannuation balance of a person is determined by their employer contributions, their own contributions and the investment earnings of their super account. However, there are still some legacy funds operating (though they are typically closed to new members). These are called defined benefit pension schemes or retirement schemes. They are very generous in the benefits they provide to members when compared with other types of funds as they use a specific formula to calculate your entitlements that can be tied to your salary or accumulation benefit—this is slightly different to a standard accumulation fund that only measures the value of the money that is invested in the fund. These schemes originated as corporate or public sector super schemes. Your end benefit is paid by the fund, and what you get is usually determined by the length of time you've worked for an eligible employer, your salary before you retire or a specific pre-determined formula. These pensions cannot be cashed out and are paid to you for the rest of your life, with a residual amount passing to a spouse in some situations. You may not be able to roll out of your fund (move your money); in addition, they are typically very generous in relation to the formula and pension outcome offered from your accumulated benefit.

Each of these superannuation vehicles have different rules, and it pays to understand the specific rules of the fund you're looking at.

How does it work?

Given legacy funds don't accept new members, they're only applicable to the people who are already within them—so if you're not already in, they're not going to be an option for you. For the rest of us with an accumulation style of fund, you should take the time to consider the different kinds of superannuation vehicles available and assess their features and benefits. For most people, doing this without seeking advice can be challenging but not impossible. If you seek personal financial planning advice from a financial planner, they will be able to assess offerings best suited to your needs. The challenge here is to find the right vehicle that helps you build your 'why'. The vehicle needs to have the right level of features and benefits so you don't overpay for things you don't require. Equally, you don't want to get caught out by a fund that doesn't offer enough options, such as a reasonable range of investment choices.

When to do it?

The Superannuation Vehicle Strategy should be considered when you first start to receive super. Most people don't think about the superannuation vehicle they want to use, even though they probably have a choice (with the exception of some legacy funds).

It's often once people have entered their working lives and started to accumulate more funds that they start thinking about whether they're using the right vehicle. That's okay too, as you can look at this strategy at any time, provided you're still eligible to hold a super account.

Do

Do consider a Superannuation Vehicle Strategy:

- When you start your first job
- If you're concerned about the performance or management of your super fund
- If you're concerned about flexibility and taxation. Different super vehicles offer different levels of control on things like investment options, insurance providers and the ability to manage the income profile of your assets. Super itself is also a very tax-effective vehicle. You only pay 15 per cent tax compared to your marginal tax rate (personal rate of tax), which is usually quite a lot higher.
- If you wish to have greater control over the use of franking credits within your fund
- If you change jobs, develop your career or become self-employed
- If you've got more than one superannuation fund or need more than one superannuation fund.

SUPER

Don't

Don't fall into these traps:

- Assuming all super funds are the same. They've all got different fees, asset types, investment offerings and features.

- Using the fund your employer offers without looking at it first—while it might not be a bad fund, it may not be the best fund for you and your 'why'

- Exiting a legacy fund without first seeking financial advice. Leaving the fund could cost you tens of thousands of dollars.

Superannuation is like a car for your 'life after work' savings

Buying your first car is a milestone. It's something to celebrate as a young person moves to independence and adulthood. If you've ever bought a car, you'll know there's a lot to think about. There are different brands, different features and options, and different likely performance outcomes. There's also the colour to think about: do you want one in black, white, blue or red—or don't you mind what colour it is? You may spend a lot of time thinking about buying a car because it's a big purchase, and you're probably emotionally invested in it because it's exciting.

Selecting your superannuation vehicle is like buying a car in some ways. There are different brands, different features and options, and different likely performance outcomes. Yet, despite it being a more important investment than your car (which will cost you money, not make you money over time), selecting the right superannuation vehicle fails to inspire or excite.

It's also important to think about the right vehicle for your stage of life, too. A MySuper fund might be a low-cost option early in your career; however, you're likely to need something with more options and features at a later date.

Using the car analogy, you need to consider the broader features of the fund. That's like taking a car tyre into a car dealership and asking what car the tyre fits. You would never do that when you buy a car, but I have seen people do this when it comes time to choosing their super vehicle. You need to consider what's important to you and the features you need in a fund. If your existing fund doesn't offer access to listed shares and you want these in your fund, it doesn't really matter what it costs—it's not appropriate. If you would like to use exchange-traded funds but your fund doesn't allow them, you need to consider a fund that does—and so on.

Tradies drive utes for a reason—it suits the job. The same must go for your super vehicle. The vehicle you choose should contribute to your 'why' to ensure it's the most effective option.

The Consolidation Strategy

With the Consolidation Strategy, you combine multiple super-annuation accounts into one structure. If you've had multiple jobs over your working life, you might have multiple super funds. With an increase in casual and part-time employment, it's not surprising. If you've taken a break from work to raise kids, you should also take a look at how many super accounts you have. There's probably some from your 'pre-kids' life you haven't given much thought to.

Each super fund you have charges fees—not only for having the account, but often insurance premiums too. Some of these premiums you might never see the benefit from, such as income protection insurance. Australian legislation requires that you replace lost income, not make money from getting hurt, so you can generally only claim on one policy anyway—so paying the premium for more than one form of income protection is a waste of money.

Make sure that prior to cancelling anything, you have medically underwritten cover with the best possible definitions and benefits as contracts differ significantly and they are NOT all the same. That's a little off-track for this topic, but ensuring constant cover is very important when changing funds; however, I talk more about insurance in Chapter 13.

How does it work?

The Consolidation Strategy works because you put all your super in one account, and review your overall fees and insurance costs—which focuses you on making decisions about your super and your 'why'. Retirement might seem a lifetime away but the more time you have on your side, the longer you have to make it grow. Think about the value of half a per cent over 30 years—it may not be much this year, but over time it could be worth a lot more. Remember: think with the end in mind as it's a marathon, not a sprint.

Combining your superannuation accounts is a relatively pain-free process once you've decided which superannuation vehicle will be your main account going forward.

What do you need to get started?

Every superannuation account has a member number. Every super fund has a number too. It's called a Unique Superfund Identifier (USI). In some cases, if the fund is a self-managed super fund, the Australian Business Number (ABN) is what you need to look for. Just check and see what your fund needs for you to roll assets into it, as each fund is different.

You can consolidate your superannuation funds by completing the roll in (or consolidation) form from your preferred superannuation provider using these identifying numbers. Some funds allow you to do this online or over the phone too, which might save you some paperwork and a trip to the post office.

When to do it?

A Consolidation Strategy should be considered when you have multiple superannuation accounts, aren't really across your super, want to reduce super paperwork, want to take it easier, and want to focus on and take control of your retirement savings. Another good time to review your super holdings is at the end of the financial year (if you haven't already done so) as the fund you are in normally sends out an end of year summary or report. This is a good time to find out what you have in your super; you can also search for 'lost super' on the Australian

SUPER

Taxation Office (ATO) website if you think you may be missing some fund information. Some funds even offer a consolidation service when you open a new account.

A useful point to note is that the government has decided to cancel any insurance within an existing fund where the fund has not been directed to maintain it or you have not made a contribution to the fund in the last 16 months. Whether this applies to you or not, it's important to know what insurance your super funds have. If you need to keep your insurance within a superannuation fund, you need to act fast to ensure that it isn't cancelled (before the super fund cancels it for you). We'll talk more about Wealth Protection Strategies in Chapter 13.

It might not be a good idea to consolidate all your super funds either, depending on what you hold. For example, you might have a fund with insurance that covers a medical condition you experienced after you opened that account, whereas it may be a pre-existing condition that's excluded from later super insurance policies. This situation might not affect you if you're fit and well, but it is worth your while to investigate the possibility before you roll into another fund. Once a super account is closed, the insurance cover disappears and you can't get it back. Never roll-over a fund until you have medically underwritten cover in place, because you can bet as soon as you move your super something will happen. Murphy's law never helped anyone—we all know that to be true!

What to look for in a super fund to consolidate your accounts will depend on your 'why'. Consider the Super Vehicle Strategy here. Features of your new super fund might include:

- Wide investment options
- Control over income and franking credits
- Access to exchange-traded funds and index-based holdings
- An ongoing admin cost of around 0.5 per cent
- Cost-effective Indirect Cost Ratio (ICR)—this is the cost of the investment option(s) you select.

Do

Do consider a Consolidation Strategy:

- When you have had multiple jobs and have accumulated multiple funds

- If you want to review and understand super fees and insurance premiums

- If you want to make it easier to manage your superannuation

- If you want to check you have selected the right superannuation vehicle to take your retirement savings forward. The selected fund gives you all the investment options you need (or may need) in the future.

Don't

Don't fall into these traps:

- Forgetting to look at insurance cover issues if you think there's a concern

- Deciding to consolidate into your first super fund or your last super fund just because it was the first or the last one you had

- Selecting a super fund on fees alone. Cheap can mean good value, but it can also mean nasty. Sometimes you do get what you pay for, even with super funds. Also, consider the fund's features and long-term performance.

- Assuming that the investment option you're moving into is the same as the one you just left. 'Balanced' can mean many different things, so check the underlying asset allocation and sector-specific weightings—don't just check that the name is the same.

Strategy Stacking Tip

The underlying allocation of your money is more important than the name of the investment option. A so-called 'balanced' super fund may allocate an 85 per cent weighting to growth assets, whereas another fund may run a more defensive 50/50 allocation for growth and defensive assets. Don't let asset allocation scare you—it's just the speed at which your super car is driving. Going back to the 'risk assessment car' from Chapter 9, a growth allocation of 85 per cent is like doing 140km/hour in a 100km/hour zone. A 50/50 allocation may be more like doing 90–110km/hour (much more comfortable—and it sounds much more balanced!).

If we are both in a BMW and doing the same speed, we should get to our destination at the same time—but with different speeds come different results. Don't assume all BMWs (or balanced super funds) give the same outcomes because of the name alone. This is also true when comparing performance—if one car is doing 140km/hour and the other is doing 100km/hour, there's no way the slower car can beat the faster one; in the same way, you can't compare performance based on the name of the investment option alone.

Keep that in mind when moving funds as it could result in you holding assets outside of your true risk tolerance (which could be good or bad), depending on markets.

Grandad only ever had two jobs

Grandad was solid when it came to his job. He started work when he was 14 and only changed jobs once over his working life before retiring. He's like most of his peers—you had job security, and part-time work really didn't exist. Superannuation only came into existence later in his working life. He and his generation also never had to worry about multiple super accounts.

How things have changed. Young Australians are now likely to have more than 10 jobs before they turn 40. It may be even more for millennials and generation Z, and some of those jobs will be in different occupations. Part-time and casual work is increasing, and some people

SUPER

have multiple jobs at a single point in time. It's not surprising then that we're likely to see an increase in the number of super funds we have.

For many, though, super is dull. Despite it being the biggest investment they're ever likely to have outside their home, their super accounts will go wanting for a little love and attention. It's a symptom of our ability not to plan for the long term and the modern need to focus on instant results.

The effort you put into something often determines what you get out of it. The same goes for your super.

The Contribution Strategies

The Contribution Strategies are strategies where you make extra contributions to your super to help you achieve the superannuation balance you require for your retirement. Simply, it's like a savings plan for your super.

If you're an employee, your employer is required to pay contributions to your superannuation no matter what you earn over your employment period. They are required to pay 10.5 per cent (from July 2022) on top of your wage, with some employers paying more than the legislated minimum (which is great for you!). For example, someone earning $60 000 a year in wages can expect to receive an employer contribution of $6300 (0.105 × $60 000) to their super. Employer contributions like this starts the first Contribution Strategy to your super, but it may not be enough to provide you with a comfortable retirement—depending on your retirement living expenses.

If you're self-employed or work in a partnership, the law says you don't have to pay yourself superannuation. Despite this, you still probably should unless you have another way to fund your retirement. It's always about weighting up your options, paying more tax on your take-home pay when you receive income, or moving over money into super to lower your overall tax payable (but not having access to the money until you meet a condition of release for super). For most people, they will pay more tax on their take-home pay than what they pay on super. You might pay 30 per cent tax on your salary but if you put it into super, you'll only pay 15 per cent.

Regardless of how you're employed, you can also make extra contributions to your super: you have the opportunity to make a real difference to your long-term superannuation balance. Additionally, you can make non-concessional contributions (contributions you make to super without claiming a tax deduction) up to the age of 75. However, the work test must be met from age 67 if you wish to make a concessional contribution to super (contributions you make to super and claim a tax deduction for). The work test says you need to work 40 hours within a 30-day period once you turn 67.

How does it work?

The Contribution Strategies can work in a number of different ways depending on how the contribution is made. Let's take a look at the different kinds of contributions. They all boost your super account balance and that's reason enough, but there are other reasons why you might make extra contributions (see table 11.1).

Table 11.1: Comparing contribution types

Contribution type	How does it work?
Employer contribution	This is the 10.5 per cent paid into your super by your employer. It's on top of your wage. Your employer claims a tax deduction for making this contribution because they've paid it.
Salary sacrifice contribution	This is where you ask your employer to make an additional contribution to your super from your before-tax pay. Your employer claims a tax deduction from this contribution because they've paid it (up to the concessional contribution cap of $27 500).
Personal concessional contribution	This is where you make a personal contribution to your super. You can claim a tax deduction from this contribution because you've paid it (up to the concessional contribution cap of $27 500).
Personal non-concessional contribution	This is also where you make a personal contribution; however, you don't claim a personal tax deduction with this type of contribution (up to the non-concessional contribution cap of $110 000).

If a tax deduction is claimed by your employer or yourself, the super contribution is taxed at 15 per cent once it goes into your super account. The 15 per cent tax rate is very favourable, given most people pay a lot more than this on their take-home pay (which is impacted by your total income each year).

Given tax deductions are lovely things to have, it's not surprising that the government has set a limit on the amount of your super contributions that can claim a tax deduction. The amount is $27 500 a year and it's called a *personal concessional contributions cap*. This applies only to contributions where a tax deduction has been claimed by yourself or by your employer.

If a tax deduction is not claimed on a super contribution (that is, it's a *personal non-concessional contribution*), then you're not taxed on that contribution once it goes into your super account. There are some provisions on this: your superannuation account balance needs to be less than $1.7 million, and the contributions need to be no more than $110 000 a year (that covers most people). In some circumstances, however, you can use a bring-forward rule to contribute more — for example, from an inheritance or the sale of a business. A *bring-forward rule* allows you to contribute more using the next three years' contributions maximum (or $330 000 in a single transaction). You need to check your total super balance prior to making large contributions as there are specific thresholds to consider.

When to do it?

Given the different contribution types, it can get a little complicated working out when to do it (see table 11.2, overleaf).

Table 11.2: Timing your Contribution Strategies

Contribution type	When to do it
Employer contribution	It will happen as part of your employment. If you're self-employed or in a partnership, you can also make contributions from your business to your super fund.
Salary sacrifice contribution	Speak to your employer about making this contribution for you. This is an easy way for some people to make additional contributions to super without any further effort. Although you can't claim a tax deduction, you will pay less income tax.
Personal concessional contribution	You make your contributions to super when you'd like to and you claim a tax deduction for the contribution yourself (rather than your employer). You must lodge a Notice of Intent with your fund to claim this, and you'll then receive confirmation from the fund. Note: your accountant will want this information for your tax return.
Personal non-concessional contribution	You make your contributions to super when you'd like to but you don't claim a tax deduction for the contribution.

You might use more than one contribution type depending on your situation. Of course, all strategies have the benefit of increasing your superannuation balance, which is the main objective.

Strategy Stacking Tip

Consider this as an example. Imagine you have a mortgage that you can't claim the interest on during the year. Most people want to own their home and limit the amount of interest they pay each year. If you're salary sacrificing because a lady at the water cooler said it's a good idea and you know no better, consider this alternative approach:

1. Direct all after-tax income to the offset account on your home during the year to lower the amount you owe the bank and the interest you incur (fantastic where you have an interest-only loan as well, as the amount the bank takes each month will go down).

2. Review your cash flow position in June each year.
3. Confirm your concessional cap space (the difference between $27500 and what your employer has directed to superannuation for you).
4. Take money from the offset account you have used to hold your after-tax income each year against your home loan, and direct your money to super in June as a personal concessional contribution.

This way, you have effectively had two uses for the money: you reduced the interest on your non-deductible home loan, and you also receive a tax deduction for 100 per cent of the money you put into super in June before the end of the financial year.

The additional tax refund you may get when your tax is lodged in July should be directed back to the offset account of your home—then you repeat the process for as long as you can.

Note—don't do this blindly; you need to make sure that making a deductible (concessional) contribution is tax-effective given your personal situation. However, if it is, the old-school strategy of salary sacrifice to super is effectively redundant when you have non-deductible debt.

SUPER

Do

Do consider a Contribution Strategy:

- When you're looking to live a more comfortable retirement and do a little more a little sooner

- If you've got savings capacity and are prepared to lock away the money until you reach retirement age

- If you have saved to your offset account all year and the end of the financial year is approaching

- As part of looking at an Appropriate Tax in Super Strategy (covered later in this chapter)

- If you receive an inheritance or sell a business or personal asset.

Don't

Don't fall into these traps:

SUPER

- Taking for granted that your employer is paying into super for you. Check that your contributions are actually getting received into your superannuation account.

- Forgetting that saving to your super means you generally can't access the money until retirement age. There are some exceptions, however, for severe financial hardship.

- Forgetting about the concessional contributions cap. Only $27 500 worth of superannuation contributions can have a tax deduction claimed (both yours and your employers). If you contribute above the cap, you'll pay more tax when you do your return.

- Forgetting about the cap on non-concessional contributions—use the bring-forward rule when you need to.

Remember: your money must be cleared and in your super fund prior to 30 June each financial year if you want to maximise your deductions. A payment made prior but not cleared in time will count in the following financial year, so you may miss out on your deduction in the current year. Don't leave it too late!

You can lead a horse to water, but you can't make it drink

If you play competitive sport, you'll go to training and may have a coach or trainer to push you that little bit further. Even the best of the best have coaches to keep them motivated and focused. What you put into something often determines what you get out of it.

The same goes for your superannuation. With the ability to claim a 100 per cent tax deduction for a personal concessional contribution to your super, the choice to contribute to super has never been so compelling. You can pay more tax to the government or save to your retirement savings and pay less tax. The choice is yours. The only limit on you reaching your goals is you. Perhaps you need a financial planner to be your coach—or perhaps this book is enough to get you started.

Doing a little more now is easier than having to make large contributions later, which can have a real impact on lifestyle that you may not enjoy—especially if you know you have to because retirement is fast approaching. I've never worked with anyone that has told me they have too much super! Starting early with a small portion of your income may also reduce the impact of an increase in the future and be more sustainable.

The Contribution Catch-up Strategy

The Contribution Catch-up Strategy is a relatively new strategy that you have been able to use since 1 July 2019 (on a rolling five-year basis). The strategy specifically deals with unused concessional contributions (from the preceding Contribution Strategies) that includes employer contributions, salary sacrifice contributions and personal concessional contributions.

Employer contributions are the legislated 10.5 per cent (or more, depending on your employer) that the employer pays to your superannuation account. Salary sacrifice contributions are where you ask your employer to make an additional contribution to your super from your before-tax pay. Personal concessional contributions are the savings you make to super yourself and on which you can claim a tax deduction. As outlined within the Contribution Strategies section, there's a limit to the concessional contributions you can make in a year ($27 500, the concessional contribution cap).

How does it work?

How might you use your unused concessional contributions to increase the balance of your superannuation account? Let's consider an example.

Paulo earned $80 000. Paulo's employer paid employer contributions of 10.5 per cent or $8400 (0.105 × $80 000) to Paulo's super account.

Paulo also makes a salary sacrifice contribution each week of $50, which equates to $2600 over the year ($50 × 52).

SUPER

Over the year, Paulo has a total of $11 000 in concessional contributions ($8400 + $2600). These are contributions where a tax deduction has been claimed.

However, Paulo could have used up to $27 500 of concessional contributions in a year. That means he has an unused concessional contribution amount. The unused amount is $16 500 ($27 500 − $11 000). In the next year, Paulo has the opportunity to use $44 000 ($16 500 + $27 500) in total as a concessional contribution.

As the name of the strategy suggests and the example shows, the strategy allows you to 'catch up' on unused concessional contributions. I believe this is one of the best pieces of legislation passed in the last 10 years and is great for the following people:

- Young people that come into money
- Parents wanting to add to super for their kids
- Mums and dads returning to the workforce after taking time out to be at home with the kids
- People who have gone from part-time to full-time work
- People finishing study who want to build their super quickly
- Contractors, whose income can vary significantly
- Employees that receive bonus payments.

When to do it?

The Contribution Catch-up Strategy can be used when you have unused concessional superannuation contributions. It provides you with the opportunity to make personal concessional contributions and receive a greater tax deduction. The tax deduction applies in the year you use the strategy. You can make a personal contribution or salary sacrifice to achieve the contribution and your taxable income would be reduced in the year the contribution is made.

What are the rules?

- You must have a super balance of less than $500 000 at the end of 30 June of the previous financial year.

SUPER

- You can only roll the unused cap space for a maximum of five years from the 2019 financial year. The emphasis here is on unused space, which means the difference between the concessional limit and the amount you added to super in that 12 month period.

Do

Do consider the Contribution Catch-up Strategy:

- When you're looking to live a more comfortable retirement

- When you've got savings capacity and are prepared to lock away the money until you reach retirement age

- If you're selling a taxable asset and want to maximise your deductions in the year the asset is sold (for example, an investment property)

- If your income has increased in recent years and you want to add that extra cash to your super and lower your taxable income

- As part of looking at an Appropriate Tax in Super Strategy (covered later in this chapter)

- If you receive an inheritance or have had a large bonus payment.

Don't

Don't fall into these traps:

- Forgetting that saving to your super means you generally can't access the money until retirement age. There are some exceptions, however, for severe financial hardship.

- Forgetting that going above your contributions cap using the Contribution Catch-up Strategy also means you'll pay more tax when you complete your tax return

- Forgetting that your salary sacrifice contributions, like personal concessional contributions and employer contributions, all count towards the $27 500 cap you have in each year

- Forgetting that you've only got five years to use your unused concessional contributions. Once they're gone, they're gone forever.

SUPER

Sometimes you have to play catch-up—and that's okay

We've probably all had times in our adult lives where we've let things slide and had to play catch-up. It might be due to work commitments, family commitments or simply running late for one appointment, which then cascades to every other appointment during the day. Those days are so frustrating.

It's okay to play catch-up. It doesn't mean you've failed; it just means there aren't enough hours in the day sometimes to achieve everything you'd like to do. It's a great opportunity to be able to play catch-up with your super.

It's also a great way to limit the tax on the sale of an asset and reduce the potential capital gains associated with it as you have increased your tax deductions by using this strategy. By holding off your contributions because you know the sale is coming, you may be able to use some of the sale proceeds from the asset, or cash, to increase your deductions in the year of sale. Again, thinking with the end in mind can provide huge taxation savings and help you build retirement assets—maximising the return on your property investment and superannuation balance at the same time.

You may wish to start a pension to gain access to capital that could be used to make additional contributions to superannuation and take advantage of available concessional cap space, therefore lowering your taxable income in the year the contribution is made. Starting a pension (provided you are able to do so) would be suitable if you don't have access to money either in an offset account or bank account.

The Super Splitting Strategy

The Super Splitting Strategy can allow you to plan improved retirement outcomes for you and your partner. As the name of the strategy suggests, one person splits their before-tax superannuation with their spouse. These concessional contributions include employer contributions, salary sacrifice contributions and concessional personal contributions. You can only split up to 85 per cent of your concessional contributions. In all these cases, you can both claim a tax deduction for making a superannuation contribution, but what you do with it next can make super look a little bit sexier.

For readers with an older spouse, this strategy is fantastic and is one of the most underused strategies out there. The simple outcome of this strategy is that it increases the retirement savings of the party that's receiving the funds (normally the older spouse, as they will reach access age for super sooner—so you both win). However, there are other beneficial outcomes too.

The strategy is only available to people who are legally married or in a relationship that's registered under certain state or territory laws. The super splitting rules are not available to someone that has already retired or met a condition of release to access their super. Remember: only concessional contributions can be split—non concessional contributions cannot be split.

How does it work?

Let's take a look at the Super Splitting Strategy in action in three different scenarios.

Splitting boost and tax scenario

Jill earns $100 000 and has $100 000 in her super, while her husband Tony has $400 000 in super. Jill had taken time off work over the years to raise the kids. Tony earns $80 000 a year and therefore receives $8400 at 10.5 per cent ($80 000 × 0.105) as an employer contribution. Tony also makes a personal concessional contribution to his super of $5000. This means that Tony has a total of $13 400 ($8400 + $5000) that he can split with Jill. Tony decides to super split $5000 with Jill.

What's the effect of this?

Jill's super is boosted by $4250, which results from $5000 less contributions tax of $750 at 15 per cent ($5000 × 0.15), which stays in Tony's super fund to pay his contribution tax. Tony receives a $5000 personal tax deduction for making a personal concessional contribution.

Boosting a lower super balance is one option; the other is to move all the concessional contribution from Jill to Tony because he will reach

SUPER

his preservation age sooner (he is 10 years older than Jill). Jill would be able to use this strategy each year, which means that if she had a total of $27 500 directed to super each year, she could split $23 375 per annum to Tony. Over a 15-year period, this could equate to $318 750 (assuming no earnings). The money could then be accessed tax-free by Tony at 60 and used to fund Jill's early retirement (or to pay off debts with tax-free capital). Either way, it's money that Jill would not be able to access for a further 10 years, so they are both far better off and have increased the flexibility of their retirement.

People want to do things together when they retire—not everything, but some things. Having access to capital that would have otherwise been locked away could let Jill reduce her work hours, take leave without pay during the year or focus on other interests, including travel.

Retirement home and tax scenario

Down the track, if Jill is looking to retire before she turns 60, she could use some of her super to put towards a retirement home in the country. However, if she withdraws more than $230 000 (called the *low cap rate*, which applies to people under the age of 60), any withdrawal above that amount is taxed at 17 per cent. In this case, Tony could access the superannuation that has been split to him over the years as he is over 60, so the capital would be tax-free.

What's the effect of this?

Both Tony and Jill can each withdraw up to $230 000 for the retirement home in the country and not pay the tax that applies with the low rate cap. Tony also receives a personal tax deduction for making a concessional contribution each year.

Centrelink benefits scenario

When Tony gets to 65 and Jill is 55, Tony decides to split his super with Jill to reduce his superannuation account balance before he retires.

What's the effect of this?

By reducing his assets, Tony could increase his Centrelink entitlement (provided he also satisfies the income test—which places a limit on the amount you can earn in a fortnight to get a full or part aged pension). Tony also receives a personal tax deduction for making a concessional contribution each year. When Tony reaches the age pension age (depending on his year of birth), the assets in Jill's name would not be included in the assets assessment as she is under the age pension age and has not started a pension from superannuation. Superannuation is not considered as part of a couple's assets test where a partner (Jill in this example) hasn't yet reached retirement.

When to do it?

The Super Splitting Strategy is something to consider when you're looking to boost the super of your partner, you wish to withdraw a larger amount from super before you turn 60, you have a partner who is older than 60 and would like to fund retirement costs tax-free, or you're looking to increase your Centrelink entitlements. It really is a case-by-case scenario as every couple's 'why' is different.

The Super Splitting Strategy is something that needs medium- to long-term planning. The benefit of time helps build up the other partner's superannuation account before you need to access the funds. Super splitting can only be completed once a year, and most superannuation funds have a form to complete.

You must split contributions each year after the end of the financial year and after your personal Notices of Intent to claim a deduction has been lodged with your respective superannuation funds. If you wish to use this strategy, you need to complete the admin every year. It's not something you can set up to keep going automatically.

Do

Do consider a Super Splitting Strategy:

- When you're looking to boost your spouse's superannuation balance over time after time out of the workforce

- If there is a difference in age between spouses

- If you want to build a capital base to help the younger spouse reduce their work hours or retire if the older spouse ceases work

- To increase the amount of capital you can access on a tax-free basis from age 60 to pay off debts

- If you're concerned about not being eligible for all your Centrelink entitlements

- If you're comfortable making a contribution to your spouse's super, which means it's locked away until they reach retirement age and it legally becomes their money.

Don't

Don't fall into these traps:

- Making decisions without running your own numbers, or asking a financial planner to run the numbers. Amending your actions can be hard or sometimes even impossible to take back.

- Forgetting about the limits you can contribute to super through concessional contributions. If you contribute above the limit of $27 500 a year, you'll pay more tax.

- Forgetting to stay on top of your admin. If you don't split one year that option is gone for that year, it's not cumulative — it must be done each year or the opportunity for that year is lost. If you forget to do it one year, you can come back and do it for the next year.

- Forgetting you can only split 85 per cent of your concessional (deductible) contributions.

- Forgetting you can't split non-concessional contributions.

Nothing says 'I love you' like super splitting

Roses are red, violets are blue. Nothing says love, like super splitting with you. I bet you didn't expect that (and I can see my wife rolling her eyes while reading this).

But couples make gestures of love all the time and in different ways. It might be something as simple as cooking dinner or taking out the rubbish; some gestures are grander, like a dozen red roses and dinner at your favourite restaurant. But can something like making a mortgage repayment or splitting super be considered romantic? After all, it's about achieving your mutual 'why'—what's most important to you both—so what could be more romantic that that? I am yet to find a younger spouse that does not want to retire at the same time as their partner, or have the option of reducing their work hours to do the things they enjoy.

There's nothing more powerful than a couple pursing their goals together and supporting each other through the journey. It's just a pity more couples don't take the time to explore what they want and get onto the same page as each other. Nothing is more frustrating than getting advice at 60 and finding out that you missed out on 10 years or more of this strategy that can make life-changing differences.

The Spouse Contribution Strategy

The Spouse Contribution Strategy, like the Super Splitting Strategy, can allow you to plan improved retirement outcomes for you and your partner. And again, as the name of the strategy suggests, you make a contribution to your spouse's superannuation.

How does it work?

Spouse contributions can be made for spouses who earn up to $40000 a year. The partner making the contribution can claim the maximum tax offset of $540 (a tax deduction) when they contribute $3000 from their take-home pay to their superannuation if their spouse earns less than $37000 a year. The more the spouse earns above $37000, the less the tax offset will be, reaching zero once their spouse earns $40000 a year. Of course, you can contribute more than $3000 a year to your spouse's super; however, you won't receive any tax benefit for doing so if the contribution is made as a spouse contribution.

When to do it?

The Spouse Contribution Strategy is something to consider when you're looking to boost the super of your partner, and it can be done before the end of the financial year. It's also a useful strategy to look at if your spouse is taking a career break, undertaking part-time work, or is a stay-at-home parent who is raising the kids.

SUPER

Do

Do consider a Spouse Contribution Strategy:

- When you're looking to boost your spouse's superannuation balance

- As part of considering an Appropriate Tax in Super Strategy (covered later in this chapter)

- If you're comfortable making a contribution to your spouse's super, which means it's locked away until they reach retirement age and it legally becomes their money.

Don't

Don't fall into these traps:

- Making decisions without running your own numbers, or asking a financial planner to run the numbers. Once you make and implement a spouse contribution decision, it's very hard to undo.

- Forgetting about the limits to the amounts you can contribute to super. In the case of a spouse contribution, the contribution is considered to be a non-concessional contribution — that is, from after-tax money.

Working together brings better outcomes

Superannuation is a great investment for focused couples. Those who work together can deliver themselves better retirement outcomes than if they only looked at their own super. It's sometimes hard to have conversations about money though, because they're usually conversations about going over a budget or not being able to spend. In my experience, the couples that look at investment using the term 'we' in place of 'I' can maximise strategies and accelerate their collective wealth a lot faster. Good cash flow and the ability to save can be the basis for using more strategies in the future.

Finding something positive for both parties is often a good way to start a conversation about money. A Spouse Contribution Strategy might be one topic. You'd be surprised how often I sit across from couples who are retiring from work who, for the first time in their lives, have a conversation about money. They're also the kind of clients that say to me, 'Gee, I wish someone had told us about that before now.' By that stage, they've missed numerous strategy stacking opportunities and are behind on where they could have been if they had done some longer-term planning.

It's not what you do, it's the consistency of what you do over time that brings the greatest rewards.

The Government Co-contribution Strategy

The Government Co-contribution Strategy is where the government will make a contribution to your superannuation account if you're eligible. This strategy was created by the government to help employees with lower income boost their superannuation for their retirement.

How does it work?

To be eligible for a government co-contribution, you must earn less than $57016 (at the time of writing). You must also make a non-concessional contribution to your superannuation account—that is, a contribution where no tax deduction is claimed. If a tax deduction has been claimed, you won't be eligible.

The maximum amount of a government co-contribution that you can receive is $500, which is available to people who make a non-concessional contribution to their super of $1000 and earn $42016 or less.

If your income is between $42016 and $57016, your maximum government co-contribution will reduce as your income rises.

When to do it?

If eligible, you need to make a personal non-concessional contribution to your super before the end of the financial year and then complete your tax return after the end of the financial year. Once your tax return has

SUPER

been completed and your eligibility has been assessed, the government will make the co-contribution to the nominated superannuation fund (the one that received your personal contribution).

Do

Do consider a Contribution Strategy:

- When you're in your first job; that is, you start work for the first time

- If you've got a part-time job and earn less than the cut-off threshold

- If you have kids or a partner earning less than $57 016. Why not gift them money so they can make an additional contribution to their retirement savings and receive the government co-contribution as well?

Don't

Don't fall into these traps:

- Forgetting about the eligibility criteria and income thresholds. These can change, so please seek advice or visit the ATO website to confirm your eligibility.

- Making a concessional contribution to your super and expecting to receive a tax deduction as well as a government co-contribution. Government co-contributions only apply when you meet the criteria, which includes making a non-concessional contribution to your super fund.

Every bit helps

Small gestures repeated often make a big difference. Let's say for 20 years of your adult life you're eligible for the maximum government contribution—that's $1500 a year, with your $1000 contribution and the government's $500 co-contribution. Over 20 years that adds up to $30 000 ($1500 × 20) without any investment earnings added. I'm sure there's a lot you could do with an extra $30 000.

The same principle goes for your everyday saving. A little bit here and a little bit there all adds up when you've got the benefit of time on your side. It's a pity that the government co-contribution only applies to super!

I also encourage parents to use the idea of co-contribution from time to time (not necessarily to superannuation) with their teenagers and young adult kids when they're saving for something. Perhaps they're saving for their first car or an overseas trip. If they put in, you put in. If they don't, then you don't. It helps reward good behaviour and helps them achieve their goal without completely relying on you.

The Re-contribution Strategy

The Re-contribution Strategy helps you plan more appropriate tax and estate planning outcomes, and possibly improve your Centrelink outcomes, by withdrawing money from your superannuation account (or account-based pension) and re-contributing it back into your super (or account-based pension). Simply, it turns taxable components into tax-free components.

The strategy is only available to people who meet a condition of release to access their super and are still eligible to make super contributions—typically, people between the ages of 55 and 75 (depending on the year they were born).

How does it work?

Let's take a look at two examples to see the Re-contribution Strategy in action.

Estate planning and tax example

Mark is 67 and has turned his super income into an account-based pension. His $800 000 account-based pension balance has two tax components. Let's keep the numbers simple as a general example:

- Taxable component: $400 000
- Tax-free component: $400 000.

If Mark dies, his adult children will pay 17 per cent (including Medicare levy) death benefits tax on the taxable component of his account balance that they receive. In this case that is $68 000 tax ($400 000 × 0.17).

Using the Re-contribution Strategy, Mark could withdraw $330 000 from his account and make a personal non-concessional superannuation contribution back to a new account-based pension. The components of the withdrawal must come out in proportion to his existing account balance from both the tax-free and taxable components (you can't just draw out the taxable amount only to get the outcome that you are after, unfortunately)—so he withdraws $165 000 from each component ($330 000/2). Mark can make this withdrawal and re-contribution as he's not previously used the bring-forward rule, so hasn't passed any contribution caps.

Taking $330 000 out and directing it back to superannuation would increase the tax-free portion of his account and also limit the tax impact for his children (Chapter 14 talks about Estate Planning Strategies in more detail). This means that Mark can start a new account-based pension along with his old one and have $565 000 as a tax-free component. This is made up of $235 000 in his old account ($400 000 – $165 000) and $330 000 in his new account. Mark may also wish to contribute the $330 000 to a new superannuation fund and lock in the tax-free status—it doesn't necessarily have to go back into the same fund.

Strategy Stacking Tip

Remember to consider your overall position and the most appropriate control of your taxable components. You can add tax-free (non-concessional) money back into a superannuation account, but to make the most of the strategy and to lock in the tax-free status long term, use a second account to maximise the value of the Re-contribution Strategy. Adding $330 000 to a new account and starting a pension ensures that any growth in the value of the new account is tax-free over the long term. Always check your contribution limits and legislation at the time to ensure you can make the most of this strategy without falling foul of the rules.

Centrelink example

In this example, Amir has the same $800000 account-based pension with two tax components:

- Taxable component: $400000
- Tax-free component: $400000.

Amir is eligible for only some Centrelink aged pension entitlements as he has assessable assets just below the asset threshold available.

However, instead of re-contributing his super back to himself, Amir can re-contribute super to his wife, Zara, who isn't eligible for Centrelink benefits because she's below her access age. As a result, Amir is able to reduce his assets and access more Centrelink benefits, and Zara has had her super account boosted (provided she is under the pension age and has not commenced a pension, her assets would not be included in Amir's Centrelink assessment).

When to do it?

The Re-contribution Strategy is something to consider when you're able to access your superannuation (you have met a condition of release) but you have not started a pension from your accumulated superannuation. Where you are under the age of 60 and have met a condition of release (met the age that you can access your superannuation), you could start a pension from your superannuation; however, increasing the tax-free percentage of your total fund would maximise the tax-free status of any pension income that you draw prior to 60 as you would have added to the tax-free components of your superannuation by making a re-contribution.

Controlling the estate planning impact of your superannuation and pension accounts is important to limit the tax impact on the transfer of assets. You should also consider the trading and tax implications of selling assets within your superannuation fund as capital gains tax may apply. If you have to sell assets to take money out of superannuation to undertake the Re-contribution Strategy, you need to consider the trading costs as well as any associated capital gains on the assets being sold before pulling the trigger.

SUPER

From a strategy perspective, it may be worth Amir starting a pension, selling his high-tax assets (as a pension account is free from capital gains tax) and withdrawing the proceeds of the sale of the asset to add back to Zara's super fund. This could help avoid unnecessary capital gains tax as part of his broader strategy.

Do

Do consider a Re-contribution Strategy:

- As part of looking at an Appropriate Tax in Super Strategy (covered later in this chapter) and an Estate Planning Strategy (Chapter 14)

- When your Centrelink benefits will help you live a more comfortable retirement

- If you're comfortable with making a contribution to your spouse's super, which means it's locked away until they reach retirement age and it legally becomes their money

- If you intend to start a pension from your superannuation when you are under the age of 60 and wish to limit the tax impact on your income stream.

Don't

Don't fall into these traps:

- Forgetting that saving to your super means you generally cannot access the money until retirement age. This especially applies if you're making a re-contribution to your spouse.

- Forgetting that the withdrawal must come out in the same proportion of your existing superannuation fund so you may have to draw out more than you need on a percentage basis to reduce your taxable component

- Forgetting to consider the tax implications when selling assets to fund the re-contribution

- Losing track of your non-concessional contributions. If you have already used your non-concessional limit, you may be

SUPER

unable to get all the funds back into superannuation. Check what has been happening in relation to non-concessional contributions in your super over the last three years.

Knowing the rules helps you play the game better

This strategy might seem a bit silly—you're taking something out just to put it back in. At no point in this book do I suggest that the rules aren't without their problems—or that they always make sense.

The art of strategy, regardless of the situation, is about knowing the rules of the game and when to use them. It could be going for that field goal or shooting a hoop just before the siren signals full-time. It could also be having set plays during key points of the match. The same goes for your financial strategies, yet most people let opportunities pass them by because they never spent any time learning the rules of the game or seeking advice from someone who did.

The basis of most people's 'why' is to maximise their overall position both now and in the future (through your children and your estate planning). Seeking financial advice can make a significant contribution to your financial life over your lifetime; it can also help the next generation on their journey, too.

The Appropriate Super Fees Strategy

The Appropriate Super Fees Strategy seeks to ensure that you're not overpaying on the operation of your super fund. Generally speaking, the more complicated your superannuation structure is, the more fees you will have to pay to manage your retirement funds.

Like most things in life, you tend to get what you pay for. I tell clients regularly that a mechanic needs a number of tools to do their job, and superannuation is no different—you need access to a wide range of assets and franking credits, and the ability to control your income, as well as the ability to use managed funds, exchange-traded funds and listed shares.

By reviewing your superannuation fund fees, you can ensure you're not overpaying. If you think you're paying too much, you can explore

SUPER

other options or talk to your existing provider to see if there's room to move, or consider another fund that is in line with your 'why' and gives you the controls you require. Cost is important, but not to the detriment of quality.

You should also consider the insurance offered through a new or existing fund if you're going to address fees and charges. Insurance premiums are a cost to the fund, and the quality of the cover may be reflected in the fees and charges taken from your account. Again, don't compromise the quality of your cover for a lower fee because insurance is about maintaining the best possible definitions and policy benefits—the term 'you get what you pay for' is never more true than when it comes to insurance though superannuation. Don't assume that industry fund insurance will be cheap either because, in my experience, there are much better ways to protect yourself and your loved ones rather than the standard option on offer within many super funds.

How does it work?

The first step to reviewing the fees you pay to run your superannuation is to understand what fees you're paying. Let's take a look at the typical fees you're likely to pay, depending on the structure that you're in (see table 11.3).

Table 11.3: Super fees for different types of super fund structure

	Industry super funds and retail super funds (accumulation phase)	Self-managed superannuation funds (SMSF) (accumulation or retirement phase)	Personal superannuation fund (Retirement phase)
Set-up costs	Nil. These funds are free to join.	These fees are charged for setting up an SMSF. These fees include: • SMSF trust deed cost • SMSF sole purpose trustee company cost.	Nil. These funds are free to join.

	Industry super funds and retail super funds (accumulation phase)	Self-managed superannuation funds (SMSF) (accumulation or retirement phase)	Personal superannuation fund (Retirement phase)
Fixed costs	Typically, these are charged for completing an ongoing function of your superannuation. These include: • Administration fees • Investment fees • Indirect costs • Insurance premiums.	Typically, these are the ongoing annual costs you'd expect to see within a self-managed super fund. These include: • Accounting and audit fees • Annual ASIC corporate fee • ATO Supervisory levy.	Typically, these are charged for completing an ongoing function of your superannuation. These include: • Administration fees • Investment fees • Indirect costs.
Variable costs	Typically, these are charged when you make a transaction on your account or invest funds. These include: • Switching fees • Brokerage • Buy-sell spread fees • Activity-based fees • Indirect fees • Super splitting fees • Family law splits • Property and borrowing costs • Insurance costs • Managed expense ratio (MER).	Typically, these are charged when you make a transaction on your account. These include: • Brokerage • Banking costs • Indirect fees • Insurance costs • MER.	Typically, these are charged when you make a transaction on your account. These include: • Switching fees • Buy-sell spread fees • Activity-based fees • Brokerage • Indirect fees • Insurance costs • MER.

SUPER

On the subject of fees, and regardless of which type of superannuation structure you choose, you might also pay a financial planner to help you make the most of your super strategies. A good adviser will deliver more value to your retirement over the long term than the fees they charge. You may also discover things about your super and other investments that you didn't even know about. After all, 'you don't know what you don't know'.

SUPER

Strategy Stacking Tip

When comparing funds, it's important that you compare apples with apples. For example, an industry fund may charge additional fees for investment costs that are in excess of the ICR for the investment option you select. Industry funds also charge property and borrowing costs that are not included in the standard ICR. These differences can make it hard to compare the fees of different superannuation products, and industry funds are very good at making it extremely difficult to work out the true cost of all of the account-based costs.

Don't forget to add up EVERYTHING when comparing fees. With that in mind, you may need to go hunting for the information as it is normally found in the fund's Product Disclosure Statement (PDS).

When to do it?

The Appropriate Super Fees Strategy is something to consider before you commit to a superannuation fund and as part of your overall superannuation strategy. It's also important to review once in a while to make sure you're still getting value for money.

Do

Do consider the Appropriate Super Fees Strategy:

- When you're selecting a new superannuation fund or joining a new employer that has a default fund
- When you commit to growing your super for the first time

- If you're concerned about the fees you're paying on your superannuation

- When you review your superannuation investment and fund performance

- If you wish to invest in exchange-traded funds, individually listed shares or specialised managed funds within your preferred risk profile.

- If you wish to maintain direct property as part of your asset allocation (in which case, an SMSF may be the right fund for you).

Don't

Don't fall into these traps:

- Making decisions on fees alone. Some structures, like self-managed superannuation funds, cost more because they offer you functionality that you can't get with other superannuation types. (Also remember that super is long term and you should consider the future value of your fund over a specific time frame. Moving and moving and moving could result in additional entry and exit fees being incurred.)

- Discounting the value of accounting and financial planning advice to simply save money. Superannuation is complicated and the rules often change. Making decisions without advice means you are taking a risk: 'You don't know what you don't know.' A wrong decision could cost you more than you realise.

- Assuming that the ICR is the only investment cost for an industry fund. Check all the associated fees and charges, which will require you to hunt through the PDS. You must compare apples with apples.

The cheapest isn't necessarily the best

Superannuation funds charge fees to cover the costs of operating their funds. They have staff wages and operating costs and there's quite a lot to do. Activities include receiving employer contributions and reporting to employers, opening and operating your account, buying and selling investments, receiving the contributions you make, managing and paying tax, reporting to you about the performance of the fund through statements and online portals, managing insurance and death claims, managing hardship and other payments, auditing costs ... and the list goes on. It's much more complicated than a bank account.

Price shouldn't be the only criteria upon which you select a superannuation product for your retirement savings. There's a real difference in features from fund to fund—investment options is one of the big ones, along with the quality of the insurance available. Some of the cheaper funds may have very limited investment options, so while you might save on fees, investment performance over the long term might not be up to scratch.

I always say to my clients that they need to lift up the hood of the vehicle and see what they're actually paying for before deciding if they have the right superannuation vehicle that works for them. The engine and features of a BMW costing $100 000 aren't going to be available in a $20 000 Kia, so check your options before you move.

The Appropriate Tax in Super Strategy

Superannuation is a tax-effective vehicle for saving for your retirement. The Appropriate Tax in Super Strategy seeks to ensure that you meet your obligations effectively and make the most of your retirement savings for your 'why'.

How does it work?

The first step to understanding the Appropriate Tax in Super Strategy is to understand what tax applies to super and when.

Most people pay tax at a rate of 32.5 per cent or more on their income when their income is in excess of around $45 000. Superannuation, however, has a much lower tax rate, which is why it's so tax-effective.

Let's take a look at the typical taxes you pay on your super, and when you pay them (see table 11.4). The type of fund that you maintain can also have an impact on when the tax is taken from the account.

Table 11.4: Taxes on superannuation contributions (figures correct at the time of writing)

Contribution types	Tax rate	When is it paid?
Employer contribution	15% of the contribution	Once the contribution arrives in your superannuation account
Salary sacrifice contribution	15% of the contribution*	Once the contribution arrives in your superannuation account
Personal concessional contribution	15% of the contribution	Once the contribution arrives in your superannuation account
Personal non-concessional contribution	No tax is payable on these contributions	Not applicable
Government co-contributions	No tax is payable on these contributions	Not applicable

* An SMSF would remit the tax when the tax return is completed; this is a key structural benefit of this fund as it lets you use the money for longer when compared to an industry or personal superannuation fund alternative.

There are a couple of special issues to note here:

- Low income earners benefit from the low income superannuation tax offset. This means that if you earn $37 000 or less, the tax you pay on superannuation contributions will be contributed back to your superannuation account, up to $500.

- High income earners, however, will pay an additional Division 293 tax. This is an extra 15 per cent tax that's charged if your adjusted taxable income is above $250 000.

Taxes on contributing too much to superannuation

There are limits on the amount of money you can put into superannuation each year. From 1 July 2021, the concessional contributions cap is $27 500 and the non-concessional contributions cap is $110 000. You might have some room to move though if you have unused contributions from previous years, or you might have no room to move if your total super balance has reached the transfer balance cap of $1.7 million (the transfer balance is simply the total value of your super).

If you go above these caps, however, you'll pay more tax. It's best to seek personal accounting advice on matters like this as everyone's personal tax situation is different. As a guide though, you might expect to pay tax as outlined in table 11.5.

Table 11.5: Tax rates for different types of super contributions (figures correct at the time of writing)

Contribution types	Tax rate	When is it paid?
Employer contributions, salary sacrifice contributions, and/or personal concessional contributions that are above the contributions limit.	The excess concessional contribution amount is included in your assessable income and the amount will be taxed at your marginal tax rate.	Generally paid when your tax return is complete and the ATO has matched the returns. A notice is issued confirming the figure due.
Personal non-concessional contributions that are above the contributions limit.	47% on the amount above the excess non-concessional contribution limit. You might alternatively have the option to withdraw the entire amount of excess non-concessional contributions and pay tax at your marginal tax rate on the excess rate earnings.	A notice is provided by the ATO on the amount due.

Taxes on earnings within superannuation

Just as tax applies to any investment income you earn, tax also applies to investment earnings within your superannuation account (see table 11.6).

Table 11.6: Tax on investment earnings within super (figures correct at the time of writing)

Tax	Tax rate	When is it paid?
Investment earnings tax	A maximum rate of 15%	When the fund's tax return is completed after the end of the financial year
Capital gains tax	A maximum of 15% or 10% where the asset is held for more than 12 months	When the fund's tax return is completed after the end of the financial year

It's important to note that your fund might pay less than 15 per cent as the amount of tax can be reduced by any tax deductions or tax credits the fund has, including franking credits. There are options for individuals who go above their superannuation contribution limits to reduce the impact of tax. It's best in this instance to seek personal tax advice as everyone's situation will be different.

Taxes on superannuation death benefits

These taxes are determined by dependency. Note, dependency under the *Income Tax Assessment Act 1997* (Tax Act) and *Superannuation Industry (Supervision) Act 1993* (SIS Act) differ. A dependant under the Tax Act is someone who relies on another party for financial support (such as a non-working spouse or children under 18 years of age). Adult children may not be deemed dependant under the SIS Act. This means they will pay tax on any superannuation death benefits they receive, as shown in table 11.7 (overleaf).

SUPER

Table 11.7: Tax on super death benefits (figures correct at the time of writing)

Benefit recipient	Taxable component of superannuation	Untaxed component of superannuation
Dependant (received as a lump sum)	No tax payable	No tax payable
Non-dependant (received as a lump sum)	15% (plus the Medicare levy)	30% (plus the Medicare levy)

Regardless of the dependency type, there is no tax payable on the tax-free component of a superannuation death benefit. I recommend that you seek advice from a financial planner and accountant should you ever need personal financial advice on tax and superannuation death benefits. It's a complicated area and if you have a mix of dependants and non-dependants involved, different outcomes will apply to them.

Strategy Stacking Tip

It is important that you understand where your superannuation would be paid in the event of your death. Having the correct nomination can ensure greater control in relation to the passing of assets and limit unnecessary tax being incurred by loved ones. Review existing nominations and your changing needs, as the age of your children could impact where your money is paid. Additionally, if you find yourself in an end of life situation and have no death insurance benefit in your super, you might consider withdrawing your account balance if you have non-dependent beneficiaries to avoid the 17 per cent tax payable or more (depending on the source of funds in your superannuation account). If you haven't given the proceeds away prior to your passing, your will would then distribute them (this could have other implications, of course).

When to do it?

You might consider an Appropriate Tax in Super Strategy as a part of your overall retirement savings plan (Chapter 12) as well as your estate planning plan (Chapter 14). You should also consider how funds are going to be invested as this can impact the tax payable within the fund. The use of franking credits can help to mitigate future liabilities, so don't forget about them either—they are very powerful. As you can see, there are a number of things to consider when selecting a fund—it's not just about the fees (or indeed tax).

Do

Do consider an Appropriate Tax in Super Strategy:

- As part of your overall superannuation strategy from the outset

- As part of your income tax planning, given that superannuation offers more favourable tax rates to save for your retirement

- As part of a superannuation review

- As part of a broader tax planning strategy in conjunction with your accountant

- When using your Estate Planning Strategies (Chapter 14) to control the distribution of funds in the event of your death

- If you're considering the Contribution Catch-up Strategy from earlier in this chapter as part of your broader tax planning strategies.

Don't

Don't fall into these traps:

- Forgetting that even if you get a tax deduction for a superannuation contribution, you generally can't access that money again until you reach retirement age

- Forgetting to keep an eye on your contribution limits. If you make excess contributions, you could incur penalty tax.

- Making decisions without understanding the consequences of your decisions

- Making a contribution because your friends do—have a plan yourself and a strategy prior to actioning the contribution.

SUPER

Managing your tax position in super

If you have a personal or an industry super fund then, as part of the fees you pay, the trustee will manage the tax outcomes for their members. This is part of the ongoing administration fee that you pay, and it's not something that you actively have to think about. Superannuation trustees have a legal obligation to act in the best interest of their members.

If you have a self-managed super fund, however, and you are a trustee of that fund, you also have the obligation to act in the best interest of the fund's members, and this includes managing tax. This is why most trustees of these kinds of funds pay financial planners and accountants to help them with this activity. It's specialist work, and unless you have relevant expertise it's probably something you won't be able to manage by yourself. Get advice, don't leave it to chance.

The Downsizing Contribution Strategy

The Downsizing Contribution Strategy is a superannuation strategy that allows senior Australians to make a contribution to their super, even if they're retired—and provided they meet some eligibility requirements.

'Wait a minute—is that really possible?' 'Can I make this kind of contribution to super even if I've stopped working?' These are the kind of questions we get asked regularly when it comes to this topic. And the basic answer is yes, you can.

The strategy is available to those 60 years or older (from 1 July 2022), working or not, who sell their home. Individuals can contribute up to $300 000 from the sale of their home to a superannuation fund (and for couples, that's up to $300 000 each). The strategy allows people to use some of the funds of the sale of their home to help fund their retirement.

SUPER

This strategy was created by the government because a lot of people have a significant amount of capital tied up in the family home. Selling, buying something smaller and using the residual funds to generate additional income is a way to increase your superannuation or add to your personal investment portfolio to fund the lifestyle that you've been aiming for in retirement.

How does it work?

The Downsizing Contribution Strategy works when you're 60 or over and want to sell the family home. You might find yourselves rattling around with too much to clean and too much lawn to mow now that the kids have grown up and moved out. So, you make the decision to move into something smaller.

To use this strategy, you need to make sure you meet the government's eligibility criteria first. To be eligible, you must answer 'yes' to all the following questions (correct at the time of writing):

- (From 1 July 2022), will you be aged 60 or more at the time you wish to make your downsizer contribution to your superannuation account?

- Was the sale contract on your home exchanged on or after 1 July 2018?

- Was your home owned by you or your spouse for 10 years or more prior to selling your home?

- Is your home a house in Australia and not a caravan, houseboat or mobile home?

- Is the capital gain or loss from the sale of the home either exempt or partially exempt from capital gains tax (CGT) under the main residence exemption, or would you be entitled to such an exemption if the home was a CGT rather than a pre-CGT (acquired before 20 September 1985) asset? In other words, is your primary home being sold?

- Have you completed the 'Downsizer contribution into superannuation' form either before or by the time you plan to make your downsizing contribution to your super fund?

SUPER

- Is the downsizer contribution you intend to make $300 000 or less as an individual? (Your spouse, if you have one, can also make a contribution of $300 000 or less to their super fund.)

- Will you make the downsizer contribution to your super fund and complete the paperwork within 90 days of the date of the settlement of the sale of your home?

- Can you confirm you have not made another downsizer contribution to your super fund from the sale of another home? (Reminder: this is a one-off opportunity.)

What if you have a spouse but only one partner owns the home? Under the downsizer contribution rules, so long as you have a spouse, you can make a downsizer contribution too provided all the requirements are met. This isn't just an opportunity for the homeowner; their partner gets the benefits, too.

You can't use your downsizer contribution to claim a tax deduction, like you can with other personal deductible contributions to your super fund. It also doesn't count towards your personal contribution limit to super either. It will, however, be taken into account when considering your eligibility for Centrelink age pension benefits as the capital added to superannuation would be included in your asset test and therefore your deemed income rate.

The downsizing contribution can also be made where you are in excess of the transfer balance cap (the total amount of money you can have in super—$1.7 million); however, the capital added to your superannuation can't be used to start a tax-free income stream as the earnings within the fund would be taxed at 15 per cent.

As you can see, downsizing is complicated. You need to consider your wider situation when making this contribution, including any Centrelink impacts. Seek financial planning advice if you need assistance.

When to do it?

The Downsizing Contribution Strategy allows you to use a superannuation vehicle to help fund your life in retirement using the proceeds of the sale of the family home.

The strategy could be considered when you (and your spouse, if applicable) are over 60 and you're looking to downsize your home for something smaller. You might move from a family home into a unit, a smaller house, a retirement village or a villa by the sea. It doesn't matter what kind of property you move into—you just need to meet the eligibility criteria.

You don't have to put all the sale proceeds into a downsizer contribution. For example, let's say Linda and Charles sell their family home for $850 000. They meet the eligibility requirements and want to use the Downsizing Contribution Strategy. They want to use $450 000 to buy a unit on the coast, which means they'll have $400 000 left. They decide to split the remaining $400 000 between them, contributing $200 000 to each of their superannuation funds. They can then use that money to generate additional income (which may be tax-free within their pension account).

SUPER

Strategy Stacking Tip

The downsizer contribution can be made in conjunction with the non-concessional contribution rules, as well as the concessional contribution rules (and don't forget the Contribution Catch-up Strategy earlier in this chapter, where applicable), to maximise the amount of money you have within superannuation (from which an income stream may be commenced). The timing of your contribution is important as you need to ensure that you meet numerous thresholds that limit the amount of money that can go into superannuation. Starting with the end in mind should ensure that you don't miss out on taking advantage of all the Super Strategies to help you reach your 'why'.

Do

Do consider a Downsizing Contribution Strategy:

- If you want to downsize your home in retirement for something smaller and invest the surplus within your super

- If there's a large amount of capital tied up in your home and it may be better used to create the lifestyle you want to have in retirement
- If your partner doesn't have much super. You might put more in one partner's account, if the other partner already has a good super balance.

Don't

Don't fall into these traps:

- Forgetting to make sure you meet all the criteria and complete the paperwork within the required time frames. Seeking professional advice before you act is always wise.
- Thinking you can claim a tax deduction for this type of super contribution—you can't
- Forgetting about the transfer balance cap. It's the limit on the amount of super you can turn into a pension, which is currently $1.7 million for each person. That limit might influence how much of a downsizer contribution you are able to make.
- Forgetting about the Centrelink age pension implications. The money from the sale of your family home will be considered when determining your entitlements. (Your new home, however, is exempt from consideration once you've purchased it and it becomes your primary home.)
- Making the downsizer contribution without considering other contribution options first—this could limit the amount of money you get to put into superannuation
- Forgetting to consider the implications of the strategy in terms of your needs and goals.

Rising home prices have made many Australians wealthy

Over the last 30 years in Australia, we have seen home prices go up and up. It's made many Australians see the value of their wealth 'on paper' skyrocket! A home in 1970 might have been bought for $40 000, yet in

2020 it could be worth $900 000. That's quite a good capital return, you'd have to agree. But what it means for many Australians is that their wealth is locked up in their primary home.

Just because you're retiring, it doesn't mean that you give up on your life goals. Retirement is when you actually have the time to do what you want to do, without the hassle of work. Retirement today looks different to our parents' idea of retirement (and certainly our grandparents' generation). We now see OPALs everywhere (older people, with active lifestyles) as well as Grey Nomads touring the country, following the sun and the seasons.

When thinking about how you'll fund your own retirement adventures, don't forget the Downsizing Contribution Strategy. You might be able unlock the value of your home to buy something smaller and fund the things you'd like to do. This strategy, in conjunction with a part-time hustle/job or contract work, could really bolster your cash flow. Remember, just because you retire, it doesn't mean that you can't work on a part-time basis doing something you enjoy—after all, is that really work?

The Super Investment Strategies

The Super Investment Strategies are simply Investment Strategies for your superannuation. You might wonder how these differ from the Investment Strategies outlined in Chapter 10? Well, many of those strategies can be applied to your superannuation too. So the purpose of this section is not to repeat those previously identified, but to uncover how your super investment strategy might be different, depending on the kind of superannuation account you have.

How does it work?

Let's take a look at the relevant Superannuation Strategies in this chapter in table 11.8 (overleaf), considering the two distinct types of superannuation structures: industry and retail super funds, and self-managed super funds (SMSFs).

Table 11.8: Investment Strategies in superannuation

Investment strategies	Industry and retail super funds	Self-managed superannuation funds (SMSFs)
The Diversification Strategy	Yes, it's available and dependent on the investment menu of a specific fund.	Yes, it's available. SMSFs can hold a wide range of assets.
The Dollar Cost Averaging Strategy	Yes, available through contributions.	Yes, available through contributions.
The Asset Allocation Strategy, the Asset Selection Strategy and the Investment Selection Strategy	Yes, they're available but they're limited to the kinds of assets and investments offered by the fund. Funds typically offer the ability to change asset allocations and investment types.	Yes, these strategies are available, with access to the widest possible range of asset classes and investments, including real estate, collectibles, artwork and shares.
The Franking Credit Strategy	Only available if the fund offers direct share investments (check the fund rules to be sure). Most super funds manage this as part of their own investment strategy.	Yes, it's available if shares are part of the investment strategy.
The Fee Reduction Strategy	Yes, it's available, depending on competitor fund offers. There are many industry and retail super funds in the marketplace to compare for a better deal.	Yes, it's available, depending on the costs to operate.
The Appropriate Tax Strategy	This is something the operator and trustee of the fund will manage for fund members.	Yes, it's available to the trustee of the SMSF to manage.
The Gearing Strategy	Not available.	Yes, it's available but subject to requirements.

Despite industry and retail super funds having some limits to the Investment Strategies available, most of them offer a wide enough range of asset classes with reasonable fees and costs to operate your super account.

There are a couple of additional special issues to note here too.

SUPER

Superannuation is a long-term investment

If you've got 30 or more years until you retire, it's fair to say that superannuation is a long-term investment. Because of this time horizon, you're likely to see several market cycles, from booms to downturns. It therefore makes sense to consider a more growth-orientated strategy to make the most of your retirement savings as well as protect against inflation. Inflation is the rising costs of goods and services, typically in an upward direction each year.

Superannuation investments aren't meant be sexy

Nowhere in the compulsory superannuation legislation does it say that super has to be sexy (by 'sexy', I mean the latest fad investments, cryptocurrencies or other exotic investments you can access in different ways). Super is a savings vehicle designed to provide you with income and funds after you decide to retire from the workforce. Taking unnecessary risks, even with a long-term investment like your super, isn't something a rational-thinking person should take part in. If all else fails, remember the KISS theory — Keep It Simple, Stupid!

When to do it?

Consider your superannuation investment strategy as often as you would your non-super investment strategy. Superannuation investment isn't a set-and-forget investment.

Do

Do consider an Additional Super Investment Strategy:

- At the point you start your superannuation

- Annually, as part of a superannuation performance and investment review

- At the time you do your tax return, and plan forward your asset allocation, asset selection and investment strategy for the coming period.

Don't

Don't fall into these traps:

- Setting and forgetting your superannuation investment strategy—although it's a long-term investment, your risk assessment might change over time

- Forgetting that if you have a self-managed superannuation fund, you need to have your investment strategy documented as part of the fund's administration

- Making superannuation investment decisions without understanding the consequences of your decisions; seek advice if you need to.

Long-term goals deserve progress celebrations

Long-term outcomes (like enjoying your superannuation benefits in retirement) are hard to focus on. They're so far away that it seems like there's no benefit to spending time on them now. But that's not the case with superannuation. If you don't set any goals and take action, you could end up costing yourself tens of thousands of dollars (if not more) over the long term.

Every goal, even superannuation retirement balance ones, can be broken down into a series of smaller steps and milestones. Having goals along the way can bring you a great sense of achievement and confirm that you're on track. Perhaps your first goal is $25 000, then $75 000, then $100 000. Perhaps you have a goal of a $50 000 increase after that. And then, just like the other financial goals you achieve, remember to celebrate achieving each goal. Crack open the champagne every $100 000 or do something else you'll enjoy. Most people wait until they retire to buy a new watch or crack a champagne bottle with friends. That approach seems too little, too late when you stop and think about it. It's much more fun to celebrate your progress towards your long-term goals at stages along the way.

Staying engaged in the goal is vital. If you need a short-term and medium-term reward, set the appropriate targets, hit them and then reward yourself, but don't go stupid—the reward should be tied to the size of the goal.

CHAPTER 12
The Retirement Strategies

Retirement means different things to different people. For some, it means giving up full-time work; for others, it means moving to part-time work or perhaps starting something new. For the purposes of strategy stacking, we define retirement as when a person is ready to access their superannuation, either as an income, a lump sum or perhaps a mix of both. Remember that this may be done in conjunction with work or contracting because, for me, as soon as you can say no to work and maintain your lifestyle with the resources you have, you have retired.

Retirement is a significant change for your financial life. You're making the decision to give up a regular pay cheque that has paid for the lifestyle you've so far enjoyed. It's a big decision, and you'll likely have questions to figure out first. Are you ready to give up your pay cheque right now? Will you be ready to give up your pay cheque in the future? How much do you need?

Unlike the retirement of our grandparents and prior generations, retirement today may not mean you give up work completely. Many Australians continue to work into their late 60s and into their 70s, often on a part-time or casual basis. By continuing to work, they can continue to earn an income and contribute to their super (covered in Chapter 11), and also turn some of their super into a pension to fund their lifestyle. Some Australians also start a pension from their super much earlier too as they choose to *transition to retirement*.

I've lost count of the number of clients who have sat in front of me talking about retirement, wishing they'd come to see me sooner and taken action to improve their superannuation savings back in their 30s, 40s and 50s. In their 60s, though, it's often too late, or the changes needed are so significant that they impact their lifestyle immediately, which they resent.

Giving up your pay cheque means you've got to live on your savings, your superannuation and any government benefits you might be able to access. Satisfactory retirement planning fundamentally means that you know what your retirement income looks like. *Great* retirement planning means that you're receiving the retirement income you want to achieve. There's often a big difference between satisfactory and great!

When it comes to retirement, retirees typically have one or more of four expectations:

1. They'll receive interest or dividends from the money invested (income).

2. They'll have their initial money returned (capital).

3. At the point of sale of the investment, they'll sell their investment for more than they paid for it (growth).

4. At the point of their passing, their investments will revert to their spouse, loved ones or estate.

Income becomes much more important in retirement. It needs to replace that regular pay cheque, and keep replacing that regular pay cheque for as long as it's required. People worry if they will have enough.

If you have a strong income stream over the years, you reduce your reliance on capital—and therefore reduce the need to 'eat into' your savings, regardless of the structure you use to hold them.

This chapter provides you with some additional strategies that can only be used to help you achieve the retirement income you need. Specifically, I explore these strategies:

- The Retirement Readiness Strategy
- The Transition to Retirement Strategy
- The Retirement Income Vehicles Strategy
- The Retirement Investment Strategies
- The Appropriate Retirement Fees Strategy
- The Appropriate Tax in Retirement Strategy.

The Retirement Readiness Strategy

A Retirement Readiness Strategy is not so much about doing something with your assets than it is about dealing with your mindset in preparation for retirement. Retirement brings change and, like all change, people deal with it differently.

Some people can't wait to pull the plug on the 9 to 5 — they've been dreaming about it for years. Others have built a career (and sometimes a business) they've invested their lives into. It can be really difficult to just let go of something you've put so much energy into. But before you get anywhere near retirement age (or perhaps even the point you've completed your career aspirations and goals), you want to make sure you're in the right headspace for retirement.

How does it work?

Over time, I've identified five steps to help people successfully complete this strategy.

Step 1: Revisit your 'why'

How does your 'why' link in with your retirement? Only you can answer this. These questions may help you look ahead in a more practical way:

- What do you want to spend your days doing?
- What does a typical week for you look like?

RETIREMENT

- Will you still go on holiday?

- Do you still want financial debt in your life?

- What hobbies, projects, sports or charities do you want to invest your time in?

- Do you expect to be a carer for your grandchildren while their parents are at work?

- Will you return to work on a part-time basis or contract? (Work can be part of your retirement too, if you want it to be.)

I also encourage you to think about the tough questions too:

- How are you going to proactively look after your health and wellbeing?

- Would you prefer to have home care or are you willing to go into an assisted living facility when you become aged?

- Who will you leave your home and other assets to?

Over our working lives we accumulate a lot of assets. These might include a family home, cars, a boat, a caravan, a holiday house, as well as things like shares and other investments. Sooner or later we will all slow down (but hopefully it is later not sooner!). Do we still need to be rattling around by ourselves or with our partners in a big family home? Do we still need the water skis and the boat when we're 85? The answer might be yes; however, it might also be no. An apartment with no lawns to mow and a new car might be more your style. Think about how these assets can be put to use to help you achieve your 'why' when your needs and your lifestyle changes. Could the assets you no longer need generate income if invested in something else?

It's essential to understand your own 'why', and only you can define it. The decision to retire creates change. I encourage my clients to revisit their short-term, medium-term and long-term goals. You may find it helpful to revisit Chapter 2, to revisit your new retirement outlook and financial life with consideration to your 'why'.

Don't expect to solve your 'why' in five minutes. You probably spent years thinking about what job you wanted to do when you grew up. So why not spend a couple of years thinking about what you want to do with your life after work? Provided you've got time on your side before you retire, you'll have some time to set yourself up however you want.

In my experience, I've found people with a clear plan for their retirement lives make the adjustment to their retirement lifestyle a little easier; however, people have told me time and time again it took them up to two years before they felt like they had a new routine that they enjoyed.

Step 2: Revisit the foundations

It makes good sense to revisit and set strong financial foundations at any point of significant change, including before you retire. Your financial life will change. You'll no longer be spending money on the commute to work, lunches out and perhaps other expenses, like drycleaning and new work clothes. Here's a reminder of the key foundations from Chapter 3.

RESPECT YOUR EARNINGS

In retirement, your income certainty becomes extremely important as you no longer have the benefit of work, overtime or a bonus to supplement your income. It's really important to understand how you're going to generate your earnings from the capital you've saved.

If you're in a superannuation fund that doesn't provide a dividend income stream, you may want to review that now because income is your best friend—having to sell units in your super fund or assets to fund a pension may not be for you. Many super funds, including both industry and retail funds, operate on a *unitised* basis. This means when you buy an investment option within the fund, you buy 'units'. The value of the units go up and down as the value of the underlying asset changes. The change in value is shown in the unit price. A bit like buying an investment property and seeing its changing value through its rental income and capital value of the house.

This is different to how shares operate. The overall value of shares is determined in two components: the price of the share and the dividend (income) it provides to the shareholder. Why may this difference be important to some retirees? When markets go down, super fund units go down—and so do share prices. To fund an income stream in retirement (pension), you need to sell units to provide you with the

RETIREMENT

cash needed to fund your lifestyle. In a retail fund that allows you to control your income, you may not need to sell units as you receive the income from your shares during the year. This way, if the market value of your fund falls, you're not selling investments at lower prices and missing out on the uplift seen when the market recovers. More of your invested capital is working for you over the longer term. Selling in a crisis can have a huge impact on the long-term value of your asset base as you have less invested during a major market event, such as the Global Financial Crisis or the COVID-19 pandemic.

PAY ATTENTION TO YOUR SPENDING

Thankfully in retirement there might be a few expenses you can say goodbye to, such as the costs of getting to and from work, work clothes, dry cleaning costs, professional association fees, and so on. It doesn't mean you can forget about your spending though. It will be important to keep planning your spending, especially on larger items like a new car, an overseas holiday, or any significant gifts to your children and grandchildren.

THE COST OF MONEY IS INTEREST

One of the first goals of many retirees is to get rid of debt—paying interest on loans or credit cards is lost money at any stage of retirement. Of equal importance is getting a decent return on the investments that will fund your retirement income—many retirees have concerns about eating into their capital too quickly.

For example, if you expect to have negatively geared properties that don't generate an income, are these assets you want to hold long term? Hardcore property lovers would say 'Yes!'—but when you retire, what you want from your assets could change. Growth is fine when you're working, but income pays the bills. It's hard to sell the kitchen of an investment property if you need to release capital to pay for a holiday.

As long as you have thought ahead, you should be able to have the best of both worlds, but it pays to look ahead to your changing financial needs.

BE REALISTIC

When you're retired and have access to super, you wouldn't be advised to go wild with your money. Of course, there's no rule to say you can't—but if you quickly burn through all your assets, you'll need to live on government benefits, which provide just the bare minimum (and even less if you don't own your own home). Being sensible with money is a lifelong skill. The reality is that Australians are living longer and more active lives in retirement than they've ever lived before. Travelling around the country in a caravan or doing a world trip are increasingly common retirement behaviours. You've still got lots of life to live in retirement, maybe another 25 years or more! Make sure you're realistic about your retirement time frame and be sensible in your approach to extracting the most from those superannuation savings that you worked over a lifetime to build. Remember: your investment time frame does not end at your retirement date—it ends when your family is throwing flowers on you at the end of your life.

REWARD YOURSELF

It is your retirement and you've worked hard, so you should aim to reward yourself. If you need to go somewhere to find yourself, that's fine too—just budget for it!

Planning future experiences is a great way to bring enjoyment into your retirement. Hitch the caravan up and take that adventure trip around Australia (or perhaps holiday offshore at a resort if that's more your speed). Go for coffee at your favourite café each week and take regular Spanish lessons. You could be retired for a pretty long time, so you may as well continue to do what you love while growing as a person.

Step 3: Revisit the Risk Assessment Strategy

When you're younger, you're more likely to be willing to take greater risks for greater rewards (often across all aspects of your life, not just your financial life). At some point, however, you may suffer a loss or injury that may make you rethink the level of risk you're willing to accept.

RETIREMENT

In retirement, with no pay cheque coming in from your work, you've got to really think about how much risk you're willing to take. Those assets you've built up over your working life need to last the rest of your life.

I hear the following comment regularly: 'I'm older now so I need to be more conservative.' However, when I ask clients what they really want, they often say one of two things:

- 'I need a strong income to fund my lifestyle without having to access or eat into too much of my capital.'

- 'I need some growth to help offset the effect of inflation, as prices keep going up.'

It's going to be a challenge to achieve both of these objectives if you have a large allocation of cash and fixed-interest assets in your portfolio. In modern times, interest rates have been at record lows and many retirees have been disappointed with their term deposit outcomes. It's important to remember that just because you'll be retired, it doesn't mean that an appropriate investment time frame no longer applies to you. Just as in your working life, you are dealing with a long time frame. You might be in retirement for 30 years or more! As a result, having an appropriate amount of growth assets in your asset allocation makes sound financial sense. I revisit the Framing Strategies to look at risk with my own clients when planning for their retirement. You can revisit them too in Chapter 9 on the Framing Strategies, which includes risk management.

Risk means different things to everyone. There are three big risks for retirees:

1. **Market volatility.** Like most retirees, you'll probably have a fixed number of assets working for you. If you invest in something that's growth-orientated (which typically has more risk), you might feel the sting of an economic downturn. The Framing Strategies (Chapter 9) and Investment Strategies (Chapter 10) become really important to minimise the risks you face. Market volatility is why many retirees choose to direct some of their investments towards defensive income assets (such as cash and fixed interest), rather than growth assets (such as property or shares).

2. **Inflation.** Inflation is like rust on your car—over time, it eats away the metal and reduces the value of your asset. In economic terms, inflation is defined as the rising cost of goods and services over time. For example, imagine a full bag of groceries. When you were younger, you got a lot more in the bag for your spend. With rising inflation, the number of things in the bag falls over the years. We've all seen the cost of living go up and up. Like rust, inflation is a hidden risk to your retirement capital. If you don't earn enough to cover the cost of rising prices, inflation will start eating into your retirement savings. This means you'll get less money to spend in your retirement. Inflation is the reason why a retiree would still have some of their investments in growth assets. Your income also allows you to fund fewer things with the same cash flow.

3. **Adult children.** Adult children can also present a risk for those approaching retirement and those who have retired. It's understandable to want to help your adult kids through financial challenges, especially if they've given you grandkids who are also affected—but don't put your own medium- to long-term financial health at risk to offer help. You shouldn't jeopardise your own financial retirement position by giving away money or chasing higher investment returns that might help them out. Perhaps the best solution for them is to restructure their debt and seek financial advice to move forward without relying on you. If you decide, however, you're going to secure an asset or lend them money, make sure you have the appropriate legal agreement drawn up so it is official. You wouldn't lend money to someone without an agreement, and your children are no different. Think carefully about loaning to your kids over giving or gifting, as you have no idea how their situation may change and impact your ability to get your money back at some point.

With consideration to all three risks, I'm not saying you have to be completely invested in growth assets in retirement to avoid each of these risks; I'm simply trying to get you to review your mindset about the duration of your investments and your own behavior when investing towards your ongoing 'why' in retirement.

Step 4: Work out your retirement income needs

If you've been keeping a budget (following the Budget Management Strategy) and monitoring your cash flow (using the Cash Flow Management Strategy), it's very easy to plug in figures to see what your retirement needs will be. Remove all the work-related costs and add in all the fun stuff you'd like to do. (Chapters 6 and 9 talk about managing your money and these core strategies in more detail.)

When looking at your cash flow, also add in those bigger purchases that you may need to make and how you're going to fund them (such as a withdrawal from your non-super investments, a lump sum withdrawal from your allocated pension, or by saving money from the government pension over time).

It can be scary to sit down and work out where your money is going now, let alone how this might look in the future. It can raise your heart rate because people tend to live on what they earn. Knowing what *your assets* will earn by comparison is very different.

People often tell me that they are 'just normal people and have an average lifestyle' and that they are 'not extravagant'. They might then go on to tell me that they can live on anything from $30 000 to $300 000 a year. In their world that may be normal, but everyone is different and has a different view on how much money is normal. Matching your assets to your income level is the next challenge because nothing in this world is free, and it may mean that you have to give something up or take additional risk to get the income you need to do what you want.

Step 5: Write down your goals for retirement and what a typical day might look like

It might sound silly to think so far ahead about the day-to-day events of your retirement, but it's an important part of preparing for and understanding what your retirement might look like:

- What does a typical day or week look like? (If you are reading this and thinking, 'I am still going to mow the lawn on a Saturday,' that's fine—not every day needs to be a big adventure!)

- What experiences do you perhaps want to re-live from your youth?

- What new adventures will you have?

There is life after work, and you can enjoy a good quality of life too. So make the most of it!

When to do it?

The Retirement Readiness Strategy should be considered well before you retire. It enables you to set the outlook for your retirement and work towards the goals and outcomes you want to achieve when you stop work. The clearer your retirement picture is, the easier it will be to make the change because there's no surprises and you'll have a 'to do' list waiting for you that won't be interrupted by work.

The sooner people engage with thinking ahead to their retirement, the greater their choices when it comes to the other strategies they might stack to build their retirement fund.

Do

Do consider a Retirement Readiness Strategy:

- When you're five to 10 years out from your retirement age—everyone needs something a little different and it means you can prepare for the shift into retirement

- If you're not sure how much income you'll need in retirement

- If you don't yet have a vision of what your retirement will look like

- If you have assets you don't know what to do with and don't know when to sell them

- If you want to make the most of other strategies prior to leaving the workforce.

RETIREMENT

255

Don't

Don't fall into these traps:

- Assuming you'll deal with change easily

- Dismissing the benefits of a retirement plan

- Going it alone—seek advice from a financial planner if you want help to understand your position and financial options

- Leaving it too late as it's getting harder and harder to get money into super—you may need longer than you think

- Missing out on contribution and splitting strategies (refer to Chapter 11) that may apply to you and help you achieve your 'why'.

Chad was ready for retirement...well, at least he thought he was

My client, let's call him Chad, was looking forward to giving up the rat race. He'd been a diligent employee all his life, working with the same employer for most of it. He also sought advice early and implemented several strategies that put him in a great position at retirement.

And retirement was great when it started. He didn't miss that commute to work. He didn't miss the deadlines. He didn't miss the unpaid overtime. He did enjoy sleep-ins. He did enjoy mornings reading the paper with coffee. He did enjoy his golf.

I was surprised then when I got a visit from Chad. Retirement wasn't going to plan at all, and it wasn't all that he'd hoped it would be. 'The thing is I'm bored. There's only so much golf you can play in a week.' The change in pace had taken Chad by surprise. So, what to do?

He asked me about turning a hobby he had into a small business. He wasn't looking for 100 clients, just a few here and there. It would give him something 'useful' to do and allow him to follow a passion. 'Why not do it!' I thought. There's nothing wrong with starting a new venture or hobby at any age, even in retirement.

The Transition to Retirement Strategy

The Transition to Retirement Strategy allows you to draw down some (a percentage) of your superannuation benefits when you reach your commonwealth preservation age while you remain in the workforce. You preservation age depends on the year you were born and ranges between the ages of 55 and 60 (see table 12.1, later in this chapter). The strategy allows you to supplement your income if you decide to work less hours. The strategy can also be used for other strategic options, such as funding contributions or paying down non-deductible debt.

How does it work?

The Transition to Retirement Strategy is available to people who have reach their preservation age. The preservation age simply means you're allowed to access your super. With the Transition to Retirement Strategy you transfer some of your superannuation to an account-based pension. An account-based pension is a vehicle like your super; however, it allows you to access your super as a regular income payment or a one-off payment in a financial year.

If you're less than 65 years of age, you're allowed to draw down between 4 and 10 per cent of your pension account balance each year. You are unable to withdraw a larger lump sum, however, given your age.

Here are a couple of examples showing how this strategy works.

Reducing working hours

Zoe has worked most of her adult life. She's not ready to retire at the age of 61, but she would like to work a five-day fortnight instead of five days a week. Zoe earns $70 000 and has $350 000 in her superannuation account.

After she moves to these part-time hours, she'll lose half of her income; so, she'll be earning $35 000 a year from work. That's not quite enough to live on as she realises she'll need $45 000 to get by. Zoe transfers $150 000 from her superannuation account to an

RETIREMENT

account-based pension. She has to draw between 4 per cent (0.04 × 150000 = $6000) and 10 per cent (0.10 × 150000 = $15000) each year from her pension. Zoe decides to draw $10000 as a pension income each year to supplement her wage until she's ready to fully retire.

This allows Zoe to ease into retirement. Additionally, Zoe still receives super contributions from her employer. The income from her account-based pension is also tax-free because she's over 60.

For an example like this, Zoe will need to keep some money within her superannuation account rather than transferring the whole balance. This is because Zoe is still working and her employer will continue to pay superannuation to her. Additionally, Zoe can't add more money to her account-based pension account once it has started. To do this she'd need to roll back her pension into super and then start a brand new pension.

Boosting your super

Doug is 55. He's not ready to retire but he's realised he does need to start planning better for his retirement. Doug earns $85000 a year and has $250000 in his super.

Doug opens an account-based pension with $150000 of his super and draws $10000 a year as pension income. Because Doug is aged between 55 and 59, he'll pay tax on a portion of his pension payments at his marginal tax rate; however, he'll receive a 15 per cent tax offset. This means he is taxed less on his pension payments than he is on his work income. The proportion of income that is taxable is impacted by the taxable and tax-free components of his superannuation fund.

Doug also wants to boost his super, so he has a couple of options.

THE SALARY SACRIFICE OPTION

Doug earns $85000 from his job. Given he's got an extra $10000 from his account-based pension, Doug decides to salary sacrifice $10000 from his work earnings to his super.

This means Doug will pay $15992 in tax instead of $19172 tax on his take-home pay. He'll also be boosting his super by $10000 before tax ($8500 after tax).

Let's crunch the numbers to see it in action in the 2021/22 financial year.

Without this strategy:

- Doug earns $85 000 before tax.

- He pays $19 792 in tax on this personal income.

- His take-home pay is $65 208 ($85 000 – $19 792).

Other than his employer contributions, Doug adds nothing extra to his super.

With this strategy:

- Doug earns $85 000 before tax.

- He makes a $10 000 salary sacrifice contribution.

- He pays $16 342 in tax on this personal income.

- He also pays $1500 tax (15 per cent × $10 000) within his super fund. The difference between the super fund tax rate and Doug's personal tax rate is what he'll save on tax.

- His take-home pay is $68 658 from his job ($85 000 – ($16 342 + $1500)), which includes $10 000 (less tax) from his account-based pension.

- In addition to his employer contributions, Doug adds $8500 to his super. If Doug repeats this over the next 10 years until he turns 65, he'll add at least $85 000 plus earnings to his super.

THE CONCESSIONAL CONTRIBUTION OPTION

Doug earns $85 000 from his job. Given he's got an extra $10 000 from his account-based pension, Doug decides to put this money back into his super as a concessional contribution.

This means Doug gets a $10 000 tax deduction on his income in addition to boosting his super by $10 000 before tax (or $8500 after tax).

The net effect in both of these examples is that Doug maintains his usual take-home pay but makes appropriate use of the tax benefits of saving to superannuation.

RETIREMENT

Without this strategy, just as for the salary sacrifice option, Doug's take-home pay is $65 208.

Other than his employer contributions, Doug adds nothing extra to his super.

With this strategy:

- Doug earns $85 000 before tax.

- He makes a $10 000 concessional contribution.

- He pays $16 342 in tax.

- His take-home pay is $58 658 from his job ($85 000 – ($10 000 + $16 342)), which includes $10 000 (less tax) from his account-based pension.

- In addition to his employer contributions, Doug adds $8500 to his super. If Doug repeats this over the next 10 years until he turns 65, he'll add at least $85 000 plus earnings to his super.

When to do it?

A Transition to Retirement Strategy could be considered from your preservation age onwards, which is determined by your date of birth and outlined in table 12.1.

Table 12.1: Your preservation age

Date of birth	Preservation age
Before 1/7/1960	55
1/7/1960–30/6/1961	56
1/7/1961–30/6/1962	57
1/7/1962–30/6/1963	58
1/7/1963–30/6/1964	59
From 1 July 1964	60

Source: © Australian Taxation Office

Working fewer hours is a great way to transition to retirement. Giving a boost to your super before you retire is also a great strategy if you're not where you want to be.

Do

Do consider a Transition to Retirement Strategy:

- When you'd like to work less hours, but maintain a similar income

- If you need to give your superannuation a kick along before you retire

- If you're looking to contribute more to your super before you retire. Often people find they can afford to contribute more than they have been.

- If you intend to use a pension payment to take advantage of the Catch-up Contribution Strategy (Chapter 11) that takes advantage of concessional contribution rules prior to retirement or when you intend to sell assets.

Don't

Don't fall into these traps:

- Taking the maximum you can from your account-based pension. You need to run the numbers or recruit a financial planner to help you. You might end up with less than more if you get it wrong.

- Rolling over to pension phase without lodging the necessary paperwork to claim deductions for contributions made prior to the change

- Forgetting to check this strategy fits with your Centrelink benefits. If you or your partner are receiving government benefits, this strategy might affect those benefits.

- Starting this strategy without checking that the life insurance within your super is unaffected. You don't want to unwittingly give up this coverage and you shouldn't have to, although it does depend on your fund's rules.

RETIREMENT

- Forgetting to maintain a small superannuation account so that you can continue to receive employer contributions while working

- Forgetting that the value of your pension account may go down over time depending on how it's invested.

The challenge of catching up when you've fallen behind

When I first started mountain bike riding in my early 40s, I wasn't very good compared to some of my friends (who had been doing it since they were kids). They'd often stop at a higher part of the mountain and give me the chance to catch up. We'd all then continue. I didn't like the fact that I was behind, but I was grateful for the opportunity to catch up to them.

The Transition to Retirement Strategy may be a good way to catch up to where you'd like to be (from an income perspective) to maintain the lifestyle you're after. You do need to run your own numbers though and be certain that what you think you're implementing is what you're actually implementing. As with any strategy, seek personal financial advice if you need guidance—everyone is different.

The Retirement Income Vehicles Strategy

A Retirement Income Vehicles Strategy investigates and determines the best way to hold and use your assets to deliver a retirement income to you. For most people, superannuation provides the central platform for funding retirement income; second to this are probably government benefits. Government benefits also often provide important support.

There are six kinds of vehicles people typically use to secure an income for their retirement years:

1. Account-based pension from accumulated superannuation (including self-managed superannuation funds, or SMSFs)

2. Fixed income annuity

3. Legacy or specific employer funds

4. Investments outside of superannuation

5. Government benefits

6. Selling the family home or reverse mortgages.

If you structure your Retirement Income Vehicles Strategy correctly, you might even be able to use multiple vehicles to fund your retirement income.

How does it work?

You've worked hard up until retirement to build your super and other assets. Superannuation for most Australians is the biggest asset they own after their family home. The Retirement Income Vehicles Strategy (or 'how to fund a pension') seeks to help you uncover how you will fund your income needs when you retire from work, taking into account the key things you are after when it comes to control and flexibility as nothing is exactly the same.

Let's take a look at each of these vehicles that can help you fund your retirement.

Account-based pension from accumulated superannuation (including SMSFs)

Using account-based pensions is effectively the same approach as the Transition to Retirement Strategy (refer to the preceding strategy), but you may see different tax rules and access thresholds.

You convert your existing super fund into an account based pension and start an income stream. Unlike a Transition to Retirement Strategy pension account, there's no maximum on the amount of money that you can take in a financial year, but it does maintain the same minimum requirements (addressed in table 12.2, overleaf). Most account-based pensions offer you a choice of how often you receive your payments: it could be fortnightly, monthly, quarterly, bi-annually or annually, depending on the pension provider. You also get to choose how the money is invested within the investment options offered by the pension product. Remember, starting a pension from your accumulated superannuation doesn't impact the existing assets you hold. You are simply taking money out of the account as opposed to putting it in.

There's a minimum amount you need to withdraw each year. Table 12.2 helps you work out the minimum you need to take.

Table 12.2: Minimum withdrawal amounts

Your age	The minimum percentage of your account balance that you need to withdraw
55–64	4%
65–74	5%
75–79	6%
80–84	7%
85–89	9%
90–94	11%
95+	14%

Source: © Australian Taxation Office

Important note: during COVID-19, these minimum amounts were reduced by 50 per cent to allow people to preserve their capital during the period of market weakness.

Payments continue until your money runs out. In the event you pass away, you can leave any remaining money to your beneficiaries or estate via a binding or non-binding nomination (which I cover in Chapter 14).

In addition to receiving pension payments, an account-based pension offers you the ability to make a lump sum withdrawal, provided you're not using the Transition to Retirement Strategy and you do want to take more than 10 per cent in any one financial year. This is useful as it allows you to pay off debt or access money for larger purchases or unexpected repairs.

RETIREMENT

Strategy Stacking Tip

An account-based pension doesn't have to be paid monthly or fortnightly—a pension payment can be made any time during the financial year. If you want to pay off debt or access a large amount of money, think about an annual payment in June and then again in July—it's a new financial year, so you can receive two years of pension payments in a matter of days or weeks during this period of the year.

Account-based pensions are very tax-effective compared to other structures, and I talk about the tax benefits later in the section on the Appropriate Tax in Retirement Strategy.

Fixed income annuity

A fixed income annuity (or lifetime annuity) is an investment that's purchased using money from your superannuation or other non-superannuation savings. Depending on the amount of money you have, you might select the annuity to provide fixed payments (perhaps with inflation added) for the rest of your life or a specific number of years.

Most providers offer a choice of how often you receive payments: monthly, quarterly, bi-annually or annually. Unlike an account-based pension or SMSF pension (refer to the preceding section for more on these vehicles), you're not able to take a lump sum withdrawal. You also don't get to choose how your money is invested, and there's no ability to increase or decrease your pension payments. You may not be able to transfer the annuity once it has started, either, which means you have less flexibility with this vehicle compared to other vehicles. On the plus side, you're paid a guaranteed income regardless of how the investment markets are performing.

Payments continue until the fixed period ends or you pass away. In the event you pass away, your annuity payments might revert to your spouse or dependant. Alternatively, you may choose at the start of the annuity to pay the remaining income payments or lump sum to your beneficiary.

RETIREMENT

Legacy or specific employer funds

In Chapter 11, I talked about legacy funds as part of the discussion around the Super Vehicle Strategy. To quickly recap, these funds are now closed to new members; they offered retirement savings schemes funded by employers or the public sector (government). At retirement, these funds operate somewhat like annuities. They pay you an ongoing pension until you pass away, and often they revert to your spouse or dependants in the case of a defined benefit.

If you have one of these vehicles to help you fund your retirement, it's very important to understand the rules to ensure you've maximised the income it can provide you at retirement, usually by making your own contributions in addition to the ones made by your employer. You might get a choice where the contributions you've made get invested, but typically you don't get a choice in how and where your employers' contributions are invested.

Most providers offer a choice of how often you receive payments: monthly, quarterly, bi-annually or annually. It's important to understand your payment options well before you retire as some funds have preset formulas to work out your benefit, and not knowing them could prevent you from maximising your final benefit (financial advice may be helpful here). This is specifically the case with the Commonwealth Superannuation Scheme (CSS) and Public Sector Superannuation Scheme (PSS) offered to long-term employees of the federal government as well as the military equivalents in the Defence Force Retirement and Death Benefits (DFRDB) and Military Superannuation and Benefits Scheme (MSBS). While the funds are closed to new members, existing members should understand how they work to make the most of the opportunities they have.

Legacy funds, like defined benefit schemes, retirement schemes, government schemes and military super schemes, are usually very generous in the pension income they provide to account holders. That's the primary reason why we don't see any of these accounts operating today—the benefits offered mean they're very expensive for employers and governments to run. All current legacy funds still operating (including CSS, PSS, DFRDB and MSBS) are closed to new members.

Strategy Stacking Tip

If you're in the PSS offered by ComSuper, aim to make a 10 per cent contribution as soon as possible. This increases your accrued benefit multiple and the figure that is used, along with your final average salary, to work out your entitlements when you retire. Check with your fund provider to ensure you're making the most of these opportunities, as I too often see people miss out on a much larger pension because they didn't understand how the fund worked. A contribution of 10 per cent each year can make a large difference to your pension entitlements when you retire.

Investments outside of superannuation

Just because you've retired, it doesn't mean you have to give up the investments you hold outside of your superannuation. You may still own an investment property you rent, a share portfolio or something as simple as a term deposit.

These investments can provide you with growth on your capital as well as an income from your underlying investments. The benefit of holding these investments is that you have a greater degree of control over them as the superannuation access rules don't apply; however, these kinds of investments tend to be taxed less favourably compared to other retirement income vehicles. I explore that more later in this chapter in the Appropriate Tax in Retirement Strategy.

Non-super assets are becoming more important as the government makes it harder and harder to get money into the superannuation system. In addition, with the introduction of the transfer balance cap ($1.7 million limit for tax-free income from super, refer to Chapter 11 for more on this), building assets outside of super is becoming an increasingly important part of your retirement asset base.

Government benefits

Traditionally (and before superannuation was introduced), most people relied on the government age pension entitlements to fund their retirement. As at December 2022, the maximum government pension

RETIREMENT

and entitlements for a single person is $1026.50 a fortnight (or $26 689 a year) and for a couple is $1547.60 a fortnight (or $40 237.60 a year). The amount of age pension you're eligible for is determined by the assets test or income tests set by the government. The test that gives you the lower pension entitlement is the one that's used.

The rules are complex and it pays to seek advice on how you might structure your personal affairs. For example, not all assets are considered as part of these tests—the home you live in is exempt, while an investment property is included in the assets test (along with rental payments under the income test). Also, superannuation isn't considered to be an asset until you reach a pensionable age, which you can factor into your strategy stacking efforts.

Strategy Stacking Tip

If one member of a couple is of pension age and their spouse is not, holding assets in the younger partner's super account means the amount is exempt for Centrelink purposes, until the younger partner either reaches age pension age themselves or starts a pension. This is a great strategy to think about where there is an age difference and you may be close to either a full pension or a part pension under the upper limit of the assets test. The older person could withdraw funds from super and contribute to their younger partner's super account (provided the younger person is eligible to make a contribution to super). Refer to Chapter 11 for more on the Contribution Strategies.

This strategy allows you to lower the asset test value for the age pension partner and also provides access to funds within superannuation (where the younger person has met a condition of release or is over 65) to meet lifestyle and retirement goals.

If I told a working couple in their 40s that they had $40 237.60 a year to live on (the same amount as a couple is entitled to from the age pension), they'd without a doubt tell me they couldn't do it. Certainly their lifestyle would suffer. At retirement, what do you want your income to be? It surprises me still that people don't choose the retirement income they want and find a way to achieve that figure. With time on your side, you've got options to realistically achieve your desired outcome.

Like all things, it requires thought and action, and an understanding of your options. Government benefits can make your retirement more comfortable, and there are other government benefits you may be eligible for—for example, if you receive a government pension payment, you're also likely to be eligible for a Pensioner Concession Card, which enables you to obtain cheaper healthcare and discounts on medicines, travel and other benefits.

Additionally, there are other benefits you might be able to access through state- and territory-based seniors cards. They provide discounts on a range of goods and services, as well as transport concessions.

Selling the family home or reverse mortgages

For many of us, our family home is the largest capital asset we'll ever own, yet it does nothing for us on the income front. When it comes to retiring though, and especially when the kids have finally moved out and are in control of their own financial lives, it's common for those thinking about retirement to sell the family home, downsize and move into something smaller. (Some people call it a sea change—or a tree change, depending on where they move to.)

Freeing up your real-estate capital means that you can add any leftover funds to your retirement income. A good strategy is to put some of that money into super, and perhaps even claim a tax deduction (so long as you don't exceed your contribution limits).

Selling the family home is a big decision, and for some people it's simply too hard to give up those memories. In cases like this, a reverse mortgage might be useful—although in my 20+ years as a financial planner, I've never recommended this strategy to a client (I think there are better ways to give yourself the retirement you deserve then give money to the bank). A *reverse mortgage* allows you to unlock part of the equity in your home as a lump sum payment (or regular income payments). There are no loan repayments to worry about; the lender recoups their money after the property owner passes on, along with any

RETIREMENT

interest, fees and charges. The issue with this is that the amount that you borrow is *capitalised*, which means that the debt gets bigger, faster.

An unintentional consequence of a reverse mortgage is that there's nothing left to pass to the next generation as the interest costs compound and eat away at the equity in your home. This strategy should be considered very carefully before you sign up as the long-term impact can be catastrophic. Other considerations include the impact of rising interest rates on the debt, the compounding of the outstanding debt over time, an inability to pay down the loan with cash flow or a pullback in the value of the house (reducing available funds for estate purposes).

When to do it?

The Retirement Income Vehicles Strategy should be considered well before you retire. This enables you to organise your assets effectively and achieve the retirement income you need.

Do

Do consider a Retirement Income Vehicles Strategy:

- When you're five years out from your retirement age
- If you're concerned about the performance of your current retirement income
- If you're concerned about control and taxation
- If you're approaching retirement (or have retired) and receive an inheritance or unexpected windfall. You could have additional funds you could add to super to start a tax free pension.
- If you have sold a large asset or downsized and wish to add capital to superannuation.

Don't

Don't fall into these traps:

- Assuming all retirement structures are the same. They've all got different fees, asset types, investment offerings and features. They're also taxed differently, which I look at in the later section on the Appropriate Tax in Retirement Strategy.

RETIREMENT

- Dismissing government benefits. Even a small government pension can give you access to the Pensioner Concession Card. This card can save you a lot of money as you age and health costs may become more of an issue for you.

- Exiting a legacy fund without first seeking financial advice. Leaving the fund could cost you tens of thousands of dollars.

Retirees love term deposits, but will they deliver the 'real return' you need?

When looking at your retirement investments, it's often useful to consider the *real return*—the interest rate you're receiving, less the cost of *inflation* (the rising cost of goods and services over time).

Term deposits have been a favourite investment of retirees for many years. They provide you with the ability to secure a return, with virtually no risk, for a given period of time. Increasingly I find myself concerned about the real return they're delivering. In the current environment, at the time of writing, the average return on a term deposit is 3.5 per cent over 12 months. At the same time, the inflation rate is 6.1 per cent over 12 months. In real return terms, the return is −2.6 per cent. In the long-term, if these kinds of returns remain (which is likely given the current policy to keep inflation between 2 and 3 per cent), retirees are likely to go backwards in real terms once they draw an income from these kinds of investments.

Interest rates are a real balancing act in Australia and often push generations into competition with each other. Events like COVID-19 and any form of economic instability in key trading partners don't help either. Young Australians want interest rates to remain low because they want to be able to afford to buy a home and pay off their mortgage; retirees, on the other hand, need an income to fund their retirement. The best way to protect your own retirement from this situation is to start early. It's one of the real benefits of having compulsory superannuation.

RETIREMENT

> ## Strategy Stacking Tip
>
> Remember that just because you've retired, your investment time frame has not stopped. A lot of people plan up to their retirement and then have the view that they need to be more conservative. In fact, you need income *and* growth as much as you did while you were working, so don't assume that you need less income and less growth (both are by-products of a more conservative risk profile). Most people tell me they want to control their income in their retirement and limit the need to draw income from their capital in order to fund their lifestyle where possible. Don't let your assumptions rob you of your ability to meet your income goals—conservative investments are suitable at the right time, but they must align with your 'why', not your assumptions.

The Retirement Investment Strategies

The Retirement Investment Strategies is simply a group of Investment Strategies for generating a reliable and ongoing income from your superannuation and other savings. You might be wondering, 'How does this strategy differ from the Investment Strategies you outlined in Chapter 10?' Well, many of those strategies can be applied to your retirement as well (just as many of them can be applied to your super—refer to Chapter 11).

I'm not going to repeat the Investment Strategies from Chapter 10 here; instead, I uncover how your Retirement Investment Strategy might be a little different.

How does it work?

Let's take a look at the key differences a Retirement Strategy has, considering three vehicles: account-based pensions, non-super investments and the pension phase of an SMSF (see table 12.3).

Table 12.3: Investment Strategies in retirement

Investment Strategies	Account-based pension (industry and retail super funds)	Non-super investments	Pension phase of an SMSF (self-managed superannuation fund)
The Diversification Strategy	Yes, it's available.	Yes, it's available.	Yes, it's available.
The Dollar Cost Averaging Strategy	May be applicable in times of volatility or the investment of new money to an already mature portfolio.	May be applicable in times of volatility or the investment of new money to an already mature portfolio.	May be applicable in times of volatility or the investment of new money to an already mature portfolio.
The Asset Allocation Strategy, The Asset Selection Strategy & The Investment Selection Strategy	Yes, they're available but they're limited to the kinds of assets and investments offered by the fund. Funds typically offer the ability to change asset allocations and investment types.	Yes, these strategies are available, with access to the widest possible asset classes and investments, including real estate, collectibles, artwork and shares.	Yes, these strategies are available, with access to the widest possible asset classes and investments, including real estate, collectibles, artwork and shares.
The Franking Credit Strategy	Only available if the fund offers direct shares or Australian-based managed funds or ETF investments. Franking credits are managed by each underlying investment.	Yes, it's available if shares are outside of retirement products. Franking credit refunds are very important to some retirees on their savings.	Yes, it's available if shares are part of the investment strategy. Franking credit refunds are very important to some retirees' income streams, depending on how their portfolio is structured.

(continued)

RETIREMENT

Table 12.3 Investment Strategies in retirement (cont'd)

Investment Strategies	Account-based pension (industry and retail super funds)	Non-super investments	Pension phase of an SMSF (self-managed superannuation fund)
The Fee Reduction Strategy	Yes, it's available, depending on competitor fund offers. There are many industry and retail super funds in the marketplace to compare for a better deal.	Yes, it's available, depending on the costs to operate.	Yes, it's available, depending on the costs to operate.
The Appropriate Tax Strategy	This is something the operator and trustee of the fund will manage for fund members.	Non-super vehicles don't offer many tax advantages to retirees.	Yes, it's available to the trustee of the SMSF to manage.
The Gearing Strategy	Generally not applicable in retirement with these super funds. Internally geared assets may be available within each respective super fund.	Available, but not applicable in retirement.	Available, but generally not applicable in retirement. Specific lending rules apply when gearing assets in self-managed super.

RETIREMENT

Despite industry and retail super funds having some limits on the strategies available, most funds offer a wide enough range of asset classes with reasonable costs to operate for most people. However, there are a few issues to keep in mind when using a couple of these strategies, as well as some additional challenges you may need to consider.

The Dollar Cost Averaging Strategy

The Dollar Cost Averaging Strategy (refer to Chapter 10) involves feeding smaller amounts of money into an investment over time. This strategy helps to smooth market volatility and therefore reduce risk. As this tends to be an accumulation strategy, it may not always be applicable within retirement planning as you're drawing down funds from an existing asset base (which is normally fully invested). That said, it can be useful where you've added money to an existing super or pension account, or used a downsizing or non-concessional super strategy to build up additional capital (refer to Chapter 11). Dollar cost averaging can also provide peace of mind during times of increased market volatility.

The Gearing Strategy

The Gearing Strategy involves both investing your own money and borrowing money to invest (refer to Chapter 10). The interest paid can then be claimed as a tax deduction.

This strategy increases the amount of money you have available to invest; of course, the loan needs to be repaid as well. This is another accumulation strategy, and it's generally not appropriate for use within retirement planning. Without an income to pay off the loan if something happens to the investment, the risk is far too high to sensibly consider in any retirement context. Other strategies can provide you with better outcomes at less risk. People generally aim to gear assets before they reach retirement while they've got ongoing income from work or other assets that are not required to meet living costs.

In retirement it's a very different story… but is it possible? Yes, it is—provided you have a suitable amount of income being generated

RETIREMENT

from your total asset base, and you are very comfortable with holding debt in retirement. Gearing can, however, impact your lifestyle or ongoing cash flow in retirement and should be considered on a case-by-case basis, taking into account all of your financial resources. Everyone is different—you need to do what is right for you and your 'why'.

Additional challenges to consider as a retiree

Retirees have some additional challenges to consider as they no longer have access to a pay cheque to fund their spending. They need to rely on the assets they've accumulated during their working life, as well as government benefits. It's important to consider these additional sub-retirement Investment Strategies as part of planning for your retirement.

THE UNEXPECTED EXPENSES STRATEGY

Life is full of surprises, even in retirement, and some of them will cost you money. Unexpected events might include the car breaking down, a leak in the kitchen or bathroom, or the hot water system giving you cold showers, all of which can interrupt your life and be a nuisance.

How do you pay for these expenses? Most people during their working lives will simply put it on their credit card and pay it off over the coming months. This approach is also open to retirees, but using credit means you pay interest. If you're on a fixed income, as most retirees are, interest stops you spending in other areas and provides no ongoing benefit to you. An alternative strategy might be the Unexpected Expenses Strategy. With this strategy, you quarantine a small amount of funds (say $3000 to $4000) to pay for unexpected expenses. By keeping this small pool of funds aside, you know you've got a rainy day account to draw upon, should you ever need to. Even retirees need to have good money habits. Setting goals (Chapter 2) and having strong foundations for your financial life (Chapter 3) are still important in your retirement.

Strategy Stacking Tip

When managing your pension account, it pays to have access to capital at short notice in both your own name as well as your investment portfolio. A good way to do this is to maintain some set-aside cash equal to 12 to 24 months of your forecasted pension drawings. This would allow you to have back-up money you can easily access; it should also prevent the need to sell assets to pay for things during times of weakness. Then, whatever happens in the markets, you have the peace of mind to know you have two years of cash flow certainty during periods of volatility or market corrections. Nobody likes selling assets that are not generating their full value, so this is a great way to get through bouncy markets and times of economic weakness without having to change the way you live or sell on valuable assets.

People were worried about retiring during the COVID-19 pandemic, saying that they couldn't afford to retire; however, they didn't think long term. You're not going to spend all your money in the first two years of your retirement; a cash back-up enables you to get through a pandemic or Global Financial Crisis and continue to live the way you want. You can invest the rest of your capital to generate an income stream for the future. Things pass, the view of an event changes, and markets will continue to go up and down. The COVID-19 pandemic saw a huge swing in value over a six-week period and the markets then returned to much higher levels over the short term.

THE AGED CARE STRATEGY

When people retire, they tend to think about what they want to do. And rightly so, as they've worked hard all their life so now it's their time. Pre-retirees, however, don't often think about their later life (another form of short-term rather than long-term thinking). How you structure your affairs might impact on how you fund any aged care you need. It's worthwhile at the very least to have a basic understanding of the rules.

The good news is that the family home isn't typically included in an aged care assessment. Many who have retired haven't thought about what will happen when they become aged and need a higher level of support. At that stage of their life they need to rely on others, most often their children or nieces and nephews. If you're comfortable with that kind of outcome then you probably don't need to do much now. If you're not, however, spend some time understanding how you might pay for aged care services. You might learn through the experience of your own parents or grandparents, too.

When to do it?

Consider your Retirement Investment Strategy as often as you would your non-super investment strategy. Be prepared to change your investments if they're not delivering you the income you expect.

Do

Do consider a Retirement Investment Strategy:

- As part of your retirement plan, before you retire
- At least annually as part of a retirement income performance and investment review
- If your living costs or needs change, as you may need more or less income
- If you've added additional funds to your portfolio or have large capital items you need to allow for
- When you're checking your ongoing investment costs to ensure they remain cost-effective
- When you know what you're going to invest in and why—not all assets pay income and not all assets provide growth, so know why you have chosen these investments.

Don't

Don't fall into these traps:

- Setting and forgetting your Retirement Investment Strategy: it's important to be confident that your strategy will deliver the income you need

- Forgetting that if you have an SMSF providing you with a pension income, you need to have your investment strategy documented as a part of the fund's ongoing compliance requirements

- Making retirement income investment decisions without understanding the consequences of your decisions; seek advice if you need to.

How far will your retirement take you?

A common goal for most retirees that I meet with is to go travelling. Some of them want to hook up the caravan and head north for winter, and I don't blame them—Canberra does freeze in winter, especially when that wind starts blowing off the slopes. Some of them, however, want to head offshore to New Zealand, Asia or Europe. And some of them love cruising on the open seas. Each year, about a million Australians enjoy a holiday cruise.

Regardless of where you want to go or how you wish to travel, the Investment Strategies you implement will play an important part in funding your income. If you need help, please seek advice from a professional financial planner to ensure you're using the right assets—and maybe even consider some investment options you've never heard of before to help you get the outcome you're after. You don't want to leave anything to chance; after all, you wait 30 years or more to get to your retirement, so you may as well enjoy it as much as possible.

The Appropriate Retirement Fees Strategy

The Appropriate Retirement Fees Strategy seeks to ensure that you're not overpaying on the ability to deliver a retirement income stream. Why might this be a concern? Well, the more complicated your retirement income structure is and the more vehicles you use, the more fees you're likely to be paying to manage your retirement funds. If you think you're paying too much, you can explore other options or talk to

RETIREMENT

a financial planner to see if there are other, more cost-effective options that might deliver comparable outcomes.

Having access to a wide range of investment options can help to limit costs; how you invest your funds will have a direct impact on the underlying costs. It's also important that you consider the investment products you use as this can limit your costs while maintaining a suitable level of diversification, as well as income and the use of franking credits. (Chapter 10 covers investment strategies, and the ways you can invest, in far more detail.)

How does it work?

The first step to reviewing the fees you pay to run your retirement income strategy is to understand what fees you're paying. Let's take a look at the typical fees you're likely to pay, depending on the retirement vehicle you're using.

A managed fund charges an ICR (Indirect Cost Ratio) when you invest. It will have a specific sector allocation depending on what you use. The costs for a managed fund can vary from 0.5 per cent in the fixed interest sector through to 2 per cent for an internally geared fund. You should consider the reason why you're holding the fund as part of your broader investment strategy.

Listed shares are a great way to maintain a specific exposure to a company without having to pay ongoing fees (such as the ICR). You do have to pay brokerage at the time you buy or sell a share, but if you're a buy-and-hold investor the costs will be minimal. Brokerage costs have come down significantly over a number of years. A wholesale brokerage account tied to a bank account can be a cost-effective way of doing it yourself. You can also engage a stockbroker to help with your investment choices—they charge a little more, but you also get the benefit of their experience.

For the fee-conscious, the use of exchange-traded funds (ETFs) can be a great way to get broad exposure to specific sectors while keeping your costs as low as possible. Like a managed fund, ETFs charge a fee for investing and using their product. For this fee, they provide you with an underlying investment option for your portfolio. They will also do the annual reporting and provide you with everything that your accountant will need at tax time. Depending on what you buy, you may also benefit from franking credits—as well as an ongoing income stream to fund pensions.

Strategy Stacking Tip

If you're constructing a portfolio, you need to confirm what's available through your selected fund or platform: not all investments are offered by all providers. If you want to use listed shares, you need to make sure your fund allows for their use. There's no point buying a Mini-Cooper if you can't fit all your tools in the boot!

Using listed shares as well as ETFs and some managed funds is a great way to diversify your portfolio, have a greater degree of control over the income generated and maximise the use of franking credits. Incorporating managed funds can also allow you to use a fund manager who specialises in specific areas you may not know much about—for example, the small-cap sector (which often includes up-and-coming young companies) or technology companies that you may not be able to purchase directly through your fund, such as Apple or Google.

You need to check what's available and then use your options wisely. A cheaper fund may not charge much in admin fees (so appear cheaper) but also it may charge a much higher ICR to make up for it, so you could lose out on their limited investment menu. You need to think big picture, considering not just the admin fee but the ICR and how your fund is invested.

A diversified portfolio of assets and products shouldn't have an ICR of more than about 0.6 per cent in total. If you're in a generic risk profile option within a fund with limited investment options, you wouldn't want to be paying more than 0.8 per cent; if it's over 1 per cent in total, you would expect that the performance will be significantly better than another option you could create by changing funds. You pay these fees every year, which could be quite a long time (depending on how old you are).

RETIREMENT

In the earlier Retirement Income Vehicles Strategy, I identified a number of vehicles that can be used to deliver you with income in retirement. Let's look at the typical fees for each of these vehicles so you have some idea about what you should be paying.

Typical fees are outlined in table 12.4 for an account-based pension, an SMSF pension and a fixed income annuity.

Regardless of which type of retirement income structures you choose, you might also pay a financial planner to help you make the most of strategy stacking at retirement and using all the appropriate strategies that stack the odds in your favour to achieve your retirement goals (refer to Chapter 4 for my strategy stacking philosophy). A good adviser will deliver more value to your retirement over the long term than the fees they charge. In addition, you may even learn about some investment options that you've never heard of that could be right for you and your preferred asset allocation.

When to do it?

The Appropriate Retirement Fees Strategy is something to consider before you retire and as part of your overall retirement income planning. Review your fees once in a while as well to make sure you're still getting value for money.

Do

Do consider an Appropriate Retirement Fees Strategy:

- When you're pre-planning your retirement and considering the right structure to use
- If you're concerned about the fees you're paying (if you're in retirement already)
- If you're looking to widen your investment universe and consider other fund options
- When you review your retirement income, investment and fund performance.

Table 12.4: Typical retirement fees

	Set-up costs	Fixed costs	Variable costs
Account-based pension (industry or retail fund)	Nil. These funds are free to join.	Typically, these are charged for completing an ongoing function of your superannuation. These include: • Administration fees • Investment fees • Indirect costs	Typically, these are charged when you make a transaction on your account. These include: • Switching fees • Buy-sell spread fees • Activity based fees • Indirect fees
Self-managed superannuation fund (SMSF) pension	These fees are charged for setting up an SMSF. These fees include: • SMSF trust deed cost • SMSF trustee company cost	Typically, these are the ongoing annual costs you'd expect to see within a self-managed super fund. These include: • Accounting and audit fees • Annual ASIC corporate fee • ATO supervisory levy	Typically, these are charged when you make a transaction on your account. These include: • Costs of investments and investment trading • Banking costs • Indirect fees

(continued)

RETIREMENT

Table 12.4 Typical retirement fees (*cont'd*)

	Set-up costs	Fixed costs	Variable costs
Fixed income annuity	Nil. These products are free to join.	Typically, these are charged for completing an ongoing function of your annuity. These include administration fees.	Typically, these are charged when you make a transaction on your account. These include: • Payment fees • Surrender fees Note: some products offer no fees and just an adviser service fee option, for advice that you might receive. They recoup their fees before providing you with a return—so in a sense, their fees are hidden. There's no such thing as a fee-free annuity.
Legacy fund	Nil. These funds were free to join but are now closed to new members.	Typically, these are charged for completing an ongoing function of your superannuation. These include: • Administration fees • Investment fees • Indirect costs	Typically, these are charged when you make a transaction on your account. These include: • Switching fees • Buy-sell spread fees • Activity based fees • Indirect fees • Exit fees

	Set-up costs	Fixed costs	Variable costs
Investments outside of superannuation	Typically, there are no set-up costs for retail investment products like term deposits or managed funds. For purchasing shares, however, there is a cost to the broker to buy them for you.	Typically, these are the ongoing annual costs of keeping your account open. These include: • Account fee • Administration fee	Depending on the kind of investment, these might include: • Investment switch or trading costs • Indirect fees • Exit costs
Government benefits	Simply your time to apply for them. No financial costs are associated with government benefits as they're part of our social welfare system.		
Selling the family home	There are no set-up costs for selling a family home. However, there are several fees likely to apply.	These include real estate agent commission (2–4%)	These include: • Auctioneer fee (if auctioned) • Advertising and marketing costs • Solicitor or conveyance fees
Reverse mortgages	Typically, you'll be charged a loan set-up fee. This covers your application costs, settlement fee and legal costs.	Providers will charge an ongoing fee to administer the loan and payments to you.	Interest rates apply, given this is a loan and different providers will offer different interest rates.

Don't

Don't fall into these traps:

- Making decisions on fees alone. Some structures (like SMSFs) can cost more depending on the overall size of your fund because they offer you functions that you can't get with other retirement types. Equally, just because some annuities don't charge fees, it doesn't mean they're right for you given they may pay less than market-linked investments and may not allow you to withdraw a lump sum if you need it.

- Discounting the value of financial planning advice to simply save money. Retirement income planning is complicated and the rules often change. Making decisions without advice is a risk. You don't know what you don't know. A wrong decision could cost you more than you realise.

Searching for value

Regardless of how old you are, no one likes overpaying for goods and services. When you're retired you might be eligible to receive government benefits and a seniors card, which offers savings on a range of goods and services. Saving a little bit a little more often could see you end up with more than you realise. For example, $10 in savings a week, over a year, keeps $520 ($10 × 52) in your bank account. That might be enough to fund a nice weekend away to visit a friend or family member. Imagine if that was 10 years of saving—what an amazing adventure you could have!

The Appropriate Tax in Retirement Strategy

The Appropriate Tax in Retirement Strategy seeks to ensure that you meet your obligations effectively and make the most of your retirement savings and income for achieving your 'why'.

How does it work?

The first step to understanding an Appropriate Tax in Retirement Strategy is to understand how tax applies to the different retirement vehicles.

Table 12.5 looks at the taxes on different retirement vehicles.

Table 12.5: Taxes on retirement vehicles (figures correct at the time of writing)

Vehicles	Tax rate	When is it paid?
Transition to retirement account-based pension or SMSF (people aged under 59)	15% on fund earnings Income—no tax is payable on the tax-free component. Tax payable on the taxable component, less a deductible amount of 15%.	At the time you complete your tax return and it's assessed.
Account-based pension or SMSF (people aged 60 and over)	Earnings are tax-free. Income is tax-free.*	N/A
Fixed income annuity	Taxed at your marginal tax rate, less a deductible amount (usually 15%).	At the time you complete your tax return and it's assessed.
Legacy funds	Will vary depending on the fund. These are usually employer or government funds—contact your fund for details. The default rate for super is 15%.	Your fund will complete the tax return and remit the tax payable from your earnings.
Investments outside of superannuation	Earnings are taxed at your marginal tax rate. There's also capital gains tax to consider if you have an applicable asset.	At the time you complete your tax return and it's assessed.
Government benefits	Taxed at your marginal tax rate.	At the time you complete your tax return and it's assessed.
Selling the family home or reverse mortgages	No capital gains tax is payable on selling a family home. There is no tax associated with taking on a reverse mortgage as it's considered debt, not income.	N/A

* Up to the transfer balance cap of $1.7 million per person

RETIREMENT

When to do it?

You might consider an Appropriate Tax in Retirement Strategy as part of your overall retirement income plan (as well as your estate planning, which is covered in Chapter 14). You should endeavour to understand the tax implications of your decisions before you implement your Retirement Strategy. Getting it right from the start can prevent the need to make changes, set up a new structure and (in some instances), with property, pay a second round of stamp duty.

> ## Strategy Stacking Tip
>
> Consider the income profile of the assets you intend to hold as well as the structures you're going to use. Tax-ineffective assets (such as fixed interest assets), as well as high-growth assets (such as the international sector), are best held within superannuation as the tax percentage may be less than your marginal tax rate. In addition, you may sell growth assets in a tax-free pension structure in the future to avoid a tax liability all together. You could then have tax-deferred property and fully franked equity income providing tax benefits in your own name These are important considerations when looking at the tax profile of the income and growth you generate from different sectors so that you pay tax at the lowest levels possible.
>
> You can also hold each asset class inside your superannuation when you don't have a family trust or joint assets to make the most of an account-based pension. Remember that there's tax on the income you receive from an account-based pension and there's no tax on the earnings the investment within the account-based pension makes.

Do

Do consider an Appropriate Tax in Retirement Strategy:

- As part of your overall Retirement Strategy from the start
- As part of your income tax planning, given that account-based pensions offer tax-free retirement outcomes

RETIREMENT

- As part of a retirement income review
- When you inherit money or sell an asset and can't add to your superannuation
- When you have reached your non-concessional limit and have to invest funds for a number of years before you can redirect them to super
- At the time you do your tax return—plan forward where you can.

Don't

Don't fall into these traps:

- Forgetting you can have $18 000 per annum tax-free income using your marginal tax rate
- Forgetting that investments outside of a super or pension environment are subject to capital gains tax, including investment properties
- Making decisions without understanding the consequences of your decisions
- Going it alone. Tax is complicated and the rules often change. Seek the advice of a professional financial planner who can help you structure the appropriate outcome for your situation.
- Assuming that all assets have the same income and growth profile. Know what you're going to buy and think about where best to hold the asset.

Retirees don't like change—and governments would do well to remember that

You've worked all your life paying taxes, and you've taken the time to strategy stack and achieve a retirement outcome that you're happy with. Your retirement income provides you with the ability to do the things you want. Life's pretty good.

Over time, we've seen proposals from both sides of government about how they might change the rules for retirees. I've even had

RETIREMENT

clients in my office crying about such changes. The effect is very real. It means what they've planned for may no longer be a reality for them, or they've been caught up in a rule change that they never expected or saw coming.

Changes to the rules around retirement (and most of them seem to be around tax) are random variables or risks. If the government announces a change before an election, your vote can help determine the outcome. Governments on all sides would do well to think about the real impact upon retirees' emotional and financial wellbeing before they change the rules: retirees live on the income from their assets and may not have the ability to boost their income mid-retirement.

CHAPTER 13
The Wealth Protection Strategies

As a society we pay close attention to protecting our cars, homes and business property. When it comes to protection, most people think insurance.

This kind of insurance is called *general insurance* and is widely available. Sure, you'd be annoyed if someone broke into your house and stole your new flat-screen TV. That's one reason why you'd take out contents insurance so you could replace your home contents if they were stolen or damaged—it's a financial protection against having to find the money for replacing the things you've lost.

Although it's important to protect your material possessions, they're not the focus of the Wealth Protection Strategies I talk about in this chapter. The Wealth Protection Strategies look at protecting your biggest asset—you. Without you, who will raise the kids? Who will earn an income? Who will pay for school expenses and pay off the mortgage? Many people have a 30-year mortgage that in some situations is secured by only two weeks' sick leave with their employer! Protecting yourself is an important part of strategy stacking, and it becomes even more important when you've got family relying on you.

When it comes to protecting yourself, there are certain situations you can insure for. The kinds of insurance I'm talking about here are *personal* insurances. They're less widely known and understood than home and contents insurances; in some cases, they even get forgotten about when they're needed most. These insurances are essential to setting up Wealth Protection Strategies to protect you and your family. The benefit of having a financial planner by your side cannot be understated here. Someone to complete the paperwork with you, lodge the paperwork and follow up to completion. That's why you've paid them and paid your premiums — to help you when you need it the most.

There's an old saying you might have heard: 'Don't cry for anything that can't cry for you.'

With today's keeping up with the Jones's mentality, it sometimes seems that we value material outcomes more than people. This old saying reminds me that the only thing a human need ever cry for is another human. As much as you might love your red sports car, house or TV, none of those things will cry for you if you pass away. Your friends and family will though. And if you have people relying on you, they'll cry and miss you even more, given the family relationship.

This chapter provides you with some Wealth Protection Strategies. Specifically, I explore the following strategies:

- The Income Protection Strategy
- The Trauma Protection Strategy
- The Total and Permanent Disability Protection Strategy
- The Life Protection Strategy
- The Key Person Protection Strategy.

The Income Protection Strategy

The Income Protection Strategy is designed to replace your income should you be unable to work if you become unwell or you're injured. Implemented correctly, the strategy will provide replacement income so you can continue to pay your ongoing expenses, such as food, household and car expenses, and even the mortgage. This for me is the most important form of insurance because we all make decisions assuming we can earn money doing something. If that choice is taken

WEALTH PROTECTION

from you by someone or something, it's the basis from which nearly all lifestyle decisions (and retirement planning) is based.

How does it work?

There are three main ways to implement the Income Protection Strategy:

1. **The self-funded option.** Within this option, an individual puts some of their income aside every payday in a rainy day account. They then draw on the money when they need it. The problem is that most people will dip into this account from time to time, so they're not able to save enough to make the self-funded option work—especially given the future value of your income over your working life.

2. **The superannuation option.** With this option, the individual takes out income protection or salary continuance insurance cover through their superannuation account. Payments for the insurance policy come out of the superannuation account. If a person ever needs to make a claim, they do so through their super fund. This option provides you with a form of cover; however, it is very inferior to a policy in your own name that you own.

3. **The retail income protection insurance or salary continuance policy option.** With this option, the individual takes out cover from a life insurance company and pays for the policy themselves. The cost of this policy is generally tax deductible, which makes this option attractive to many people who like to get a benefit rather than just pay more tax. The premium payable reduces your taxable income when your tax return is completed each year. It still shocks me how many people are unaware of this benefit, especially because Australians love a tax deduction—and claiming a tax deduction at your marginal rate is normally far better than that of the superannuation tax rate of 15 per cent. You also pay less income tax. If you're going to pay tax and get nothing, why not pay for an insurance policy and have the security of knowing your lifestyle could continue if you can't work?

WEALTH PROTECTION

293

Some key features and insurance policy terms and conditions to look for when comparing any existing policy to a new contract to ensure you are comparing apples with apples include:

- **The policy definition of 'pre-disability income':** Depending on your employment status, this may refer to your income in the 12 months prior to a claim or (if you're self-employed) an average of your income over two years prior to the claim.

- **Benefit indexation:** This feature ensures your sum insured keeps pace with inflation over time.

- **Claims indexation:** This feature ensures your claim payment is indexed or increased with the Consumer Price Index (CPI) over the time you are unable to work, to keep pace with inflation.

- **Crisis benefit:** This can be a payment of up to six times your monthly benefit on the diagnosis of specific conditions or events. There's no waiting period applicable here so you're paid immediately, which is great. (Note: the government removed this feature on new contracts from October 2021.)

- **Rehabilitation benefit:** This may be up to 12 times your monthly benefit to cover rehabilitation costs to get you back to work.

- **Specified injury:** This is an immediate payment, which is normally a multiple of your monthly benefit (depending on what has happened) that isn't impacted by your waiting period. An example of this would be a broken arm—you can get one month's benefit even though you may not be off work at all. (Note: the government removed this feature on new contracts from October 2021.)

- **Waiting periods:** Often, insurance policies will make you wait a number of days before they start to pay your claim. Typical waiting periods include 30, 60, 90 and 120 days. Typically, the longer the waiting period, the cheaper your premiums should be.

Strategy Stacking Tip

Policies in force prior to October 2021 may include features no longer available in the open market following government intervention in the sector (a couple of examples are noted in the preceding list). New policies aren't eligible for a range of included benefits, so make sure you consider what you have before you move: you may be going backwards.

Let's consider an example. Andrew is an accountant and earns $200 000, which would see him entitled to a monthly income protection payment of $11 667 (which is based on 70 per cent of his income). Taking into account some of the listed benefits that may be included in his policy with an existing contract (prior to October 2021), here are some different scenarios and their payment outcomes that his insurance protection policy might provide for:

- Andrew falls off his bike and breaks his arm mountain biking with his mates and receives a $12 500 specified injury benefit.

- Andrew has a heart attack after riding his mountain bike off some jumps; $75 000 is paid on diagnosis, with no waiting period or tax payable.

- If Andrew cannot work more than 10 hours a week due to an injury that stops him from working, he may be able to claim his monthly benefit and do some work during the week (provided he has a contract that offers this benefit).

- If Andrew is off work for an extended period of time, his $12 500 monthly benefit would index with CPI to keep pace with inflation over time (where he has benefit indexation in his contract).

It's paramount that you understand the terms and conditions of the income protection insurance policy you hold. A new policy taken out after October 2021 may only secure 70 per cent of Andrew's

WEALTH PROTECTION

pre-disability income and offer very few lump sum benefits. All policies are different, and it's important you understand what you're paying for. It's also important that you understand what you get for your money because cover inside and outside of superannuation (the difference between the second and third option in the earlier list) can be very different.

When you're choosing a policy, consider the following questions:

- **What's your occupation?** Occupations are treated differently by insurance companies. Some occupations are considered more high risk than others, and each different insurance company will make their own assessment on how risky your occupation is.

- **How much will this income protection insurance cover?** Most policies pay a maximum of 70 per cent of your income. Most good indemnity contracts will offer the best 12 months of income in the two or three years prior to your claim. This is normally not offered through a superannuation-based contract, so check your terms carefully.

- **What's the waiting period?** This is the time frame you select before a payment will commence. You need to be able to service this period with your own funds, accumulated leave with your employer or another form of assistance. Some policies make you wait 30 days, others might make you wait 60, 90 or even 120 days before you can receive funds. It's a time frame that you choose, taking into account what you need.

- **How long will the policy replace your income for?** Some policies offer a fixed period of payment or two, five or six years of payments; other policies will pay you until you turn 65. This can also be impacted by your occupation and the overall risk appetite of the insurance company.

- **Does the insurance company offer an 'own occupation' definition to age 65 or does it revert to 'any occupation' after a two-year period?** *Own occupation* means you can't work again in the occupation in which you trained. *Any occupation* means you can't work again in any occupation that you are suited by education or training. This is an important policy definition to be aware of. If your policy has an 'any occupation' definition, it means that if you're still capable of doing work in a different role after your accident or injury, the policy may not pay you any benefits. The 'own occupation' definition policy may pay you in the event you can no longer do the job you had before the accident or injury.

Strategy Stacking Tip

Income protection is paid monthly in arrears, so a waiting period of 30 days is actually 60 days without money. Factor this into your waiting period, just in case.

When to do it?

You should consider an Income Protection Strategy from the day that you first start work. If you have expenses you need to pay when you're unwell, sick leave will only cover so much.

If you're a parent and still have adult children that think they are bulletproof and know everything, take cover out for them to protect yourself, as the 'bank of Mum and Dad' can come under significant pressure because a child didn't think ahead (and your children can still claim the premium as a tax deduction). A $2000 insurance premium (an example annual cost of an income protection policy) could be a lot less than $25 000 of interest on a $600 000 home loan for 12 months because your son had a bike accident and can't work. And if you think your adult children need to start taking full responsibility for their financial lives, encourage them to protect their own income with this kind of insurance so they don't rely on you.

Do

Do consider an Income Protection Strategy:

- As part of your overall Wealth Protection Strategy

- When considering your tax return. Decide on how you want to claim a tax deduction—in your own name or in super. Where your marginal tax rate is greater than 15 per cent, it makes a lot

WEALTH
PROTECTION

of sense to hold the policy in your own name to maximise your available tax deduction.

- If you're evaluating your income protection options. Consider your waiting period and any ongoing costs to ensure the policy is appropriate for you. Understand what is included in your policy, and remember that superannuation contracts are generally inferior to personal policies.

- When you have dependants or financial commitments, like a mortgage

- If you have a job and would find it hard to live without a salary over the longer term (that's nearly everyone!)

- If you're looking to maximise your tax deduction. Consider pre-paying a year's premium just prior to 30 June so you can claim the entire year's premium as a tax deduction when you lodge your tax return in July.

- Even if you have sick leave. If you've accumulated two months of sick leave, you can extend your waiting period and pay less insurance premiums for your cover.

- If your salary changes. Review your cover because your ability to work is one of your greatest assets.

Don't

Don't fall into these traps:

- Purchasing an income protection insurance policy without understanding the terms and conditions

- Assuming a default insurance policy within your superannuation fund is the best option

- Missing out on cover if you do self-fund this strategy rather than take out a policy. Make sure you consider the other Wealth Protection Strategies within this chapter, as most people are unlikely to be able to fully fund all the Wealth Protection Strategies themselves.

WEALTH PROTECTION

- Cancelling any existing cover before a new medically underwritten contract is in force and complete

- Changing jobs without having cover in force, especially if you're moving to a more manual occupation.

A reality check for you, your friends and your family

I've often said you don't know what you don't know. I had a client tell me a story about his brother, who was a schoolteacher and was diagnosed with cancer. After going through several treatments and being away from work, things at home started getting tough financially for him and his family. It was only after he passed that his wife realised he'd had income protection in his superannuation all along. This was heartbreaking. They'd been doing it tough and barely making ends meet. So much financial stress could have been avoided at what was already a very difficult time.

I was thankful to learn in this case that the superannuation fund back-paid out some (not all) of the cover to his wife, along with the husband's superannuation and death benefits. If you know someone who is really ill, please tell them to look into their super and check if they have default income protection insurance in place. In times like this, something is better than nothing. I genuinely hope that by sharing this sad story, I never again hear of this happening to anyone else.

The Trauma Protection Strategy

The Trauma Protection Strategy is designed to provide you with access to a pre-determined sum of money if you are diagnosed with a specific major illness such as cancer or you experience a critical health event such as a stroke. The strategy can be used to provide replacement income if you can no longer work (as income protection will only cover 70 per cent of your gross income for contracts taken out after October 2021) and cover medical costs and other expenses you may incur. What you spend your trauma payment on is completely up to you.

How does it work?

There is only one way to implement the Trauma Protection Strategy and that's through purchasing a kind of insurance called trauma cover. Trauma cover is also known as recovery insurance or critical illness insurance, depending on the provider. Payment of the benefit occurs once a diagnosis covered by the trauma policy has been made and a claim has been made and assessed. There is also generally a 14-day survival period after the traumatic event (otherwise it's a death claim; for more information on this strategy, see the Life Protection Strategy later in this chapter).

Today, superannuation providers aren't allowed to offer trauma cover through their funds. However, if you held a superannuation fund prior to 2014 and you still hold this fund, check to see if you already have trauma cover in place.

Like income protection cover, it's important that you understand the terms and conditions of the trauma insurance policy before you purchase it. All policies are different, and it's important you understand what you're paying for.

When you're choosing a policy, consider the following questions:

- **What serious illnesses does the policy cover?** Cancer, stroke, heart disease, and loss of sight, speech or sound are usually included, as are extended stays in intensive care due to injury or illness.

- **How much will the policy pay you as a lump sum if you experience one of the traumas covered by the policy?** It's important to think about how much cover you need as you will be able to choose your level of cover. Of course, the greater the cover, the higher trauma insurance premiums you will pay.

- **Do you have any pre-existing conditions?** If so, the policy is unlikely to cover them. These are called *exclusions* and would have been agreed to in writing when the cover was taken out.

- **How will you pay for the policy—stepped or level premiums?** *Stepped premiums* are determined by your age.

When you're younger, the premiums cost less, but with every birthday the cost of your premiums rises. *Level premiums* are priced using the age you were when the policy was taken out, not your age next birthday (stepped). Level premiums were removed from the open market and are no longer available to new customers. So if you have an existing contract priced in this manner, check your options carefully before changing as you cannot replace it.

When to do it?

Cancer, stroke, heart disease and other major illnesses such as multiple sclerosis are becoming more common and would all impact your ability to continue working on a full-time or part-time basis. You should consider trauma insurance if you're concerned about how you'd pay for your expenses if you were to experience one of these major health events. It's particularly important for those with partners and children, or those with debts like mortgages. You may wish to cover the 30 per cent of gross income that you can't cover with income protection insurance, plus a year or more of a spouse's gross income (in case they need to stay home and care for you), as well as the prepayment of school fees or mortgage payments to give you some breathing space.

Trauma insurance is *slump money* — by that I mean I have seen many a client slump down in their chair with a huge sigh of relief when they realise they will receive a large sum of money after a traumatic health event. All they have really done is buy themselves some breathing space during a horribly difficult time in their life — so they don't have to replace a large capital sum with after-tax income over the next 10 years and delay a range of financial decisions.

Trauma is normally a linked or standalone structure — linked meaning it's tied to life insurance or total and permanent disability (TPD) cover (both of which are discussed later in this chapter), so in the event of a claim, a TPD policy that is linked is removed (you have the option of buying back the cover in your contract structure if you wish). Standalone is exactly that — it is a policy that doesn't impact any other insurance cover you have. Standalone cover is normally more expensive than linked cover — to continue the example, trauma cover would be paid out with a standalone policy while the TPD cover remains in place.

Strategy Stacking Tip

There is no perfect answer to how much cover you should maintain, but think about the key things that would impact your lifestyle or family: is it paying off debt, replacing income, paying school fees, covering a year's wages for a spouse if they need time off to care for you? Your 'why' is vital here because you don't want to race back to work to pay your mortgage if your work contributed to your trauma event occurring.

Do

Do consider a Trauma Protection Strategy:

- As part of your overall Wealth Protection Strategy

- When you have dependants or financial commitments, such as a mortgage

- Even if you have sick leave. No matter how much sick leave you have, it's unlikely to be enough to ever cover a serious trauma.

- Even if you don't work full-time — even stay-at-home parents can benefit from trauma cover should such a situation arise

- If you are in an occupation where you can't get income protection insurance. Trauma cover can give you a multiple of your annual income.

- Whether you have other Wealth Protection Strategies in place or not, as your trauma cover may be linked to other policies or held as a standalone contract.

Don't

Don't fall into these traps:

- Purchasing a trauma insurance policy without understanding the terms and conditions

WEALTH PROTECTION

- Lying to an insurance company about your medical history or any pre-existing medical condition if they request information at the time of application. This might void your policy at the time you need to make a claim.

- Setting and forgetting your trauma insurance. Policy options change over time, and sometimes better policies become available.

A trauma might be serious...but you're not dead yet!

I've spent enough time with clients over the years to realise that most of us want the same things. We all want the love of our families. We strive to buy and pay off a home. We prefer laughing with friends than going to funerals. And when things don't go as we want them to, we want to know we're not going to be placed in financial hardship.

Trauma might be serious, but you're not dead yet and there's still a good amount of life to be lived, even if recovery is challenging. Financial stress is likely to erode and not add to your recovery when you or a loved one is faced with a serious illness.

The Total and Permanent Disability Protection Strategy

The Total and Permanent Disability (TPD) Protection Strategy is designed to provide you with access to a pre-determined sum of money if you were to become totally and permanently disabled. Implemented well, the strategy provides a lump sum payment or equivalent instalments paid over time. The level of cover you decide could take into account things like the repayment of debt (such as a mortgage) and education expenses for your kids, as well as the ability to replace lost income in the event that you can't work again. Remember that income protection can only protect up to 70 per cent of your pre-disability income for contracts taken out after October 2021, so you may think about topping up the part that's missing because you will have a tax impost as well. Thinking through your 'why' in relation to cover can ensure that you get the best outcome possible. I am yet to meet anyone that is upset about having too much money to spend at claim time!

How does it work?

There are three main ways to implement the Total and Permanent Disability Protection Strategy:

- **The superannuation option:** With this option, the individual takes out 'any occupation' TPD insurance cover through their superannuation account. Payments for the insurance policy come out of your super. If a person ever needs to make a claim, they do so through their super fund.

- **The TPD insurance policy option:** With this option, the individual takes out cover and pays for the policy themselves. If a person ever needs to make a claim, they do so with their insurance company. The 'any occupation' or 'own occupation' definition can be selected by the life insured.

- **The super-linking option:** With this option, the individual uses their own superannuation account to pay and own the 'any occupation' TPD insurance. The 'own occupation' definition is linked and owned by the life insured.

It's really important that you understand the terms and conditions of your TPD insurance policy, whether through super or paid for separately. All policies are different and it's important you understand what you're paying for.

When you're choosing a policy, consider the following questions:

- **Does the TPD insurance policy use an 'own occupation' or 'any occupation' definition?** Own occupation means you can't work again in the occupation in which you were trained; any occupation means you can't work again in any occupation. Own occupation or any occupation is a primary consideration. If you have an 'any occupation' definition, it might mean that you can do any job, even though you can't do your 'own' usual job. If this is assessed to be the case, your policy is unlikely to pay you a benefit. For this reason, 'own occupation' policy wording provides additional peace of mind when assessing different options. Where you have a specific skillset or education that's industry-specific, the own occupation definition is the most secure definition available. I generally recommend that you opt for 'own' over 'any'; however, this can be impacted by your job, as the own occupation option isn't always available.

- **How much will the policy pay you as a lump sum or equivalent instalments if you experience one of the disabilities covered by the insurance?** Think about your own financial situation and your likely financial needs if you experience a TPD event when working out your cover amount. TPD is great for paying off mortgages and covering fixed costs (like education), living costs, lost wages for a spouse and the 30 per cent of your income that you can't insure with income protection.

- **Do you have any pre-existing conditions?** If so, the policy is unlikely to cover them. These are called exclusions.

How your cover is held may impact the potential tax implications of your benefit. For example, a TPD contract owned within a superannuation fund may have a taxable component, depending on your age when you claim. A personal policy is generally tax-free and paid to the person insured.

Understanding how you own the policy and how you pay for your premiums is essential as it can impact the amount you're paid, and nobody likes nasty tax surprises. The TPD benefit out of super can be taxed at up to 22 per cent on the taxable component if taken out in one go. Consider how the benefit is taken as you may be able to reduce the amount of tax paid on your benefit.

Keep in mind that an 'any occupation' TPD claim held via your superannuation fund can also provide you with early access to your total super balance as well as the insurance proceeds (where the trustee has agreed).

Instead of taking a lump sum, you can also use the capital from the policy paid to the fund to start an account-based pension from your super if you wish (refer to Chapter 12 for more on account-based pensions within the Retirement Vehicles Strategy). By taking your benefit as a pension you can benefit from a 15 per cent tax rebate on the taxable component.

Managing the potential tax payable on your benefit is important—getting advice on how to take your funds can save you a lot more than you realise.

To work out the tax-free and taxable component of a superannuation-based contract, use this formula:

$$\frac{\text{Amount of benefit} \times \text{days to retirement}}{(\text{Service days} + \text{days to retirement})}$$

The hybrid option of having a TPD insurance policy inside and outside of superannuation is also sometimes known as *super-linking*. This is where you have the majority of the TPD definition held and paid for by your superannuation (people like to limit the cost to themselves directly) with the 'own occupation' portion of your cover held in your own name (and paid personally). This can help to limit the impact on personal cash flow by using your super capital to pay the cost and allowing you to maintain the best 'own occupation' definition at the same time. A key benefit here is that the 'own occupation' benefit is a tax-free payment to the life insured.

The reason super-linking is required is because the own occupation TPD definition cannot be held in superannuation for new contracts issued. Practically, this means that if you want an own occupation definition, you need to hold this insurance outside your super account.

When thinking about TPD cover, you should decide on how much you need and what the proceeds will be used for, and who is going to own the cover and therefore how it will be paid for, as well as the potential tax implications.

Strategy Stacking Tip

If you're going to use superannuation to fund the premium, think about increasing the level of cover you have to allow for the potential tax payable on a benefit. By doing this, the increased cover can fund the tax payable, should you ever need to make a claim. This can prevent the amount you get being reduced and also ensure that you can meet your specific objectives when you need the money most. Remember: a small deduction may not be worth the tax impact at claim time, so think with the end in mind.

When to do it?

You should consider the Total and Permanent Disability Protection Strategy if you're concerned about how you'd pay for your expenses if you were subject to a disability. It's particularly important for those with partners and children, or debts like mortgages. It's also something you might consider for non-working spouses, too.

If you're self-employed, TPD cover can be a great way to secure your business value and create an amount of money that could be paid to a shareholder in the place of shares. This may be known as *key person cover* or *buy-sell protection* as most business don't have the available funds on hand to pay out a stakeholder (the Key Person Protection Strategy is discussed later in this chapter).

Do

Do consider a Total and Permanent Disability Protection Strategy:

- As part of your overall Wealth Protection Strategy

- When you have dependants or financial commitments like a mortgage or other ongoing costs

- Even if you have sick leave. No matter how much sick leave you have, it's unlikely to be enough to ever cover a disability.

- Even if you don't work full-time — even stay-at-home parents can benefit from TPD cover should such a situation arise

WEALTH PROTECTION

307

- When you are a shareholder in a business and want to ensure the value is paid to you if you can no longer operate that business.

Don't

Don't fall into these traps:

- Purchasing a TPD insurance policy without understanding the terms and conditions

- Lying to an insurance company about your medical history or any pre-existing medical condition if they request information at the time of application. This might void your policy at the time you need to make a claim.

- Forgetting about the potential tax liability if superannuation funds your contract

- Trying to 'do it yourself' if you're unsure—seek financial advice first!

- Forgetting to consider the ownership structure (super, own name or super-linked) so you understand the tax impact

- Missing the distinction between any occupation and own occupation. Be sure to understand your policy's TPD definition as they're not the same.

- Forgetting to check that your superannuation fund has the necessary paperwork to be able to pay a benefit to you

- Setting and forgetting your TPD insurance. Policy options change over time and sometimes better policies become available.

Change and disability

Learning to live with a disability is probably one of the biggest challenges you're ever likely to face, if you find yourself in that situation. It might require changes to your home to make everyday living more practical. Most of us never think about what it would be like to live life in a wheelchair, for example. What would need to change in your house? How would your life change as a result?

While change like this can be hard mentally and physically, it's not a change people typically expect or plan for, often because they're fit and healthy and they don't think it will ever happen to them. Many superannuation funds have some automatic or default TPD cover as a part of their product offering. Unfortunately the terms of these policies aren't widely understood by their members. Many of the policies also have an 'any occupation' definition. So do your homework, and explore what you have and what you need. Having Wealth Protection Strategies in place means that you are taking action to deal with all kinds of outcomes.

Over time, most people learn to live with their disability. They still have active and social lives. Life does go on — and having adequate cover in place means the process will be less stressful and better supported.

The Life Protection Strategy

The Life Protection Strategy is designed to provide your spouse or dependants with access to a pre-determined sum of money if you were to pass away.

Life cover ensures that your family can still live the way they were used to prior to your passing. The money could be used to repay debt, cover education costs or provide a capital base from which income may be generated over the longer term. You may also wish to give the kids a deposit on a house. The options are endless, but starting with your 'why' (refer to Chapter 2) will ensure that you can still meet your objectives, whatever happens.

Life cover can also be held to create a capital base that may be used to pay out a shareholder in a business. The value of the contract would be equal to the market value of a shareholding. If you pass, you may want your family to receive the value of your shares. Most businesses don't have the cash lying around to pay out a significant sum, which is something I address later in this chapter in the Key Person Protection Strategy.

WEALTH PROTECTION

How does it work?

There are two main ways to implement the Life Protection Strategy:

- **The superannuation option:** With this option, the individual takes out cover through their superannuation account. Life insurance may also be called 'term life insurance' or 'death cover'. Payments for the insurance policy come out of your superannuation account. If a party ever needs to make a claim, they do so through their super fund.

- **The life insurance policy option:** With this option, the individual takes out cover and pays for the policy themselves. Many people seek financial planning advice to help identify their life insurance needs and find appropriate and affordable products to meet those needs, rather than buy a policy directly from an insurance company. Insurance policies are often hard to compare when you're doing it yourself.

It's really important that you understand the terms and conditions of your life insurance policy. All policies are different, and it's important you understand what you're paying for.

When you're choosing a policy, consider the following questions:

- **How much cover do you need?** The amount should consider what debts and living expenses need to be taken care of if you were to pass away.

- **What events are covered by the policy—or not covered?** As an example, suicide is excluded in many policies for a specified period of time.

- **How will you pay for the policy—inside or outside superannuation?** You can hold life cover through your super fund where your superannuation capital pays the annual premium. You could also own it in your own name and pay the premium yourself.

If you ever decide to change your cover, make sure you have your new policy in place before you cancel your existing policy. This will ensure that you have continued coverage and won't be caught in between any waiting periods that might apply to the new life insurance cover.

Cover held through super is generally deductible to your super fund. You also have the option of using an insurance company to provide the policy in the super environment. This would see the premium rolled over from the super fund holding your investments to the insurance provider. You also have the option of paying the premium personally (not paying through your super cover) and claiming the cost of the premium as a personal tax deduction.

Keep in mind that the value of the premium would also count towards your concessional contribution cap (so don't go over the limit) and remember to include the premium amount in any pre-June contribution to superannuation. Structuring and paying your premium in this way is great for people in a defined benefit scheme that doesn't allow for the rollover of superannuation benefits to pay the premium. It's also great if you don't want to reduce your superannuation capital by taking money from the fund to meet the annual premium. You can use personal money to pay a life premium and benefit from a tax deduction.

You should consider where the money will end up in the event of a claim. Money paid from superannuation to a dependant is generally tax-free; however, money paid to a non-dependant (usually an adult child over 18) can incur tax.

Strategy Stacking Tip

If you're going to pay funds to a non-dependant and you want to use superannuation to hold the contract, think about increasing the sum insured to cover for the tax payable on any benefit that's paid.

When to do it?

You should consider the Life Protection Strategy if you're concerned about how your spouse, partner or dependants would manage financially if you were to pass away. It's particularly important for those with partners and children, or with debts such as mortgages. Future education costs or just having enough money to keep the household going may also be factors as your family won't have the income from your wage any longer. It's also something you might consider for non-working spouses as it is very hard to care for young children and work full-time without any help. It's easy to undervalue the activity that's required to keep a home going and forget about the money it would cost to hire in extra help if needed.

Do

Do consider a Life Protection Strategy:

- As part of your overall Wealth Protection Strategy
- When you have dependants or future financial commitments, like a mortgage
- Even if you don't work full-time — even stay-at-home parents can benefit from life cover should a need for capital arise.

Don't

Don't fall into these traps:

- Purchasing a life insurance policy without understanding the terms and conditions
- Discounting the benefit of financial advice to help you identify your needs and select appropriate options
- Forgetting about the transfer balance cap implications of having money within superannuation for the surviving spouse
- Forgetting that your personal objectives are not what your friends say or think they are. We're all very different and have different 'must haves' when it comes to our loved ones.

WEALTH PROTECTION

- Forgetting to consider how the contract will be owned and how the premium will be paid

- Forgetting to consider the tax implications. Remember that the premium can be tax deductible. Consider where the proceeds will be paid—dependants are tax-free, with non-dependants potentially incurring a tax liability. Sometimes the tax impost can negate the benefits of a tax deduction, so make sure you know where the money will end up.

- Lying to an insurance company about your medical history or any pre-existing medical condition if they request information at the time of application. This might void your policy at the time a claim needs to be made.

- Setting and forgetting life insurance. Policy options change over time and sometimes better policies become available.

It's a challenging thing

Reflecting on not being here is challenging. It's so challenging, in fact, that it stops many people implementing any kind of Wealth Protection Strategy for themselves or their family. But the Life Protection Strategy is the ultimate gift you can provide for your loved ones. You might already have default coverage in your superannuation, so take 30 minutes to understand what cover you have and seek financial advice if you need to get better cover in place.

The world will still continue to turn when we're not here. Debts like mortgages and children's education will still need to be paid for. The time you spend getting your life cover sorted might just be the best legacy you provide to your nearest and dearest—one that impacts the quality of their lives for years to come. It's important to consider the cost of not having enough cover over the actual cost of the premium.

The Key Person Protection Strategy

The Key Person Protection Strategy is designed for partnerships and businesses where key people, like a business owner, founder, or important staff or income generators, are really important to the

WEALTH PROTECTION

ongoing success of the business. If a key person passes away, the strategy provides a pre-determined sum of money to the partnership or business. Key person insurance is also historically known as 'key man insurance' but today is more often called *buy-sell protection*. It isn't just men who run businesses!

The two sides to key person insurance are:

- **Capital protection:** Here, the policy transfers the value of the company shareholding to your family to represent all of your hard work and hours of deduction.

- **Revenue:** This protects the income generated by key staff, which underpins the profitability and sustainability of the business if someone is unable to work due to illness or injury.

How does it work?

Typically, you implement the Key Person Protection Strategy using life insurance and total and permanent disability insurance (which I cover earlier in this section under the related strategies). However, I have also seen trauma cover being used to further secure the lifeblood of the business when it comes to revenue.

Unlike taking out insurance policies for your spouse and children, in this strategy the individuals or business take out a policy on the 'key person', and it's the owner of the policy that makes a claim should that person become totally and permanently disabled or pass away. Businesses often seek the help of a financial planner to help identify and implement their key person needs.

Key person *capital protection* policies can be held via a trust structure or in the individual's name. A buy-sell agreement is used to confirm the transfer of shares in place of the shares owned. A buy-sell agreement is a formal agreement between business partners or parties that's written by a solicitor. The buy-sell agreement controls how shares within the business are transferred in the event of an insurance event. The agreement protects the spouse or partner of the person affected. The agreement also covers the remaining shareholders who have control in the future and are able to pay out the affected spouse or partner with the money paid from the life insurance or TPD insurance.

The buy-sell agreement would also address the rules set by the business owners in relation to trigger events, time frames and so on in relation to the circumstances around a claim on the policies held. Having a well-worded agreement removes any confusion or misunderstanding when you need clarity the most. You should attain legal advice to put parameters around where the proceeds of the policy are paid in lieu of the shares of the business. This is also called an *equitable charge* and you should always obtain specialist advice.

Key person *revenue* policies are generally owned by the trading entity that would have otherwise generated the income through employment of the life insured. Capital considerations for cover might include:

- Passing the agreed value of the shares owned by those involved to their loved ones

- Evaluating capital gains tax for the transfer of shares in the business and the cover you take out

- Understanding how the business is valued to attain the correct level of cover

- Setting up a buy-sell agreement to control the transfer of shares and money

- Repaying existing loans and debts held by the business.

Revenue considerations for cover might include:

- Sustaining the business revenue and offsetting decreased profits with income that would otherwise have been generated by the insured individual income

- Finding and funding a key person replacement or locum costs to cover the work done by the individual that has been injured or passed

- Clarifying the time frame within which the person making the claim has to return to work (especially for where trauma cover is maintained)

- Identifying the tax implications of the policy as the benefits are generally taxable to the recipient where a deduction for the premium is claimed

- Checking the potential benefits of claiming the premium as a deduction against the tax payable to the policy owner (generally the trading entity or company) on the benefit paid. Make sure you check as the tax can far outweigh the deduction over time.

Key person strategies are important if you have a significant part of your future earning or capital invested within a business. For business owners, their company can be seen as another child—it's a labour of love over many years, and the value of this love should be protected as your family may have given up a lot to let you chase your dreams.

When you're choosing a policy, consider the following questions:

- **What does the cover need to fund and how much cover will be needed?** Are you securing business loans that need to be repaid in the event of a claim, which may be a capital purpose (like business machinery loans) or income generated by a key staff member which is of a revenue nature?

- **What are the time frames under which the shares may be transferred in the event of a claim?** As an example, you may need to stipulate in your buy-sell agreement a time frame for a staff member to return to work in the event of a claim for trauma.

- **Does the person have any pre-existing conditions?** If so, the policy is unlikely to cover them. These are called exclusions.

- **Do waiting periods apply?** Some policies don't provide benefits immediately. These waiting periods mean that there might be a delay in the start of your coverage.

- **Who will own the policy and who needs to receive the proceeds?** A policy could be owned by the company (revenue) to replace income. A policy to remove debt may be owned personally or through a trust structure. You must consider the best outcome from a strategy and tax perspective with your financial adviser and accountant when it comes to how your policies are set up.

Taxation should also be considered as a part of the decision-making. Premiums are generally tax deductible if the funds would be used to replace lost business income and to pay for the cost of hiring or training a new staff member. If the premiums are tax deductible, it's important to note that the payment received from a policy would be subject to tax. Taxation then can also impact on the amount of cover sought. Where a capital-based contract (that is used to provide a sum of money to repay debt secured by a director, for example) is paid to the estate of the deceased or the life insurance in the case of TPD injured, the premiums may not be tax deductible and no tax is payable on the money received.

Strategy Stacking Tip

Consider the potential capital gains tax realised from the sale of shares in the business. *Capital gains tax* is the tax that needs to be paid on the profits of selling an asset, such as a business. Most people who use this strategy don't want to pass a tax liability to their estate as this would reduce the capital that the estate has to distribute. Make sure your spouse, partner and family is protected from capital gains tax as well, in the event of a claim—this may require you to increase the level of cover to allow for the pending tax issue on the triggered sale of your asset (shares in the business, for example).

When to do it?

You should consider a Key Person Protection Strategy if you own and operate a small- to medium-sized business and have multiple owners and key income providers within your organisation. You could also cover the cost of lost staff. You're likely to be relying on the business for your income and have money invested in your business. If you have key people that are very important to the ongoing success of your business, you might also consider this strategy.

WEALTH PROTECTION

Do

Do consider a Key Person Protection Strategy:

- As part of your overall Wealth Protection Strategy

- When you co-own and operate a business

- When seeking to mitigate lost income from key staff

- To provide a funding mechanism that could be a lot cheaper than borrowing money and paying interest to pay out the deceased or injured individual

- To maintain sufficient cover to pay out the value of business partners' shares in the business, which would allow you to control the transfer of the business's shares. Without key person protection, you may end up in business with your business partner's spouse, who may not have the skills to be a shareholder or decision-maker.

- If you have debts to repay in the event of a death or injury.

Don't

Don't fall into these traps:

- Purchasing a life insurance or total and permanent disability policy without understanding the terms and conditions

- Forgetting to consider the tax implications

- Forgetting to consider the correct ownership structure

- Forgetting a buy-sell agreement. Without appropriate paperwork (that is, the buy-sell agreement), you could end up paying the estate of your business partner a large capital sum while being unable to force the sale of shares in your business and therefore losing control.

- Discounting the benefit of financial advice to help you identify your needs and select appropriate options

- Lying to an insurance company about your medical history or any pre-existing medical condition if they request information at the time of application. This might void your policy at the time a claim needs to be made.

- Setting and forgetting your key person insurance. Policy options change over time and sometimes better policies become available. Review the level of cover to reflect the value of your company and its ongoing income.

- Forgetting your 'why'—it's ever-changing.

Business is all about mitigating risk

Losing a key person or business partner can have a real financial impact on you. Even if you're not related to them, they end up being like family given the time you spend together in the workplace. Increasingly, owners of small- and medium-sized businesses are thinking about the future of the business if they or one of their key people suddenly weren't there.

Sure, these might be difficult conversations to have, but they offer everyone involved peace of mind. Identifying key people and putting in place strategies that protect everyone's interests provides more certain business outcomes at what will undoubtedly be a very difficult time.

WEALTH PROTECTION

CHAPTER 14

The Estate Planning Strategies

Estate planning. What a cheerless topic to have to read about! It's not something we like to talk about, let alone have to do—yet it's an essential part of managing our finances and planning for the future. You might not realise it, but it also links to your 'why'. Estate planning provides you with the opportunity to plan and record what you want done with your assets, less any liabilities or debts, after you've passed.

I've never seen anything good come from a situation where there's been no estate planning. Nobody wins. Even those who end up receiving something from the person who has passed have had to go through some sort of emotional torment and gut-wrenching hell to get it. It doesn't bring families together. It rips them apart in some situations and may even make people resentful of each other and the person who has died.

So, I encourage you to get over the fear of dealing with your estate planning. *Not* doing it should scare you more. If you're a parent, you have even more reason to make it a priority—estate planning is about more than your assets and possessions. If something were to happen, who is going to look after your kids and have their interests looked after? Would you be happy for your kids to be split up and put into foster care?

How about tax? It is important to consider the outcome of your objectives. The tax payable on a benefit is impacted by the tax status of the person that receives the money or benefit. The ATO considers who is and is not a dependant, or if they are under the age of 18 (a minor) when it comes to the tax payable. A family solicitor can add a lot of value with regard to this by ensuring your objectives are met These issues can be addressed with a well-worded Will and the use of a Testamentary Trust (both of which I cover in this chapter).

When I ask new clients if they have a Will in place, the conversation tends to go like this:

ME: *'Have you got a Will and Enduring Power of Attorney in place?'*

CLIENT: *'No, but we have been meaning to do that since the kids were born.'*

ME: *'Oh really, how old are your kids?'*

CLIENT: *'They are 27 and 30.'*

Enough said. We all mean to get around to it, but life is so busy that more often than not it's overlooked as it's 'too hard' or 'we don't know a lawyer'. Both responses are valid—but also easily rectified.

I know I'm being harsh here—and I mean to be, because this is so important. Not planning your estate is so much worse than just doing it. Trust me—I've seen what happens when there's no plan in place. At the very least, call a solicitor and make a Will. If you have complex financial affairs, including owning your own business, it really pays to seek advice to secure the outcomes you wish to achieve (in line with your 'why'). You might wish to protect assets, review their ownership or change your investment structures, which are more complex strategies spanning several chapters in this book.

To help you understand the essentials of estate planning, there are four key things we all should be looking at:

- The Last Will and Testament Strategy
- The Testamentary Trust Strategy

ESTATE PLANNING

- The Power of Attorney Strategy

- The Superannuation Nomination Strategy and the Reversionary Pension Strategy.

In this chapter, I aim to lay the groundwork so you can ensure your estate planning protects those you value most. Much like the Framing Strategies (Chapter 9) that determine the stacks you build to enhance your financial life, the strategies here seek to enhance the outcomes of your financial life through the financial gifts and property that you leave to others.

The Last Will and Testament Strategy

The Last Will and Testament, or more simply a Will, outlines how a person would like their financial assets and possessions to be distributed when they pass away. The Will takes effect after a person dies. The executors of the Will, who are appointed by the late person, have the responsibility to ensure the instructions within the Will are carried out.

How does it work?

Most people make their Will with the assistance of a solicitor or a public trustee. While you can buy 'do it yourself' Will kits online and even at some newsagents, I'd never encourage one of my financial planning clients to use these as there may be a range of jurisdictional and state-based issues that need to be addressed that you don't know about (while we live in one country, state- and territory-based anomalies are becoming increasingly common). Seeking professional advice is the only way to be confident you've got your Will in good order.

A Will should cover:

- How your financial and material assets will be distributed

- Who will look after your children (if applicable)

- What structures or vehicles you might establish to look after young children—for example, a Testamentary Trust

- Charitable gifts you wish to make.

> ## Strategy Stacking Tip
>
> Your Will does NOT cover your superannuation and pension benefits. Make sure that your super wishes are addressed through a binding nomination or a reversionary pension form that you complete and lodge with your super fund (I cover the Superannuation Nomination Strategy and the Reversionary Pension Strategy later in this chapter).

When to do it?

You should make a Will as soon as you start accumulating assets. You never know what life is going to throw at you, so even if you've just started working or you're in your 20s then you've got something to gift should something dire happen to you.

You can update your Will at any time, too — it's not set in stone.

It's advisable to update your Will:

- When your financial situation changes significantly
- When you buy a home
- When you enter a permanent relationship or get married
- If your partner passes away
- If you and your partner separate or divorce
- If you have children or grandchildren.

Do

Do consider the Last Will and Testament Strategy:

- As the first step and cornerstone of your estate planning
- Regularly during your adult life, or at significant life milestones
- Even if you don't have any living relatives. If you were to die, your assets could be impacted by state or territory government legislation. Why not consider passing your assets to a charity or cause that you care about? The choice is yours.

ESTATE PLANNING

- To leave gifts or specific items to others. Speak with a solicitor about making provisions for people that you want to receive your assets, as well as those that you don't want to receive anything. You may be looking beyond your immediate family to distant relatives, family friends or godchildren.

- To ensure a Testamentary Trust is included where appropriate. A good solicitor would address this and inform you of their benefit.

- To make sure you have identified what you want to happen to shareholdings in companies and other entities that hold assets. This is even more important where you have owned the assets as an individual and don't have others like business partners or co-owners who are able to step in.

Don't

Don't fall into these traps:

- Using a 'do it yourself' Will kit without seeking professional advice

- Forgetting to tell your executors that you've nominated them to be executors and where they can find a copy of your Will (it is usually held with the solicitor you use or somewhere in your home)

- Forgetting to update your Will. I've seen situations where a person has separated and remarried and then unexpectedly passed away. As a result of the Will not being updated, the new partner and child weren't included. Situations like this can be challenged in the courts but the process can be costly, both financially and emotionally.

- Excluding people without getting advice—the outcome may be much worse than if you had included them. A good solicitor can help resolve this for you.

What happens if there's no Will?

It frustrates me no end as a financial planner that people work hard all their lives but never take the time to make a Will. If a person dies

ESTATE PLANNING

without a Will, legally they are said to have died 'intestate'. Each state and territory has its own intestate laws that spell out how the property of the deceased is to be distributed based on family relationships. If there are no family relationships, the proceeds of the estate usually go to the state or territory government.

So the key question is: would you be happy with someone else's rules determining how your property is distributed or do you want to have your own say? If you want to have your own say, make sure you have a Will in place.

The Testamentary Trust Strategy

In the Investment Structure Strategy (refer to Chapter 10), I talked about *trusts*—a type of ownership structure. A Testamentary Trust is just a special kind of trust that is specified in a Will to be used for the distribution of assets to a beneficiary. The Testamentary Trust is then established by your solicitor and executors after you pass away.

Why would you request to use a trust in your Will? There are several reasons, including:

- Managing and protecting assets for a minor who is not yet 18

- Managing and protecting assets for a beneficiary living with a disability, regardless of their age

- Managing and protecting assets for a child who is at risk due to a drug or gambling addiction, has debt or spending issues, or is in an unstable relationship (where another party might benefit from a relationship breakdown)

- Managing and protecting the assets for a spouse who may re-marry and have another party interested in their finances

- Managing and protecting the assets of a beneficiary for any reason—it can be used as an investment structure by the beneficiary, which is handy if they are ever at risk of being sued

- Distributing income to secondary beneficiaries as required.

In all these cases, a Testamentary Trust can help the beneficiary manage and protect the gift provided in your Last Will and Testament.

How does it work?

In creating your last Will and Testament, your legal adviser will be able to include a clause that provides for the establishment of a suitable Testamentary Trust after you pass away, depending on the goals you're trying to achieve.

A trust can be created for a single or multiple beneficiaries, and there can also be more than one trust. How the trust structure works is defined in your Last Will and Testament. It's increasingly common to see a solicitor, a financial planner and an accountant at an estate planning meeting, especially if you have a complex estate or it is of a significant size.

When to do it?

You should make a Will as soon as you start accumulating assets (refer to the earlier section on the Last Will and Testament Strategy). You should talk to your legal adviser about using a Testamentary Trust as part of the process of making a Will, should you have estate planning goals that you can achieve by using this kind of trust.

Do

Do consider using a Testamentary Trust Strategy:

- If you have children or grandchildren you are leaving assets to, or if you have beneficiaries living with a disability or who are in some way at risk

- When you are assessing the tax implications of your Will. In addition to acquiring legal advice, seek advice from your financial planner or accountant about the tax implications of your estate plan before you finalise the details.

ESTATE PLANNING

Don't

Don't fall into these traps:

- Using a 'do it yourself' Will kit or going it alone without professional advice

- Relying on what your friends or family do—seek your own advice.

What happens when there's no Testamentary Trust?

If you have a Will but no Testamentary Trust, the money will be paid directly to the beneficiary that you nominate.

There are some cases, however, where beneficiaries may need to be protected—for example, a child, a person with a cognitive disability (unless a guardian is appointed) or a person who is at risk, such as a beneficiary with a gambling or drug addiction health issue. In cases such as these, the beneficiary may be taken advantage of and lose control of the benefit that you've provided to them.

By distributing your estate to your beneficiaries by way of one or more Testamentary Trusts, your assets are safe from attack and your beneficiary is more protected.

If the beneficiary is a minor, the Will stipulates that the money will be held by the executor or trust for the beneficiary until the beneficiary turns the age specified in the Will, after which time it will be distributed directly to them.

So please, if you only take one action as a result of reading this book, talk to your legal adviser about this strategy (as part of setting up a Will) if you have children. I hope you see how important it is.

The Power of Attorney Strategy

A Power of Attorney is a legal document that allows you to appoint another person while you're still alive to act on your behalf in the management of your financial affairs (for example, managing your bank account, managing your investments and paying your bills).

We never know what life is going to throw in our direction. In the event that you need someone to act for you and you don't have a Power of Attorney in place, a trusted family member or friend will need to apply to your state or territory's trustee to appoint them to act for you, as well as monitor what they do. It's much simpler for all concerned to have a Power of Attorney already in place.

One of the greatest misconceptions I see from clients is that a Power of Attorney is a document for old people that you have for your own parents. Control has nothing to do with age, and choosing who can act for you is a very important, very personal decision.

There are two kinds of Power of Attorney:

- The Power of Attorney (also known as the General Power of Attorney)
- The Enduring Power of Attorney.

The Power of Attorney allows you to give another person the power to act on your behalf. For example, they can buy or sell things for you and make transactions for you on your bank accounts. The Enduring Power of Attorney allows you to give the authority for someone to make legal and financial decisions for you, should you not be able to. This may apply to health events where you lose the capacity to act for yourself, such as in the case of serious illness or injury.

The difference between the two kinds depends on the powers that you choose to give to someone else to protect you when you can't make an informed decision yourself. If you lose the capacity to deal with your own financial affairs, the General Power of Attorney may no longer be used. In cases like this an Enduring Power of Attorney may be required.

How does it work?

When a person makes a Will, they will be asked by their solicitor if they wish to appoint a Power of Attorney or Enduring Power of Attorney. The appointment takes the form of a legal document that outlines the kinds of decisions and actions someone can make for you. Both you and your attorney must sign the document, which says they agree to act for you.

ESTATE PLANNING

Seeking professional advice from a solicitor is the only way to be confident you're implementing the right kind of power of attorney for your needs. Each state and territory has its own legislation around these documents, so how they work can vary.

When someone is appointed as having Power of Attorney, they can act only in the areas outlined in the Power of Attorney document. Power of Attorney obligations include:

- Acting only in the areas outline in the Power of Attorney where they have the authority to act

- Making medical or financial decisions with regard to you

- Obeying your instructions while you're mentally able to provide them

- Keeping their finances separate from yours

- Keeping accurate and proper records.

Your solicitor will be able to provide you and the person you appoint as your Power of Attorney with complete information about the obligations involved.

When to do it?

You should consider making a Power of Attorney at the time you make a Will, if not before. You might appoint a Power of Attorney (either General or Enduring) if:

- You're going overseas or travelling for an extended period

- You need help to look after your financial affairs (perhaps you're sick or ageing)

- You have assets in your own name and want to know someone else can assist you if you can't manage your finances for any reason.

Do

Do consider the Power of Attorney Strategy:

- If you're making or updating your Will

- Regularly during your adult life, or at significant life milestones and changes

- Even if you don't have any living relatives. If you weren't able to act for yourself, who would you like to act for you? State and territory governments offer trustee services and can act for you if required. Perhaps close friends could act for you too — it might be a better outcome with someone you know and trust rather than a government trustee service.

Don't

Don't fall into these traps:

- Using a 'do it yourself' Power of Attorney without seeking professional advice
- Appointing people that you don't trust to act in your best interest
- Forgetting to update or cancel your Power of Attorney if your situation changes. Separation from a spouse or partner is a common reason to update a Power of Attorney.

Who do you choose to act on your behalf?

Some people ask their financial planner or solicitor to act as a Power of Attorney. While the vote of confidence and trust is appreciated, I don't tend to recommend this and would suggest any professional adviser worth their weight wouldn't either. The role of a professional adviser is to give you advice.

You need to choose someone who you trust and who is willing to take on the role. It might be:

- A spouse or partner
- One of your children
- A niece of nephew
- A trusted friend
- Your state or territory trustee services.

Keep in mind that if you use a state-based service there may be fees and charges involved to manage the estate, which may make any family involvement difficult. It's a big decision to hand over power of your

ESTATE PLANNING

financial affairs. Seek advice and think carefully about who you choose to act for you. Good advice will help you tailor your documentation to ensure your interests are protected.

The Superannuation Nomination Strategy and the Reversionary Pension Strategy

What happens to your superannuation or pension is not covered by your Will. The Superannuation Nomination Strategy and the Reversionary Pension Strategy enable a person to select who they would like their superannuation (or pension) to go to when they pass away, as well as other death benefits that might be included in the fund (such as life insurance).

Superannuation operates within a trust structure (refer to Chapter 11), rather than being an asset that is individually owned. Regardless of whether you are already receiving funds from your super (or pension), you need to provide a nomination to your super fund on what you'd like to happen.

How does it work?

A person with superannuation typically has two different types of nominations to make—a binding nomination or a non-binding nomination—to consider when determining who gets the proceeds of their superannuation and death benefits.

With a binding nomination, the trustee of the superannuation fund must follow the instructions outlined in your nomination form and distribute the funds as per your wishes.

A non-binding nomination is more of a 'guideline' of sorts and not as secure by comparison. You get to choose who the funds should be delivered to, but the trustee of the superannuation fund is not obligated to follow your instructions and may pay your entitlements to other people or to your estate. For example, if you get re-married and have children with a new partner, the superannuation trustee can make the decision to provide for your spouse and your children. A binding nomination is a great way to ensure that money does not reach the estate as this can see the payment of money quickly and easily without the need for probate and the legal fraternity. Again, while a benefit in some situations, the implications must be considered with your trusted adviser.

Some funds only offer nominations of either kind that last for three years, which means you need to make sure your nomination is up to date. It's a good idea to check your superannuation statement to see when your nomination will lapse. This will allow you to make a new nomination and of course make any changes that are required, such as appointing a different person to receive your funds (for example, if you were to separate and re-marry).

Some funds offer non-lapsing binding nominations. You're also able to change the person that you have nominated for this non-lapsing option by completing the necessary paperwork and ensuring it is witnessed by two individuals over the age of 18.

You can't make a binding nomination to just anyone. It can only be made to:

- A spouse
- A child
- A dependant
- An estate or legal personal representative.

Keep in mind that a nomination made to an adult child may have a taxable element depending on the underlying components of the superannuation fund (which is a good reason to get financial advice when selecting your nomination). Tax at a rate of 17 per cent (including the Medicare levy) is incurred when money is paid to a non-dependant—this includes via the estate, as the proceeds are taxed in the hands of the recipient.

If you're in the pension stage of superannuation, you have another option: the Reversionary Pension Strategy, which is different from the superannuation nominations covered so far. A *reversionary pension* takes the money left in the pension and starts paying it to your spouse, partner or child. The pension income continues to the nominated person and generally enjoys the tax benefits offered to the member that has passed (in that account-based pensions are tax-free inside the fund). A new pension is started in the recipient's name, with the same underlying assets, and the pension payments continue. A reversionary pension is a great way to keep capital within the tax-effective environment that superannuation offers, stop money going to the estate, and continue an income stream for continuity for a surviving spouse during an already difficult time.

It's possible to get your superannuation or death benefits paid to your estate and distributed according to the instructions of your Will. When you complete your binding nomination form, you can make an election to pay the benefits to your personal legal representative. The super fund will be obligated to pay the funds to your estate bank account (details will be provided by your legal representative) and then once out of the superannuation fund the assets may be distributed according to your Will.

You need to complete a binding nomination and nominate your 'personal legal representative'. Your personal legal representative is your executor(s), if you have a Will, or your administrator, if you die intestate (that is, without a Will). Who is an administrator in this circumstance? An administrator is a usually a family member or close personal friend. Often with legal assistance, they apply to be appointed by a court to take charge of the deceased estate. As there is no Will, state- and territory-based legislation will determine who receives the proceeds from the estate.

If you don't complete any nomination, the trustee of your super fund will make their own assessment about where the funds from the superannuation or pension should go. This is an uncertain outcome that most people aren't happy with, so make choosing and implementing a nomination a priority if you haven't done so already. Most superannuation funds don't charge any extra fees for making a binding or non-binding nomination.

With the introduction of the transfer balance cap (which is a limit on how much superannuation can be transferred from your super into a 'tax-free' account-based pension), getting specific legal and financial advice in relation to your reversionary pension or binding nominations is becoming increasingly important. Ensure that your family solicitor and financial planner are both across your superannuation nominations and that they have made you aware of the implications of both options, given your specific circumstances.

When to do it?

You should make a binding or non-binding nomination when you first open a superannuation account, which will be when you first start working. Even though you might have a low superannuation balance, many superannuation funds offer default insurance like life cover (refer to the Life Protection Strategy in Chapter 13), which can be a significant amount of money.

You should update your binding and non-binding nomination every time there is a significant change in your finances or your life stage, such as getting married, having children or experiencing the death of a family member.

Strategy Stacking Tip

Taking into account the value of your super account, you may wish to keep the funds within the superannuation environment by using a reversionary pension, as the value of the fund may be more than the recipient could recontribute back to superannuation under the non-concessional contribution limits (Chapter 11 talks more about these limits). A reversionary pension option could keep them in a tax-effective environment for a much longer period of time.

Do

Do consider a binding or non-binding Superannuation Nomination Strategy for your super account and/or a Reversionary Pension Strategy for your account-based pension:

- When you create or update your Will

- Every three years of your adult life if it's a lapsing nomination, or when you reach a significant life milestone, such as getting married or having children

ESTATE PLANNING

- Even if you don't have any living relatives. You deserve to get to decide where your money goes.

- If you don't have a spouse or children, in which case a binding nomination to your estate may be a good option

- If you want to confirm where your funds end up. A binding nomination would see them leave the super environment; a reversionary pension could keep them in the super environment.

- To limit the impact on Centrelink assessments and calculations (a correctly structured reversionary pension can achieve this)

- If the deceased is over their preservation age (the age you are allowed to access your super), when the reversion of a pension to someone younger would continue to offer tax-free earnings as well as access to capital each year.

Don't

Don't fall into these traps:

- Forgetting to tell your executors or your solicitor which funds you have superannuation or pensions with, especially if you don't have a financial planner who can point them in the right direction. A lot of time can be wasted in settling estates because people don't know where to start looking for your assets.

- Making a nomination without considering where the funds will end up. Avoiding a tax bill can be very important when you have spent your lifetime building an asset base for the benefit of your retirement, and your family and beneficiaries.

- Being sloppy with your paperwork—errors can make your nomination invalid and undo all of your hard work

- Forgetting to work out the implications of the transfer balance cap as you may push the total value of your superannuation over the $1.7 million dollar limit, which could have broader strategic implications

ESTATE
PLANNING

336

- Forgetting to consider where the proceeds from your superannuation-based life insurance will be paid. Again, managing any associated tax is vital where non-dependants are involved.

What happens if you don't have a super fund or pension nomination on your account?

If you don't have a nomination on your superannuation or pension, the trustee of the fund has the discretion to decide where your money goes (including any benefits from life protection cover attached to your superannuation fund). Each superannuation fund has its own rules and process around how to determine the most appropriate beneficiary for your retirement savings.

In cases like this, you're handing over the decision-making responsibility to someone who may not follow your exact wishes— because they won't know what they are! This has in the past caused fights and disputes among family members, as well as delays in settling the estate. Having a nomination in place gives everyone involved peace of mind—including you.

— PART IV —

PUTTING YOUR FINANCIAL PLAN INTO ACTION

This book has covered a lot of ground, and now is the time to talk about implementation. It would be remiss of me if I didn't spend some time talking about the role of a financial planner and why people use them. Many people think that financial planning is only for the wealthy. That's not actually the case, and I hope you have seen the truth of this as you've worked your way through this book. Financial planning advice offers lots of value to people from all walks of life.

If you've never used a financial planner before, you might not know what to expect—so here, I take the mystery out of the process. I also outline what you can expect to see in a typical financial plan.

So, how will you put your financial plan into action? Read on to find out!

CHAPTER 15

Why Seek Personal Financial Advice?

When I first started thinking about writing a book about how to stack financial planning strategies, my motivation was twofold. I wanted a book I could give to some of my clients who were interested in learning more about financial planning strategies on a deeper level. I also wanted to give more people the opportunity to make the most of their financial lives in line with their own 'why', and perhaps engage with financial planning like they'd never engaged with it before—in a way that makes a real and significant difference to the financial and other outcomes they'll achieve across their lives. This is an ambitious book in that regard, as everyone has different needs and goals and they will change at different life stages. However, I believe that the strategy stacking philosophy holds true regardless of where a person is at in their life, or how old they are.

We've all got some money in our pockets, but it doesn't mean we're experts when it comes to managing it. That's why seeking the help of a qualified and licensed financial planner can make a real difference. If you have doubts about seeking personal financial advice, I share some reasons in this chapter why you should consider working with a financial planner.

You don't know what you don't know

Here is the most common thing I hear from my clients who are approaching retirement: 'I wish someone had told me that years ago.' I wish younger people could hear the missed opportunities and regret in their voices: it might prompt them to act sooner.

The more time you give yourself, the more options you have. Time is your friend and you can make a big difference with small changes, without having to change your lifestyle in your later years because you left it too late to get the right amount of money into superannuation. Seeking personal financial advice also provides you with access to options you may not even be aware of. The cost of not finding out what's possible is normally outweighed by the value of a few simple strategy stacks over the longer term. You may not need to pay for ongoing advice as you could have a few basic strategies that could work for five years or more. A check-in to make sure you're on track or to hold you accountable may be enough to do the trick.

Things change—you'll never keep up with the latest options

Most people don't realise what it takes to provide financial planning advice. There's a lot of study. In addition to your initial qualifications, you need to complete 40 hours of extra training every year. Why? Because things change—things like investment and super rules, tax, and other regulations, not to mention investment vehicles and returns. Seeking personal financial advice means you have access to up-to-date information.

Just because something worked well in the past, it doesn't mean it will continue to be the best option for your money. Changing your view of how things may be done can accelerate what you do over time and potentially provide benefits along the way. I have people coming in all the time who listen to my radio show and say, 'I had no idea you could do that' or 'I have done that since you talked about it on the show and it works great.' Finding out what's new can open the door to a range of options you may have never considered or thought possible.

Asking family and friends for financial advice is a risky idea

One of the biggest dangers to a person's financial health is relying on family or friends for advice. What works for them might not actually work for you. You can't count the money in someone else's pocket; in the same vein, you shouldn't use strategies that work for others without making sure that they're right for you. You don't have their 'why', so you may need to take a different approach entirely.

Seeking personal financial advice means you keep your relationships with family and friends intact as you're not blaming them for any bad, though well-intentioned, advice they share with you. Your sister's risk profile may be totally different to yours so you may hold different assets—everyone's situation is different.

The outcomes of a previous generation's experience shouldn't cloud your own options either. We all know things change!

Trying to go it alone is just too difficult

On any journey, having someone to travel with makes it easier. The same can be said for managing your financial journey. Seeking personal financial advice means that you have access to a sounding board—someone who can provide advice and help keep you motivated. Your financial planner can also identify new opportunities as well as highlight the risks, which means you can get on with doing the things you'd rather be doing instead of doing your own research and risk analysis.

Used correctly, you can figure out a number of strategies for yourself and execute them to get a better super fund, with better contribution and pension options. You can arrange for a mortgage review and set up or restructure a loan for yourself too. But with a professional adviser on board, you can run your plans past someone else and get a second opinion—just in case they can make them a little better, faster or stronger.

Just like speaking to a specialist doctor about your physical health, you might speak to a financial expert to get a second opinion about your financial health. Seeking personal financial advice can help you confirm your options and get you on a pathway to achieving your goals.

Advice is not just for the ultra-rich

It is a common belief that you need to be wealthy already to need a financial planner working for you—but that's not actually the case. Everyone can benefit from financial advice—it's just a case of finding the right planner for you.

Consider how many kinds of milk there are in the supermarket. There's full cream, low fat, calcium-enriched, almond, soy … and the list goes on. Financial planners are in some ways like milk brands—there's someone suitable for every situation, depending on who you are and what you need.

You've got goals you want to achieve

It's great working with someone who has a clear goal. If you've got a goal but don't know how to achieve it, a financial planner can fill the gap. It might be a savings goal, a debt reduction goal or a retirement goal—or perhaps you have multiple things you'd like to achieve. By seeking personal financial advice, you learn about your options and can find a sensible way to achieve your goals.

Sometimes the advice process can provide you with clarity about your goals and help you prioritise them if you have more than one. People often say to me, 'I just want to make sure I am not missing out on anything', which is a great way to start your relationship with your financial planner because you're willing to accept that you don't know everything and you could benefit from their help.

I should stress the 'help' aspect as you still have to do the work—you can't outsource your financial behaviours, such as saving your income as planned or curbing your spending as required.

You don't want financial stress

Financial stress is a particular kind of pain unlike any other. It's hard to deal with, and when you're stressed you are prone to making rushed and sometimes bad decisions. Many couples experience financial stress at some point in their lives, which can put pressure on the relationship. Personal advice helps take the stress out of your decision-making so you can focus on getting better value from your money.

Seeking personal financial advice can help you clearly understand where you are, where you want to be and the journey between the two points. In some ways it might feel like you've left it too late to get started. There's always time, regardless of what stage of life you're at, to make the most of what you have—and to educate the next generation, if you're inclined to do so.

Setting strong foundations (as outlined in Chapter 3) applies to every stage of life too. You always have options, you just might not realise what they are. Don't leave seeking financial planning advice till later if you have fears or doubts. If you have got this far through the book, you must want to change your behaviour or consider other options—and you're now in a far better position to do so.

You're looking for a better way to manage your money

Many people earn enough to pay for what they need, but they might want to save a little bit more or perhaps retire from work just a little bit sooner. Seeking personal financial advice can help you better manage your money day to day and work towards something bigger.

Time is often a major factor if you have a busy life, with family commitments, a demanding job and other responsibilities. A planner is someone that you can outsource the decision-making to and who will help you along the way, leaving you to focus your time on the things that are most important to you. This is something we do in all areas of life—we do what we can with the time we have free and then get help with the rest, especially when something is not our area of expertise. It's no different when it comes to your finances.

You're facing a redundancy

It's a fact of modern working life that positions get made redundant and organisations change. Change like this can be hard to deal with, and often the outcome is a sum of money that you need to manage. Redundancy can open the door to accessing your super, depending on your age and the type of fund you belong to. There are tax and investment implications that you may wish to consider as a part of your decision-making, regardless of your age. Seeking personal advice can help you make financial sense of going through a redundancy. Being financially more confident can also help you move on with your career.

Redundancy may also allow you to do something new or simply take a break and recharge. What about study? It could be for an interest or your next role. Make the most of the opportunity!

If you learn of a strategy that could help you return to work on a part-time basis without having to work full-time, you could make that your short-term goal. When presented with the opportunity to do things a little differently, why not explore it rather than jumping back into full-time work because you think you have to—you may find you already have the resources to support your choice.

You want certainty when you retire

Some people love their jobs, some not so much. One thing for certain is that everyone in work will eventually want to retire and spend less time on the tools, talking to clients or in front of a computer screen. Seeking personal financial advice can help you understand how much you'll need in retirement and how you can get there before your last payday arrives.

You've had an unexpected windfall

Coming into a lot of money quickly can be a positive experience, but it can also be fraught with risk. It's most often an inheritance (which may also come with complicated emotions, such as feelings of loss and sorrow)—and less often, it's a lottery win (which may come with feelings of excitement and joy). It's common for people to lose their heads and become more carefree and perhaps even unintentionally reckless, which is likely to be a marked departure from their usual spending habits.

Seeking personal financial advice can help keep you grounded—regardless of what your emotional state is—and focused on your 'why', given the financial resources you now have available. It might also allow you to increase your tax deductions in line with your broader 'why' and give you access to additional financial strategies that you hadn't yet been using.

You've gone as far as you can by yourself

Many of my clients have done well to figure out their finances by themselves. However, they eventually reached a point where they'd paid off their house and were looking for additional options, possibly as a result of feeling like they're paying too much tax. Seeking personal financial advice can help you explore where to go next when your financial situation changes, helping you focus on your goals as well as explore new options.

It's all too complicated!

We've all had times in our lives where we've thrown our hands in the air and said, 'It's just all too hard!' Sometimes these words relate to your financial life. Don't be embarrassed or frustrated. The complexity of making the most of your financial life is probably the greatest it has ever been. It's not easy. If it were, everyone would be doing it and you wouldn't need a book like this—or, indeed, a financial planner. Seeking personal financial advice can help you simplify the complication and put in place strategy stacks that make sense for you.

You think you're paying too much tax

One of the five truths about money in Chapter 1 is, 'Most people plan for a tax deduction, not a lifestyle.' Seeking advice simply to find another tax deduction is probably not a good reason by itself to speak with a financial planner or accountant, but when coupled with other reasons it might make sense. Remember, the Appropriate Tax Strategy (Chapter 10) is just one strategy and therefore one component to help stack the odds in your favour, so make sure you think more broadly about your 'why'. This may also lead to a discussion in relation to your investment structures to help you manage your overall tax position, as well as introduce other strategies.

You want to stack strategies in your favour for a better life

Stacking strategies is a great reason for seeking personal advice to help you achieve your 'why'. Sometimes, multiple stacks can accelerate the impact of the advice, improve your ongoing financial behaviour and advance your progress towards your 'why'. You want to understand your financial options and how to put strategies together, given your own personal situation. This book can help you line up your strategy stacks with the help of a qualified financial planner.

—————— CHAPTER 16 ——————

What to Expect from the Financial Planning Process

If you've never met with a financial planner before, you're probably not aware of the process they follow. It's important that clients understand the financial planning process so they get the most out of seeking personal financial advice.

In this final chapter, I take you through the financial planning process step by step, and look at what you can expect your resulting financial plan to cover. Many Australians have never met with a financial planner before and don't know how the process works. By sharing this with you, I hope to take the mystery (and any uncertainty you might feel) out of the financial planning process.

The financial planning process in six steps

Like all interactions you have with advice providers in your life, it's okay to ask a financial planner about how they work with their clients. While there might be differences in how each financial planner works, the following financial planning process is general enough to cover off how the majority of Australians receive financial planning advice. You can use this as a starting point for a conversation with a financial planner, should you decide to seek advice.

Figure 16.1 outlines the six steps of a typical financial planning process.

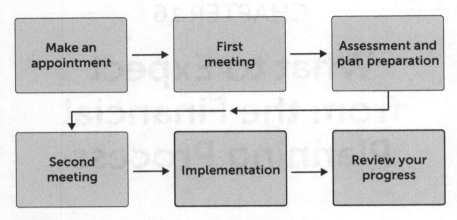

Figure 16.1: The six-step financial planning process

1. Make an appointment

The first step in the financial planning process is to make an appointment to meet with the financial planner (usually arranged over the phone). At this stage, you're likely to be asked a little bit about the reason for making the appointment, so be prepared to provide your reason. You're also likely to be asked to pull together some key information before the meeting, which will help your financial planner provide you with personal advice.

This information typically includes:

- Details about your employment and income
- Your budget (if you have one)
- Your latest superannuation statements
- Details about assets and investments you own, including current valuations
- Details about your debts, including personal loans, credit cards or mortgages

- Details about any personal insurance you hold
- Your most recent tax return.

If you've completed the Strategy Stacker's Starting Position exercise from Chapter 6, take that along too—it will contain many of the details listed here, as well as a wider picture of your financial position.

2. First meeting

The first meeting is where you sit down with the financial planner and start talking about who they are and how they can help you, as well as your financial situation. Some financial planners have a different name for this meeting—it might be called 'The fact find meeting', 'The discovery meeting' or 'The kick-off meeting', for example.

Your financial planner will likely lead the conversation, and you can expect to cover these areas:

- Who the financial planner is and more about their business
- How their specific financial planning process works
- Your short-term goals (one to two years), your medium-term goals (three to four years) and long-term goals (five + years)
- Your current financial situation, based on the information you brought along to the meeting and any additional questions your financial planner might ask
- Your attitudes towards risk and return
- The strategies they might consider to help you.

Of course, this is your opportunity to find out information too, so don't be afraid to ask questions about their areas of advice and service, their process, their qualifications and experience, and how they charge their clients for the advice and service that they may also provide to you.

As technology improves, it's likely that an increasing number of financial planners will offer internet video meetings rather than face-to-face meetings. However, I'd always recommend that your initial meeting is face to face so you can start to build a strong relationship. I do use video-conferencing technology in my business where possible—it's easy to use once you know how—but there's a lot to be said for the face-to-face meeting.

Finally, make sure the financial planner provides you with a Financial Services Guide (FSG) and Adviser Profile. It's a legal requirement to do so, and if they don't I'd suggest you find an alternative financial planner. (An FSG provides you with information about the entity and financial planner that will be providing the financial advice. It should explain the advice and services offered to clients, how they charge for the advice and service provided, and how any complaints are dealt with.)

3. Assessment and plan preparation

This step in the process happens largely without you being present. In this stage, the financial planner looks at your goals and reviews your financial life on paper to assess your position. They will spend time looking at appropriate financial planning strategies and how they can put them together to help you achieve your goals. Simply, they are working out the best strategy stacks for you. If the financial planner needs any more information or wants to clarify something, they may contact you during this stage.

Once they have the strategies in place, they will then consider appropriate structures and financial products (if required) that can be used to help you realise your goals. These are often referred as *product recommendations*. They could cover specific vehicles, investments, superannuation funds or insurance products.

Product recommendations should never come before a financial planner has done a thorough assessment of your situation, so be alarmed if they do. It's about finding the right product for you, not making you fit into a product. You'd never purchase a brand of tyres and later try to fit them to your car!

The kind of planner you use will determine how widely they look at suitable financial products. Bank financial planners, for example, may recommend their own bank's financial products. More independent financial planners will look more widely at the marketplace to find the best products available. Be sure your advice can be implemented using assets and products appropriate to you and with appropriate costs. Refer to the Framing Strategies (Chapter 9), Investment Strategies (Chapter 10), Superannuation Strategies (Chapter 11), Retirement Strategies (Chapter 12), Wealth Protection Strategies (Chapter 13) and Estate Planning Strategies (Chapter 14) as you need to.

A good financial planner should be able to provide you with an understanding of how the assets, products and policies they've chosen help you achieve your goals. They should also provide comfort that the costs are appropriate when compared to other similar products or policies within the marketplace. One of the objectives of me writing this book was to enable you to have better informed and more productive conversations about financial planning strategies with your financial planner. The chapters in Part 3 (chapters 9–14) might be a great starting point for a conversation about your personal situation and can be a useful reference point to come back to over time.

4. Second meeting

The second meeting is where you meet the financial planner again to hear the strategies they recommend you use to achieve your goals. Some planners have a different name for this meeting —it might be called 'The plan meeting', 'The strategy meeting' or 'The presentation meeting', for example.

The primary objective of this meeting is for the financial planner to demonstrate to you what your options are, based on your current financial situation. They will offer one or more specific personal financial advice recommendations. These will include financial planning strategies and, depending on the kind of advice, they might also make specific financial product recommendations for your personal situation.

It's very important that you understand the strategies being implemented and how they will help you achieve your goals. Don't be afraid to ask questions if you don't understand something. It's also a good idea to put the strategies in your own words and play them back to the financial planner to check your understanding. You might do this by saying something like: 'Okay, what I think you're saying is that if we do "X", we'll increase the likelihood of reaching "Y". Is that correct?'

The financial planner is likely to walk you through the key elements of the financial plan as well as provide you with a copy of the financial plan in writing (I guide you through a typical financial plan later in this chapter).

It's important that you understand the plan and that you're comfortable with the strategies and recommendations before you implement any of them. If financial products have been recommended to you, your financial planner should also provide you with a Product Disclosure Statement (PDS) for each investment, superannuation or insurance product they've suggested. The PDS is a document provided by the product provider and details how their product works, including any fees and charges.

5. Implementation

If you're happy with the advice that your financial planner has provided in the second meeting, the next stage of the financial planning process is where you put the plan into action. Your financial planner should guide you through this process, including the paperwork that needs to be completed before you can proceed. You will need to sign the paperwork before implementation can take place. This may occur at the end of or after the second meeting.

This stage is also an opportunity to ask questions if you still have them. If there's something you don't understand, make sure you don't implement your financial plan until you do. It is essential you understand the advice before you implement it. You should be comfortable that the advice provided will help you achieve your goals.

It's important to also note that implementation doesn't mean that you invest all your money right now. It could take a while to implement your overall plan, depending on the structures you're using and the market conditions at the time. For example, if your financial planner recommends investing through a trust, or setting up a new account-based pension at retirement, it's going to take some time to set up before you can make an investment through it. A good financial planner will outline to you how and when implementation will occur so you have certainty throughout the process.

Often, the financial planner or their staff will check in with you from time to time if it's a particularly long or complex implementation process. They also will let you know when implementation is completed.

6. Review your progress

Assessing and reviewing progress is an important part of your financial plan. Some planners have a different name for this step—they might call it 'The review meeting', 'The progress meeting' or 'The assessment meeting', for example.

Without this step, you won't know how much progress you've made towards your goals. Your financial planner will suggest an appropriate time frame in which to review your progress. An annual review for investment performance is the industry standard; however, if your financial affairs are more complex, you might expect quarterly or half-yearly reviews. Reviews may also arise due to legislation changes or if a specific life event occurs that creates a need for an additional meeting.

At the review meeting, your financial planner will identify the progress made towards your previously stated goals. This usually includes reviewing your superannuation and investment performance, as well as the insurance you have in place. If the planner believes something needs to change, they will provide you with new recommendations for your review and consideration. This might include new or modified strategies, or new or alternative financial products. Just like the second meeting, it's important that you understand any changes before you agree to implement them. Implementing any new recommendations can occur at the end of your review meeting or shortly thereafter once you've provided the go ahead.

It's also important to share with your financial planner at this meeting any changes to your situation that are likely to impact on the achievement of your goals. Sometimes your circumstances in life will change, and these changes need to be considered. If a major change has occurred, like a marriage or divorce, your financial planner might need to revisit your original financial plan and re-cast the plan. Smaller changes or additions can usually be dealt with through a 'record of advice', which simply documents the reason for the change to your strategy, the strategy itself and any new personal financial advice recommendations.

The financial plan: What should it cover?

The financial plan your financial planner creates for you must be given to you in writing. It's vital that you understand all the strategy and product recommendations made to you before you make the decision to implement them.

Table 16.1 provides an overview of a typical financial plan so you know what to look out for in your own.

Table 16.1: The elements of a financial plan

Component	What it covers
Cover page	Highlights who the plan is for and the name of the financial planner providing the personal financial advice, as well as their contact details.
Executive summary	Summarises the plan and highlights the key elements of the financial plan, including your goals and the financial planner's recommendations.
Key personal information	Highlights your key personal information in detail. This includes your name, age, contact details and key relationships (if applicable). It should also detail your current financial position.
Detailed strategies	Provides you with detailed information about the strategies your financial planner is recommending to help you meet your goals. Depending on your goals, this might include strategies on: • Budget management (refer to Chapter 9) • Cash flow management (refer to Chapter 9) • Debt reduction (refer to Chapter 9) • Risk assessment (refer to Chapter 9) • Investment (refer to Chapter 10) • Superannuation (refer to Chapter 11) • Retirement (refer to Chapter 12) • Protection/insurance (refer to Chapter 13) • Estate planning (refer to Chapter 14) When outlining the recommended strategies, the risks should also be noted.

Component	What it covers
Product recommendations	Provides you with information about the products your financial planner is recommending for you. These should clearly relate to one or more of the strategies provided.
Implementation checklist	Provides the steps required to implement the plan.
Authority to proceed	Requires you to sign an Authority to Proceed document and return it to your financial planner so they can implement the plan. It will usually ask you to confirm that you have received a personal financial plan and any applicable Product Disclosure Statements (PDSs), which are found in the 'Additional enclosures' section, and that you authorise the financial planner to implement your plan. You might also have to sign forms from PDS documents, depending on the products and policies recommended to you, to implement your plan.
Ongoing service agreement	Confirms the services provided to you if an ongoing service is part of the plan. Typical ongoing service agreements include review meetings to assess your progress towards your goals.
Disclaimers and important notices	As you might expect, there are some legal notices relating to the financial plan you receive. It is important you understand these disclaimers and notices.
Appendices	The financial plan might include additional reading material or research information to support the strategies recommended.
Additional enclosures	The financial plan might come with additional enclosures, such as investment, superannuation or insurance PDSs or research. These might be provided as additional printed enclosures, but more often they are provided electronically as we move towards a more online world.

Of course, the example offered here is only a typical financial plan, and everyone's goals and circumstances will be different. For example, if you're only seeking advice for a particular issue, the advice document provided to you may not include all the elements suggested for a full financial plan. For single-issue advice, such as an assessment of a client's existing super fund or their investment choice within a fund, the paperwork provided is likely to be a lot shorter. However, there should still be an Authority to Proceed you need to sign. There's not likely to be any ongoing review meetings for single-issue advice unless you request a meeting. (Single-issue advice is called 'Topic-based advice' by some financial planners.)

Now that you know what's included in a financial plan, you know what to look out for and ask questions about when you're seeking personal financial planning advice. Whether you're looking for single-issue advice or more comprehensive advice that covers a range of areas in your financial life, you should expect to receive that advice in writing. This provides you with the opportunity to review the information and strategies provided to you and ask questions about anything that you don't understand or issues you'd like more information on. Good financial planners will always take their obligations seriously to ensure you understand their advice before they implement it.

ENDINGS AND NEW BEGINNINGS

Although you've reached the end of the book, it's only the start of your strategy stacking journey—a new beginning. You might have even started making some proactive and positive changes as you worked your way through the book—if you have, that's great. Keep going!

Before you start your journey, it's worth reflecting once more on the five truths about money (Chapter 1). The reality is very few of us will have had the perfect start to our financial lives—or have a perfect relationship with money. But with some focus and thought, we can explore our own attitudes to money and our relationship to money—both the good and bad aspects—to re-evaluate what we're doing with our financial lives and make changes.

If you decide to make changes in your financial life, they should be changes that reflect your own 'why'. So much of what we do in life has a financial consequence—but do we take the time to set goals? Your short-, medium- and long-term goals should drive the strategy stacks that you decide to build for yourself. It's easy to get caught up with trying to keep up with others, but when we do so we don't put ourselves first. Setting goals requires you to focus upon what's most important to you, so your financial strategy should be about you and what matters to you.

The stronger your financial foundations, the sturdier your strategy stack. My strategy stacking philosophy helps you to put together different financial planning strategies in a way that works for your 'why'. The strategies you choose to stack (or don't stack) will have an impact on your financial life.

Sound budget management (the Basic Stack in Chapter 4, where earnings meet spending) is essential if you want to genuinely stack the odds in your favour. Having the ability to save something each week, fortnight or month affords you the opportunity to achieve your goals. And of course, this thing called life is going to happen to you along the way, which might include getting made redundant from a job, getting married or divorced, receiving an unexpected windfall ... or all manner of other significant events.

When you're ready to get started, you would be wise to assess your starting position so you know what you already have in place and you understand what your outgoings are. Much like driving a car, it's easier to plan a journey to a destination if you know where you're starting from. The Strategy Stacker's Starting Position exercise in Chapter 6 provides you with an overview of your financial life and allows you to reflect on what's actually happening within it so you can take practical steps forward.

Any strategy stack you build should consider the Framing Strategies in Chapter 9, which cover budgeting, cash flow management, debt reduction and your appetite for risk. Combined, these strategies frame your stack, in much the same way that the frame of a house structures its walls and rooms.

The core of this book (Part 3) explores an array of additional strategies that financial planners use with their clients, covering investment, superannuation, retirement, wealth protection and estate planning. It's these strategies that you may find you need to revisit again and again. Remember—your strategy stack should change as your life and goals change.

If you're still wondering how strategy stacking works in practice, you may find it helpful to review the example strategy stacking scenarios in Chapter 8. Of course, the strategy stacks you build for yourself, perhaps with advice from a financial planner, should reflect your goals—but these examples are a great starting point for understanding how strategy stacking can support you and your family throughout your lives. And if you feel ready to seek personal financial advice, chapters 15 and 16 give you a place to start to understand how financial advice works. I hope they help take the mystery out of what's involved in the financial planning process.

Thank you for reading *Smart Money Strategy*. I hope it's been an educational experience, and I hope it motivates and inspires you to take real action so you can achieve more confident outcomes in your own financial life.

I wish you all the best on your strategy stacking journey as you start your new beginning, and I wish you well if you decide to seek personal financial advice. If you have enjoyed the book, please do recommend it to your family and friends. I'd love to see more people taking control of their financial lives and stacking the odds in their favour!

I sincerely hope this book has provided you with many insights and perhaps even some revelations about money. For additional resources, including how to access my podcast, please join me at thestrategystacker.com.au.

INDEX